GAVRILO PRINCIP

The Assassin who started the
First World War

Peter Villiers

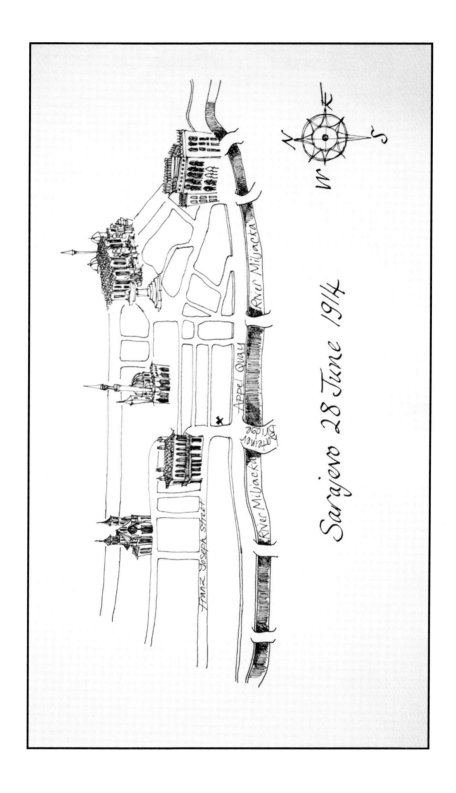

Sarajevo 28 June 1914

GAVRILO PRINCIP

The Assassin who started the
First World War

PETER VILLIERS

The Fawler Press

ISBN 978-0-95662110-8

First published in 2010 by The Fawler Press

Printed and bound in England by CPI Antony Rowe, Chippenham, Wiltshire

Dedication

To the Masters at the King's School,
Canterbury 1961-1965

Who attempted to teach me history

Preface

I first became interested in Gavrilo Princip when researching the history of assassination, at the national police library in Hampshire. (The comma in this sentence, as Lynne Truss might have pointed out, is important.) In the account of what happened in Sarajevo in 1914 by Joachim Remak (Remak, 1959) Princip springs to life in all his youthful vulnerability and murderousness; and from there on I was hooked. Further research followed; a play or two; and then this book.

I am not an historian by profession, and have wrestled with the challenges of that occupation since I first became absorbed with the events of 28 June 1914 and my need to write about them. Princip himself, the young Bosnian dreamer who made his dream into a reality, had captured my attention, and I was to discover a good deal of information on him—much of which proved to be speculative, biassed, or of doubtful veracity, including what I learned when I finally visited the city of Saraejvo itself, for he remains a controversial character about whom people have firm opinions, not always backed by fact. My interest expanded to the mysterious Colonel 'Apis', who had supported and equipped the assassins, if not actually planned and directed the whole thing himself; and to the character and ambitions of the Archduke Franz Ferdinand, the happily married *paterfamilias* with his volcanic temper and impossible inheritance.

Issues as well as people entered the arena, and I found myself contemplating the history of Bosnia within the context of the Roman, Ottoman and Austro-Hungarian empires of which it had been a part. In 1919, the province became part of the Kingdom of the Serbs, Croats and Slovenes, which was later renamed Yugoslavia. Yugoslavia was invaded by the Axis powers in the Second World War, and a fierce and divided struggle took place to restore its independence. Under Tito, and under its official title of Bosnia and Herzegovina, Bosnia became one of the six republics of the new Yugoslavia. The federal republic of Yugoslavia began to fall apart in the 1980s. At that point we reach contemporary times, and the post-communist settlement of the Balkans in which we are still absorbed. The reader will find some very brief comments on the situation in Bosnia in 2010, which concludes with a hope but not a prediction.

The chapter headings suggested themselves. As I researched the subject, it became clear that I should attempt some sort of comparative account of revolutionary violence in Russia, by which 'Young Bosnia' was inspired. That account, and its influence, has been included in Chapter Three.

In the main, I have attempted to produce a 'proper' text. My aim has been to find out the facts and to make it clear when I am shifting from fact to assumption, interpretation or commentary, although the difference is not always an easy one to mark. I have tried not to make things up, for example conversations that could not possibly have been recorded: this is a biography and not an historical novel. In Chapter Seven, The Fatal Day, I write without constraint, and have allowed myself to imagine what some of the main characters might have been thinking and feeling on that day. I must apologize for having been carried away. Readers may choose to read this chapter first, if they so wish: it will not spoil the narrative for them. Many will already know what happened in Sarajevo in 1914, at least in outline; but that is neither the beginning nor the end of this story.

I have tried to turn my own experience to advantage, as when writing about the principles of military intelligence, or planning an ambush; and I have assumed that my readers will have the good sense to be able to identify for themselves whatever anachronisms I may have introduced, and to decide whether or not their presence is legitimate. To attempt to judge the past by the priorities, standards and values of the present is to attempt the wrong quest; but comparisons are still possible.

Some questions can never be answered definitively, and the enjoyment is in the quality and liveliness of the debate. What would have happened to the Austro-Hungarian empire, if Franz Ferdinand had not been assassinated? And what would have become of Bosnia? We cannot know; but we can discuss possibilities. Such an exploration may lead to more fundamental questions about the nature of state and society, and ultimately our views on human nature itself. There is a place for such issues in a biography, but it is a limited one. The author has no more insight into human nature than any of his readers: and they will bring their own interpretation to the story.

Gavrilo Princip was born a Bosnian Serb in a remote corner of a province that had only recently become a part of the Austro-Hungarian empire. He was raised as a peasant of peasant stock. Peasant families used to belong to a *zadruga*, and would gather in the extended farmhouse to listen to the tales of the past and what it meant to be a Serb. These tales were told in verse, and commemorated the events that were significant for them all: tales of heroic actions, and love requited or spurned, and the greatest achievement of all—the survival of the group. Gavrilo Princip listened to such tales as a boy, and they made a profound impression on him. His tale deserves to be told.

Acknowledgements

In researching and writing this book I am much obliged to a wide variety of people who have assisted my research and deepened my understanding. Mistakes remain my own. The written sources are listed in full under references. Two have been of especial use.

Sarajevo, the story of a political murder, Joachim Remak, 1959.

The Road to Sarajevo, Vladimir Dedijer, 1967.

I am grateful to Professor Robert Evans, of Oxford University, and to Professor Alan Sked, of the London School of Economics, both of whom offered expert commentary on parts of the text; to the Director and Staff of the Ashmolean Museum in Oxford who furnished me with further information on Sir Arthur Evans, the first director of the Ashmolean Museum and previously a special correspondent in the Balkans; to the Chief Historian of the Information Management Group of the Foreign and Commonwealth Office, for advice; to the National Records Office in Kew, for advice; to Michael Molnar of the Freud Museum in London, for information on the Austro-Hungarian psychiatrist Dr Martin Pappenheim, who interviewed Gavrilo Pricnip in prison; to Dr Eran Rolnik of Tel Aviv, who provided information on his daughter, Dr Elsa Pappenheim; to His Royal Highness Crown Prince Alexander II and his Privy Counsellor Dusan Babac, in Belgrade, for information; and to Commander Allan Gibson of the Metropolitan Police Service, for advice. I am extraordinarily grateful to Max Hohenberg, the great grandson of the Archduke Franz Ferdinand, for his invaluable information on family history and for his perspective into what it means to be a Hapsburg. I must, as always, acknowledge my debt to Carolyn, who has tolerated with patience and good humour my long obsession with Gavrilo Princip. She accompanied me to Sarajevo in 2009 and upgraded us to the Hotel Europa, which gave us a much better perspective into the heart of that fascinating city.

Finally, I am greatly indebted for the skills, enthusiasm and energy that Mr Geoffrey Fisher of Antony Rowe Publishing has shown, in turning a raw manuscript into a book.

MBTI acknowledgement

"MBTI", "Myers-Briggs Type Indicator", "Myers-Briggs", the "MBTI" logo and "Introduction to Type" are registered trademarks of the MBTI Trust, Inc. in the European Union and USA. CPP Inc. is exclusively licensed to distribute publications bearing these trademarks worldwide, and OPP Limited is licensed by CPP Inc. to use the MBTI trademarks in Europe and is the exclusive distributor of the MBTI instrument through-out Europe.

I am grateful to Fiona Balfour for the six charcoal drawings of the life and death of Gavrilo Princip, which were commissioned and created for this project; and to Kate Barker for the map of Sarajevo. The three photographs of Sarajevo in 1910 are reproduced with kind permission of the Royal Geographical Society of London.

Contents

CHAPTER ONE

The Age of Empire

In the modern view of the world, imperialism is not a popular concept, and London's Imperial War Museum combines in its splendidly robust title three of the most unpopular words in the English language.

Empires, it is assumed, mean conquest, exploitation and the removal of what it means to be an independent nation with a pride in its own history, culture and identity. They are a bad thing both for those who are colonised and those who colonise them.

This view was not always in fashion. Empirically speaking, empires are a commonplace if not a natural state of affairs. Indeed, it might be argued that the majority of peoples in the world have lived as members or subjects of an empire for much of recorded history. Empires have existed for a very long time, and very few peoples have never been conquered and colonised. Nor have those who have been colonised necessarily resented that status, or indeed perceived it as anything other than the natural order of things. Indeed, from an historical perspective, it is the absence of empire which is unusual; and the nation-state, if we take that to be the opposite of an empire, is a very recent phenomenon.

The Roman Empire

For the West the archetypal empire is Rome[1]. Rome, as far as the Romans were concerned, was the centre of the civilised world, if not of the world itself; and it had both duty and right to conquer and exploit the rest of the world. That world included the province of Illyria, which contained modern-day Croatia, Bosnia and Serbia as well as other territories and became an important possession of the Roman Empire. Some of its inhabitants prospered in imperial service, including the Emperor Constantine (274-337) who was born in what is now Serbia, and who declared the empire to Christianity—a measure, according to the historian Edward Gibbon, which was a major cause of its decline and fall.

In the fourth century AD the Roman Empire was divided between a western empire based in Rome and an eastern empire based in Byzantium, which was renamed Constantinople and became the centre for orthodox Christianity[2]. The western empire collapsed in 476, whereas the eastern or Byzantine empire survived until 1453 when Constantinople/Byzantium was conquered by the Ottoman Turks under Mehmet 11 [3].

The Ottoman Empire

The Ottoman Empire was to occupy not only most of the near East, but also a substantial part of what is now referred to as the Balkans. It was to find itself in conflict with the Hapsburg Empire, which established the Austrian Military Frontier as a defensive measure—a military frontier which Gavrilo Princip's forbears were later to defend as peasant-gendarmes.

The Ottoman Empire was to pose a significant threat not only to the Hapsburgs but to the security of Europe in general. Indeed, it was far from impossible that the Ottoman Turks would conquer Europe as a whole, and in 1683 they were defeated at the gates of Vienna itself—a significant threat indeed! The leader of the forces against them, Jan 111 Sobieski, King of Poland and Grand Duke of Lithuania, was not a Hapsburg, but was in command of Polish, German and Austrian troops: and this was not the only time that Europe needed to defend itself against an encroaching Ottoman menace.

All empires follow a pattern of growth, development, decline and fall, although not on the same time scale. By the nineteenth century the Ottoman Empire was in serious if not irreversible decline. Although it still remained a formidable military force it was no longer the power it had once been, and could no longer easily defeat the other major powers in battle. Moreover, the Ottoman Turks were followers of Islam, although they did not insist that their subjects convert to that faith, and the rest of Europe was Christian. Islam was seen as a threat, and the Osmanli Turks, despite their military prowess, large cities and impressive architecture, were perceived as not really civilised, or at least as not really members of the club[4]. The great powers were prepared to support the Turks, from time to time, as they were a regional force for stability: but that did not mean that they were loved[5].

The British Empire

The British Empire is conventionally dated from the colonisation of Newfoundland in 1583. Arguably, there were two British Empires. As David Cannadine (Cannadine, 2001, page 11) puts it: 'The first British Empire consisted primarily of a western Atlantic dominion extending from Canada, via the thirteen American colonies, to the Caribbean, and reached its peak in the brief years between 1763 and 1776. Out of its post-Yorktown wreckage was born its successor, which was a much more far-flung and varied realm.'

Part of this new empire, Cannadine explains, would become the colonies of settlement such as Australia and New Zealand, which would eventually develop into self-governing democracies. Part of it would be the colonies of conquest, 'which would eventually be abruptly terminated by nationalist agitation and independence.' (op. cit., page 12.)

The (second) British Empire reached its zenith after other European powers, such as the Spanish and Portuguese, and to some extent the Dutch, had already created and lost their own empires, and in some cases moved to a post-imperial phase; and the great age of British imperialism was from 1815 to 1914, which coincided with the scramble for Africa. (Last into the race for colonies overseas were the Germans and the Italians who, having united their own countries, began to look elsewhere to expand their interests: both created African colonies. Austria-Hungary had no colonial interest in Africa, as it had already more than enough territory to administer and defend in Europe. Moreover, by the mid-nineteenth century this very long-lived empire was in decline.)

At its greatest extent, the British Empire was the largest empire in the world and included about a quarter of its total surface. However, much of that expanse was commercially worthless, and it is significant that trade between Great Britain and continental Europe was always of more value than trade with the empire further afield. The empire was neglected or ignored rather more than it was worshipped; and the imperial ideal was never popular with more than a small minority[6].

The Austro-Hungarian Empire: An Hapsburg Dynasty

The Austrian Empire, or the Austro-Hungarian empire as it became in 1867, was of a different character to the Roman, Ottoman and British Empires which we have briefly considered. In the first place, it was the personal possession of the Hapsburgs, and destined to remain in their hands for ever. Or so the Hapsburgs believed, for they believed in divine right; and if they could have had their way, they would have ruled by absolute power, for ever and ever, amen.

Charles V: The ultimate Hapsburg

Charles V (1500 to 1558) was the ultimate Hapsburg, and under his rule the Hapsburg possessions, titles and power reached their greatest extent. Charles V, under various titles and variations, was King of Spain, and therefore ruler of its huge possessions in the Americas. (Spanish conquistadors had conquered both Mexico and Peru, and the Spanish created an empire in Hispanic America that lasted for 300 years. The Spanish American colonies provided fantastic wealth for the ruling dynasty at home.)

In addition, Charles V ruled the Spanish Netherlands, or what is now Belgium and Holland; part of what is now Italy; Sardinia; and other lands and possessions, besides Austria. He was also Holy Roman Emperor.

After his reign, the Hapsburg dynasty was separated between the Austrian and Spanish branches. The Hapsburgs remained Holy Roman Emperors, a post that was technically fulfilled by election rather than inheritance, until that empire itself dissolved into history.

Mother and Son: Maria Theresa and Joseph II

Great Hapsburgs included the Empress Maria Theresa, the only woman to rule the Hapsburg empire in 650 years: she came to the throne in 1740 under her father's wishes, won a war of succession, and ruled until she died in 1780, during part of this period sharing power with her son Joseph, and acting as a very necessary restraining influence upon him. Joseph ruled alone as Joseph II from 1780 until his death in 1790, and during this short but frenzied decade was finally able to put in place all the reforms on which his mother had urged caution.

Claiming to be an enlightened despot, he was certainly despotic. Joseph did not believe in moderation, and unlike his mother, had no conception of timing. If his reforms had lasted and born fruit, he might have been one of the most respected emperors in history. Sadly, they did not, and his rule ended in chaos and confusion, with little of permanent achievement: although he did lay the foundations for the Hapsburg equivalent of a welfare state. According to Sked (op. cit., page 281), the essence of 'Josephinism' was:

'An attempt to create a centralised monarchy in which the link between the absolute ruler on the one hand, and a materially contented and intellectually and spiritually supervised people on the other, was a well-trained and educated bureaucracy, not, as had been the case previously, a feudal nobility and powerful Church. This system was to be based, however, on principles of natural law under the guidance of a paternal and enlightened monarch.'

A well-trained and educated bureaucracy was achieved, and was to be a characteristic of the Austro-Hungarian Empire until its final collapse. To ensure a paternal and enlightened monarch was a greater challenge.

Joseph II's successor Franz I believed in the need for both firm and fair administration in which the sovereign demonstrated his interest in his subjects by personal example, adjusting his behaviour to the requirements of the time. According to one account (op. cit., page 292):

'In the days of Francis (the Emperor Francis 1, 1804-1835; also Holy Roman Emperor until 1806) every farmer or petty proprietor or shopkeeper for hundreds of miles around Vienna, who had a grievance to complain of against any member of the government, used to get into his cart, drive himself to the capital and tell his story to 'Kaiser Franz'... (If wronged he usually got redress)... Upper and lower Austria and Styria abound with stories of simple-minded men, who, in their domestic difficulties, their differences with each other, their doubts as to their daughters' marriages or their own testaments, used to go up to have a friendly conversation with the emperor, and were certain to receive from him plain straightforward sensible advice.'

However, Franz I's contribution to posterity was not wholly a beneficial one. One of the disadvantages of the Hapsburg system of rule was that supreme power was limited to a closed circle. That system led to the problems of a limited gene pool. The family of the last Holy Roman Emperor and first Austrian Emperor, Franz 1, was dangerously inbred. As Van der Kiste points out (Van der Kiste, 2005):

'(The) Emperor Franz had been married four times and fathered thirteen children, but only two sons and five daughters survived infancy. All were the issue of his second wife (who was his) first cousin twice over.

'The elder son and heir, Crown Prince Ferdinand, was a well-meaning, simple-minded soul and a victim of epilepsy. With his ugly shrunken figure and unnaturally large head, he could barely utter two connected sentences, lift a glass with one hand, or descend a staircase without assistance.'

His younger brother, the Archduke Franz Karl, was clumsy, shy and slow on the uptake, but in better shape than Crown Prince Ferdinand. Luckily, he was to produce another possible contender for the poisoned chalice of the throne of Austria, who was in better condition than either his father or uncle.

The Emperor Franz Joseph

Franz Karl married his cousin Sophie in November 1824 and she promptly suffered the first of five miscarriages. However, Sophie was a woman of great determination who went on to play a major role in imperial politics, and in August 1830 she finally gave birth to a son. He was to be named Franz Joseph, and to be followed by three brothers who all reached maturity, and a sister who died of epilepsy at the age of four. They were, in order of appearance:

Franz Joseph	1830
Ferdinand Maximilian	1832
Karl Ludwig	1833
Maria Anna	1835
Ludwig Victor	1842

The three older brothers were strong enough, but Ludwig Victor was very much a late-comer and was a sickly child. He was favoured by his mother and grew up to be effeminate, if not camp. He enjoyed dressing in women's clothes and chasing pretty boys, although he eventually married.

His three older brothers were more conventional. Franz Joseph made a fetish of conventionality: the imperial guard changed outside his nursery window every day, and he grew up to worship the military. He was given the strictest possible education, learning by rote from early morning until late at night, and was never encouraged or even allowed to think for himself. Other children might have resented and rebelled against this rigid upbringing. Franz Joseph did not. Instead, he taught himself to conquer his fears, as far as possible, and never to concede to an apparent obstacle unless absolutely necessary; and he was to retain this habit throughout his life.

Although naturally a nervous and shy child who was by instinct scared of horses, Franz Joseph taught himself to be a good rider, and finally an excellent one, still capable of providing a display of accomplished horsemanship in his eighties. He also proved an acceptable soldier, although it was noticeable that it was the predictability of peace-time drill and manoeuvres that really appealed to this cautious collector, never happier than when assembling his massive collection of model soldiers and putting them out in perfect display, rather than dreaming of death or glory on the battlefield for himself. His attitude was commonplace. European armies were full of officers like Franz Joseph, more addicted to ceremony and drill than the reality of war.

In 1835 Franz Joseph's uncle the emperor Franz 1 died, to be succeeded by the epileptic Ferdinand. Ferdinand's reign as emperor lasted a respectable 13 years, although it is to be doubted that he made any decisions. However, by 1848 the empire was in crisis, and it was necessary that Ferdinand resign. Rather than that he should be succeeded by the well-meaning but incompetent Franz Karl, his younger brother, it was decided to elevate Franz Joseph to be emperor at the age of 18; a decision in which his mother Sophie, the 'only man in the Hofburg', played a considerable part.

What began as an accession in crisis became the longest period of unbroken dynastic rule in contemporary Europe, for Franz Joseph was to last in power for an astonishing 68 years, from 1848 to 1916[7], when he died of natural causes—unlike his brother Maximilian, his son Rudolf, and his wife Elizabeth, as well as other relatives, including the heir apparent. However, almost no-one would have predicted, in 1848, that Franz Joseph was a contender who would last the course.

1848 was a significant year in European history, not so much for what it achieved but for what it threatened, which was nothing less than the stability and indeed the survival of many of the crowned heads of Europe. Demonstrations began, as was often the case, in Paris, and rapidly became riots, leading to insurrection. It was a spontaneous movement, not orchestrated by intellectuals seeking planned political change, and therefore, perhaps, all the stronger for it; for when the mob rose, as it had arisen before in Paris in 1789, the establishment trembled.

The mob was unpredictable. The mob had a character of its own. The mob fed on its own behaviour, and manufactured its own grievances, if there were not enough to hand, and created its own demands. The mob was insatiable. It could only be controlled by violence: the superior violence of the state. But if too much violence was used, the consequences would be disastrous for the regime, which would lose its legitimacy. Moreover, those who exercised the violence—the soldiers, gendarmes and policemen of the ancient regime—came from the same background as the rioters themselves. If they themselves could be 'radicalised'—a word which was not to come into common use for another century and a half, but which perfectly describes what needed to occur—then they would cease to fire on the rioters, and join them behind the barricades.

In February 1848 the situation in France reached melt-down, and King Louis-Philippe abdicated. The young firebrands Karl Marx and Friedrich Engels published the Communist Manifesto—*Workers, unite! You have nothing to lose but your chains!*—but this was not to have an immediate effect. The workers of Vienna and Budapest had more than their chains to lose, and had no intention of uniting as the international proletariat of which Marx dreamed, and which he was never to see successful in his lifetime. Although Viennese workers sought to achieve political change, the 1848 events were led more by bourgeois radicals than the proletariat itself.

Trouble was not restricted to Austria. Major demonstrations took place in Italy, which had yet to be united, and much of which was under Austrian rule. If that were not enough, there was major trouble in Hungary, always a potential source of danger to the Hapsburgs. The Magyars, the dominant race in Hungary, and originally a tribe of central Asian origin, had always chafed under Hapsburg restraint, and believed that Hungary deserved to play a far more important role in the empire.

In March 1848 the Hungarian patriot Lajos Kossuth made a speech in the Hungarian diet or parliament, calling for a restructuring of the empire and the virtual autonomy of Hungary. Major agitation followed in Vienna, and Count Metternich, who had in effect controlled the Austrian Empire and certainly its foreign policy since resettling Europe at the Congress of Vienna in 1815, was forced to resign. He fled to England.

By the autumn of 1848 there was major violence in Vienna, which was put down with great brutality by the army, still loyal to the Hapsburgs. Ferdinand abdicated and Franz Karl renounced his turn to succeed. Franz Joseph, untainted by recent events, and having briefly proved his courage on the Italian front in the neighbourhood of artillery fire, became emperor.

It seemed unlikely that he would remain in office for very long. He was very young; he was almost wholly inexperienced; and he had no Count Metternich to rely upon. The agitations in Vienna might die down, especially if he took a firm hand in repressing them; but Hungary was quite another matter. However, Franz Joseph dealt with this problem by inviting Russian intervention, and showed himself a firm believer in the strong hand; 'between 1848 and 1853 Franz Joseph signed and confirmed more death sentences than any other European ruler throughout the whole of the 19th century.' (Op. cit., page 20).

Death sentences, of course, were not enough. A ruler had to be respected as well as feared, and it were better still if he were loved (although Machiavelli disagreed.) But this Franz Joseph, with his cold, dry, manner and inability to communicate with his people, was unable to achieve. As Van der Kiste notes (op.cit., page 21):

'Those who worked with Franz Joseph noticed that he had an excellent memory, a keen desire to solve problems as soon as possible, and a lack of patience with people who would have liked him to consider decisions more deeply.' These characteristics were to remain with him.

Franz Joseph survived a serious attempt at assassination in 1853, and married in 1854, having fallen in love with the beautiful and fascinating but unsuitable Elizabeth of Bavaria. His marriage was a disaster, for the self-centred and dangerously obsessive Empress Elizabeth proved wholly incapable of fulfilling any imperial role; but the couple were able to produce four children altogether, three girls and a boy, the Crown Prince Rudolf. On his slender shoulders rested the hopes of the Hapsburgs for the future of the dynasty. It was to prove a false hope.

In 1866, Austria was defeated by the Prussians at the battle of Koniggratz, and lost its leadership of the German-speaking world. That role was taken over by the Prussians under Bismarck, who went on to unify the German states and to make Germany itself become the dominant Germanic power in Europe—a position held for so long by the Hapsburgs.

The troubles with the Hungarians continued, and in 1867 the emperor Franz Joseph was forced to reach an accommodation with his rebellious Magyar subjects, so that the Austrian Empire became the dual monarchy of Austria and Hungary. Franz Joseph made sure that the new imperial arrangements included joint ministries for finance, foreign affairs and war, and in those areas Vienna ruled and the empire spoke with one voice. As a true Hapsburg, Franz Joseph was determined to continue to rule by absolute power and not democratic consultation; and a dual monarchy did not necessarily impede this process. One parliament would have diluted his powers. Two imperial parliaments allowed him, on occasion, to play off one against the other.

Franz Joseph's imperial inheritance

As we have seen, Franz Joseph came to the throne as a raw eighteen years old youth in 1848, when the Austrian Empire was in crisis. What did he inherit? As Professor Alan Sked summarises the facts (Sked, 2001, page 1) Franz Josef inherited in 1848 an empire of about one quarter of a million square miles, which amounted to the largest area in Europe, after Russia, to be ruled by a single sovereign. The empire contained 37.5 million inhabitants, who could be further sub-classified as follows:

Germans	8 million
Magyars	5.5
Italians	5
Czechs	4
Ruthenes	3
Rumanians	2.5

Poles	2
Slovaks	Almost 2
Serbs	1.5
Croats	Almost 1.5
Slovenes	Over 1
Jews	.75

And over half a million others, including Gypsies, Armenians, Bulgars and Greeks.

Although Germans were therefore the largest single group in the Hapsburg Empire, they were easily outnumbered by other groups in combination. It is noteworthy that the Hapsburg empire in 1848 contained a large number of Italians, people who were neither Slav nor German, and with whom the empire tended to be very unpopular; and that the Magyars, with only 5.5 million people, were disproportionately successful in their quest for power within the empire, compared with other non-German groups. We may also note that the Magyars were extraordinarily successful in dominating Hungarian politics.

Hungary is supposedly the land of the Magyars, who are to be distinguished both by their racial origins and their language which is almost unique in Europe, being related only to Finnish and Estonian. However, the Magyars are not the only race to live in Hungary, which throughout the 19th century contained substantial racial and ethnic minorities, including Gypsies and Jews as well as other ethnic minorities such as Rumanians. All these groups were systematically under-represented in the Hungarian Diet or Parliament, which was a Magyar stronghold; and the gypsies, then as (almost) now, were not represented at all.

Magyars and Slavs

If the Magyars were a constant thorn in the flesh of the emperor's Austrian-German subjects, the Slavs were the major problem in the empire, which always rested on the achievement of a precarious balance between opposing forces. That balance was sometimes so difficult to achieve that it became an end in itself. The task of the emperor, or his chief minister, was not so much to set policy but to create a means whereby this multi-cultural phenomenon could continue to survive; and the Ausgleich or compromise as set up by Franz Joseph in 1867, was depending on one's point of view, either a masterpiece of constitutional engineering or a recipe for disaster, since it was almost certain to ensure that no clear policy was achieved by the empire as a unity.

Kakania

The late Hapsburg Empire was a ramshackle affair, a broken pot held together by wire. Cynics believed that the empire was not something to be reformed, lest the pot disintegrate altogether; and there were plenty of cynics in the last days of the Austro-Hungarian Empire, within the administration as well as outside it. Indeed, it was fashionable to be cynical, and a romantic pessimism conveyed the spirit of the times and was reflected in the literature of such writers as Stephan Zweig (one of whose short stories is named simply, *Beware of Pity*) and Robert Musil (whose lengthy magnum opus, *A Man Without Qualities*, is set in the allegorical empire of Kakania—a land of lost content. Kakania derives its name from the description of the top army regiments as kaiserlich und koeniglich— imperial and royal, or in abbreviation, k. und k.)

Franz Joseph as father figure

In 1914, Franz Joseph had been in power for so long that he had become a national institution in his own right, and it was impossible for the ordinary person to imagine the empire without him. The aged emperor still worked a full day in his simple office in the imperial palace, and kept to the same timetable throughout the year. Rather like a piece of very old but still robust furniture, he still served a purpose. He was conversant with the different habits, customs and practices of his empire, and did not discriminate between its citizens. Indeed, he was just as happy in talking to an Orthodox priest, Jewish rabbi, or Islamic cleric, even though he was a practising Roman Catholic. In Franz Joseph's simple creed, he was the emperor for everyone: a sort of universal father[8].

However, not all of his subjects accepted that relationship; and although much of his time was spent dealing with problems raised by Hungary and the Hungarians, it was the Slavs who were to prove the most dangerous threat to the peace and stability of Franz Joseph's empire.

NOTES

[1]Rome began as a republic in 509 BC and became an empire in 27 BC.

[2]The Holy Roman Empire, of which many Hapsburg rulers were also emperors, was an extraordinary intuition that had little or nothing to do with ancient Rome, and was essentially Germanic. It was conventionally dated from 962 to 1806 and collapsed during the Napoleonic Wars.

[3]Constantinople remained the capital of the Ottoman Empire until that empire came to an end in 1923. Constantinople then became the capital of the Turkish republic and was renamed Istanbul in 1930. The capital of Turkey is now Ankara, in Anatolia, but Istanbul, on the Bosphorus, remains Turkey's largest and most cosmopolitan city.

[4]There is a need, as always, to distinguish between prejudice and facts. Byzantium/Constantinople, the capital of the eastern Roman Empire, was a highly civilised city; and its conquest by the Ottoman Turks in 1453 did not make it any less civilised. It remained a highly cultured and sophisticated metropolis, in which Greek was the language of choice and a very large number of officials, including a large proportion of the Grand Viziers, were not Osmanli Turks. The Ottoman Empire tended to have a bad press, and was certainly capable of extreme brutality in crushing rebellion within its territories; but it also showed some surprising features, for example in its absence of an hereditary aristocracy of Osmanli origin. The Sultan was a Turk, but his officials need not be.

[5]British foreign policy varied. The realist Disraeli tended to support the Turks, although that did not stop him from acquiring the former Turkish colony of Cyprus in 1870. The more idealistic Gladstone condemned the Turkish massacres of their Christian subjects in Bulgaria, in pursuit of an apparently more ethical foreign policy.

[6]In this context it is significant to note that an imperial hero such as Colonel Nicolson, whose efforts, perhaps more than those of any other single soldier, were responsible for crushing the Indian Mutiny of 1857, was an Ulster protestant from Lisburn in what is now Northern Ireland. Successful empires practise divide-and-rule: and some of their most effective operatives come from transplanted minorities. Like the Osmanli Janissaries, they are the servants of the state.
For a searing account of what it was actually like to live as an ordinary citizen in the capital city of the greatest empire in the world, the reader is encouraged to consider 'The People of the Abyss', by Jack London, published in 1903.

[7]Queen Victoria reigned for 63 years, from 1837 to 1901. George III reigned from 1760 to 1820, although his rule included periods of madness and for the last ten years his son was regent. Louis XIV (1638-1715), the 'sun-king', ruled France as an absolute monarch for 72 years, and achieved the longest European reign.

[8]Perhaps it was not entirely a coincidence that the psycho-analyst Sigmud Freud (1856-1939), who was born in Moravia and practised in Vienna, believed that a

healthy son should rebel against his father. Freud himself had little time for the Hapsburgs, whom he is reported to have described as having left behind them 'nothing but a pile of shit.'

CHAPTER TWO

Geography, history and politics:
Serbia and Bosnia

Serbia is the archetypal Balkan state, and its present, if not its future, is to some extent dominated by its past. We begin with the battle of Kosovo on 28 June 1389, which is the key to the Serbian history, the construction of Serbian identity, and the Serbian soul.

The Battle of Kosovo: History, legend and myth

The battle of Kosovo marked an Ottoman victory over the Serbs and resulted in the absorption of Serbia into the Ottoman Empire for 400 years. It is of epochal significance in Serbian history, and has been cited as evidence that:

    a.   Serbia was an independent kingdom before 1389, and
            deserved to be so once again;
    b.   Kosovo was an historic part of Serbia; and
    c.   Serbia had an heroic tradition of sacrificial assassination
            which could and should inspire future generations.

Legend asserts that during the battle, a Serbian nobleman found his way into the Sultan's tent and was able to assassinate the Turkish military commander with a dagger, being put to death afterwards. Whether or not this really occurred is something over which historians can and do argue. Its effect on the outcome of the battle was nil. However, its significance as myth is beyond question.

The raw facts of Serbian history are easily summarised. In the third century BC, the Romans arrived in the area. In AD 305 the emperor Theodosius divided the Roman Empire between Rome and Byzantium. Serbia went to the eastern Roman Empire (the dividing line was the River Drina, which put Bosnia in the western empire.) During the sixth century, Slavic tribes crossed the Danube and occupied much of the Balkan peninsula, including Serbia. In 879 the Serbs were converted to Christianity by Saints Cyril and Methodius. Serbian Christianity allied itself with Byzantium and evolved into the Eastern Orthodox Church, which holds its services in Old Slavonic.

Serbia was briefly independent from 1217, with a golden age under King Stefan Dusan, 1346-55; but Turkish rule followed the battle of Kosovo in 1389, and the Turks occupied and ruled Serbia for the next 400 years. In 1815, the Serbs rebelled against a Turkish empire in decline, and achieved a *de facto* independence. Complete independence followed in 1878, as a result of the Treaty of San Stefano which concluded a short war between Russia and Turkey from 1877 to 1878, and which was accompanied by a Serbian uprising in both Serbia and Montenegro against Ottoman rule. Russian victory led to a major loss of territory for the Ottoman Empire in Europe. The Treaty of San Stefano was modified by the Treaty of Berlin which followed later in the same year, but the latter treaty did not alter Serbia's independence[1].

Regicide and its consequences

Serbia, which had declared itself a monarchy in 1882, contained two rival dynasties: the Obrenovic family and their Karageorgevic opponents. They had been locked in a struggle as to who was to rule Serbia, whether as prince or king, for the whole of the nineteenth century; and the two rival families had conspired against each other as well as against the Turks.

In 1903, as a result of a bloody regicide which shocked the rest of Europe, King Alexander (Obrenovic) and his wife were savagely murdered in a military coup and King Peter I (Karageorgevic) came to power. He was to rule Serbia and then the new state of Yugoslavia until his death in 1921, when the Obrenovic dynasty was vanquished.

Despite the international unpopularity of the new regime as installed in 1903, Serbia managed to retain its independence and to ward off the economic domination of the Austro-Hungarian Empire. The dual monarchy thought that it could dominate under-developed Serbia by controlling her market for exports, but proved unable to do so. An economic boycott of Serbian goods (the so-called pig war of 1906) failed to damage the Serbian economy as expected, and to drive them back into the Austrian economic fold: the Serbs were able to find both new customers for their products and new means by which to export them, and Serbia's lack of access to the sea did not prove a crippling disadvantage on this occasion[2].

In 1908, the dual monarchy formally accessed Bosnia. This was a source of huge resentment amongst the protesting classes in Belgrade, who identified themselves with their Serb brethren across the Drina, and believed that the proper future for Bosnia was in a closer relationship with Serbia. However, the Serbian government took no action against its stronger neighbour, and the annexation was in effect accepted as a *fait accompli*.

Serbia played a major role in the First and Second Balkan Wars (1912-1913), which resulted in the further decline of the Ottoman Empire in Europe and a substantial victory for local nationalism and nation-building in the Balkans. In the First Balkan War, the Serbs and others were able to achieve major victories over the Turks. In the Second Balkan War, the victors of the previous conflict fought each other for the spoils[3].

In summary, at the beginning of the twentieth century Serbia could be seen as a small and poor but independent country with some useful allies and some prospects of economic and political development.

On the plus side, it had defeated the Turks and achieved (or re-achieved, depending on one's interpretation of history) national independence. It had resisted Austro-Hungarian domination and it had established useful relationships with both Russia and Germany. It was beginning to develop an educated middle class who would be capable of acting as a competent bureaucracy[4]. It was not bedevilled, as other Balkan nations, by religious and ethnic division. Serbia had a clear identity and a relatively homogeneous population (with the exception of areas such as Kosovo.) It had both pride and prospects.

On the other hand, Serbia's internal politics were much too volatile; the army was far too deeply involved in politics; and the existence and activities of secret societies such as the Black Hand, which had arisen out of national resentment at the Austrian annexation of Bosnia in 1908, were a major force for destabilisation5. Economic development was possible, despite the lack of access to the sea. But economic development rested, as always, on political stability and the absence of war, both of which were necessary if capital investment were to be achieved from abroad. Left to themselves, Serbian politicians might have been capable of ensuring the continuing independence and economic growth of their country: but they were not to be left to themselves.

Bosnia

As with Serbia, we begin with the Roman Empire. The Romans conquered Illyria in AD 9, and it became an important province of the empire, in demand both for its minerals and the usefulness of its inhabitants as soldiers. The coastal part of Illyria, Dalmatia, became an important trading centre for the Roman Empire and was to acquire an international population; and the port of Ragusa (now Dubrovnic) established the reputation as a centre of both commerce and culture for which it is still known.

By whom was Illyria inhabited, what languages did they speak, and what religions did they follow? The answers to these questions are not entirely clear; but we may be sure that the native 'Illyrians' were not Slavs, did not speak Serbo-Croat, were gradually converted to various forms of Christianity from earlier faiths, including paganism; and were not Moslem.

Racial origins and movements

The Slavs were a Eurasian race, some of whom had migrated into central Europe, and who moved into the Balkans as the western Roman Empire collapsed. Russia (as opposed to the former USSR, which contained a huge variety of ethnic groups) is essentially a Slav nation, although its capital, Moscow, had been founded by roving Norse invaders who travelled to what was to become Moscow by river.

Some Slavs gradually moved into the Balkans, including what is now Bosnia, from the sixth century AD onwards. The name Yugoslavia refers to the nation of the South Slavs, and nineteenth century Russians were wont to refer to the South Slavs as their 'little brothers'[6].

Language

Serbo-Croat was a much later development, a politically motivated combination of the officially separate languages of Serb and Croat (which were in fact closely related). It became an official language only when the Serbs, Croats and Slovenes joined forces to become a new kingdom as a result of the Treaty of Versailles in 1919. (We must note that both Serbs and Croats are Slavs, the result of the Slav population shift from Asia to Europe. If racial classification means anything, they are members of the same race.)

Religion

As for religion, the Roman Empire had been slowly impregnated by the new religion of Christianity from the first century AD onwards, although Pontius Pilate had agreed the execution of its Founder; and the emperor Constantine, (272-337 AD), who had been born in what is now Serbia, had officially proclaimed the empire to be Christian after establishing his new eastern capital in Byzantium.[7]

Constantine's conversion and proclamation did not mean that Illyria became Christian overnight, although Christianity in various forms, including the fascinating paradox of the Bogomil heresy, did eventually take hold there.[8] The two forms of Christianity most popular in the Balkans were Roman Catholicism and the Eastern Orthodox faith. They emerged from the division of the Roman Empire between Rome and Constantinople in 1054 AD. The later-to-be-recognised state of Serbia was (and is) predominantly Eastern Orthodox, whereas Croatia, which has been associated with Hungary since 1102, is predominantly Roman Catholic. Bosnia has three main faiths, including Islam.

Islam was a post-Roman development that may be precisely dated to the life and teachings of the Prophet Mohammed, whose 'combination of qualities enabled him to build up out of nothing in ten years [during the decade from 622 to 632 AD] an empire that was ready to conquer the world' (Runciman, 1951.)

Independence

After the Romans ceased to rule Illyria, the area corresponding to modern Bosnia came under the rule of local chieftains, of whom the most signifcant were Ban Kulin (1180 to 1204), Ban Stephen Kotromaric (1322 to 1353) and King Stefan Tvrtko 1 (1353 to 1391) who crowned himself as King of Bosnia in 1377.

Although medieval Bosnia achieved both peace and prosperity for part of this period, and although its area corresponded to some extent to modern Bosnia's boundaries, it was not a golden age to be looked back upon with nostalgia and longing.

Serbia had its dreams of the past, real, mythical and a combination of both, to look back upon and use as the basis for nineteenth century nationalism and independence: for Serbia had once been, if only for a brief period, a large, powerful, independent and united kingdom.

Bosnia had no such past on which to draw. Bosnia's history was largely one of subjection, to the Romans, the Turks, and finally the dual monarchy of Austria-Hungary; and its periods of independence from any empire could simply if cynically be described as one of uncertainty for those alive at the time, and confusion for those historians who later attempted to analyse what had been going on—whether or not they had axes to grind.

The Ottoman Conquest of Bosnia

In 1483 the whole area of the western Balkans was invaded and conquered by the Ottoman Turks.[9] They were an Asiatic peoples who had moved westwards out of Asia into Anatolia; conquered the Byzantine empire and seized its capital, Constantinople; absorbed the Islamic faith which was up till then Arabic; threatened to conquer the whole of Europe itself; and went on to maintain Bosnia as part of the Ottoman Empire for the next 400 years.

Characteristics of the Ottoman Empire and Ottoman Bosnia

The chief characteristic of the Ottoman Empire in its expansionist phase was its unquenchable urge to conquer. The Turks were an invincible military force, but unlike the Romans they were not inspired by an imperial ideal. There was no mission to put the Sublime Porte at the centre of a new civilisation. Instead, the Turks were prepared to deploy the accomplishments, skills and talents of those whom they conquered, in order to make the Ottoman empire itself still larger and more successful—on an eclectic basis.

The Turks were not, on the whole, organisers, and the records of their empire do not show a genius for administration. Their method of organising was not to organise, but to leave it to others; and if the Sublime Porte, under the influence of some new and ambitious Sultan, did attempt reform, it was difficult if not impossible for an edict from Constantinople to reach the farthest parts of the empire and to be applied there.

The Ottoman Turks decorated the towns in which they preferred to live, and the minarets of their mosques were graceful and inspiring. They administered, a little, and they traded, to some extent. They practised a form of justice, although it remained mysterious to the adherents of Roman law. They farmed; or at least they made sure that the native peasants did so on their behalf. In other words, they did what they needed to do, in order to lead comfortable and often indolent lives, at least judged by western standards.

Those standards were culturally biased. The later spectators of the Ottoman Empire such as Arthur Evans were the product of an industrial civilisation based on the protestant work ethic: a concept which would have been incomprehensible to the Turks. Evans, moreover, was experiencing an Ottoman Empire which had already been in existence for 500 years, and was showing many signs of wear and tear.

The Ottoman Turks believed in Islam, but like the Arabs before them were tolerant of other faiths, at least those of the Book (which meant the Jews and the Christians. Under Arab rule, tolerance had extended to Zoroastrianism.) The Ottoman Turks did not set out to destroy Christianity, nor to convert the majority of Bosnians to Islam. [10] Over time, Bosnia did gain a substantial Moslem minority. They tended to be Serbs who had converted to Islam, rather than Osmanli Turks who had moved to Bosnia; and their motives were probably on the whole economic rather than religious. Under Turkish rule, Moslems had some advantages.

The Janissary System

The Turks were conquerors. A major asset was the Janissary system, a process almost unique to the Ottoman empire: the key to its success during its expansionist phase, which became a threat to its stability and even continued survival, once conquest turned to stagnation and then decay.

Janissaries were professional soldiers, forbidden to marry, who lived in barracks and served the Sultan in his wars of conquest and retention. They had been seized as small boys from throughout the empire, and were of any race or background. Having been forcibly conscripted, they were raised as Moslem soldiers, with a fanatical loyalty to the Sultan who had become their substitute father.[11] They were able to rise on their merits to the highest positions in an empire in which there was no official preference for Osmanli Turks, and many of the Sublime Porte's most senior officials were of Balkan origin. As they reached maturity, they were able to contact their original families once again; but the familial link had been broken.

This was the force that conquered the Balkans, and threatened Vienna and the whole of Europe. As the Turkish empire changed from growth to maturity to decline, so that the traditions of the Janissaries changed also: they became corrupt and self-serving, and decided for themselves the right to choose the next sultan. In 1826, they were destroyed by a sultan who had finally had enough, and used other army units to massacre them. But for hundreds of years they had been the mainstay of the most powerful empire in the world, whose capital had been its largest city.

Indirect rule

Generally speaking, the Ottoman Turks ruled Bosnia from afar, and did not prove especially oppressive conquerors. They acted through intermediaries, and their main demand was for revenue, which was raised by a host of what were in effect tax-farmers, operating at both local and regional levels. The ordinary peasant was able to survive under these circumstances, and even to achieve a modest wealth if that were within his capabilities, provided that he did not criticise or oppose the system.

The peasant paid taxes on almost everything, and the officials who raised those taxes were on the whole corrupt, venal and inefficient; but they knew enough not to kill the source that fed them, and the peasant was able to cope with their demands, both for taxation and forced labour on occasion. He was not forced to convert to Islam, but was able to continue his traditional religious practices: Christianity was an accepted practice in the Ottoman empire, and the Christians were not persecuted but tolerated.

They were, after all, people of the Book (the Koran), and Jesus had been accepted as a prophet by the Prophet. Bosnian Christians were not allowed to ride on horseback, or carry arms, or wear the colour green (which was sacred to Islam), and they could not bring a case against a Moslem in court. But they were able to build their own dwellings, to grow crops, work as craftsmen, and trade; and to marry and raise their families in peace, provided that they accepted their place in the empire.

Decline and unrest

Gradually this tolerable state of affairs was to decline, and the life of the peasant in Bosnia (and especially in Herzegovina) was to become unbearable. There was a tradition of agrarian uprisings in the Balkans, in which increasingly desperate peasants confronted increasingly oppressive landlords and tax-farmers; and as the Ottoman empire declined, so the demands for revenue from the centre became more pressing, and its control over the venality and corruption of its administrators less and less effective.

The Ottoman empire had been created by force; and it relied on force for its survival. The forces at the hand of the Sultan and his administrators were considerable. There were the janissaries; and in the provinces, there was a tradition of unleashing irregular forces in order to enforce the will of the local bey, who were accountable to no-one save themselves. These attack dogs were known as the bashi-bazouks, and their ferocious reputation was a deserved one. They were able to sustain Ottoman rule by force, if not terror; but their actions had consequences.

The Great Eastern Uprising (1875-1878) and its consequences

Peasants in Herzegovina began an agrarian uprising in 1875 and were soon joined by their Bosnian fellow-sufferers. Rural uprisings were relatively common in the more remote regions of the Ottoman Empire as it entered its phase of inexorable decline. They usually arose because peasant life had become unbearable as a result of poor harvests and crippling taxation; and they were usually put down with great severity— until the next time.

This uprising was different.

Firstly, it was on a much greater scale than the usual uprising, and having started, it continued, with the rural population of Herzegovina and Bosnia declaring liberated areas where they attempted to regulate their own affairs.

Secondly, it attracted significant international attention. The Balkans were not quite as remote as they had once been, and travellers from Western Europe were beginning to explore their dusty plains and mountain fortresses and to report on what they found. The carefully-researched and strongly written reports of the investigative journalist Arthur Evans were published in that fountain of liberal opinion, the *Manchester Guardian*, and sympathy was easily aroused for the Christian victims of Muslim oppressors.

Sympathy led to practical outcome, in support for the humanitarian work of the redoubtable Miss A. P. (Pauline) Irby, a Victorian traveller and philanthropist who had founded a school for girls in Sarajevo in 1870, and went on to organize famine relief. [12]

Partly as a result of this exposure, and partly because the Foreign Office had an abiding interest in the balance of power in an area where four major international players had an interest[13], the situation in the Balkans became an important issue in British politics.

Disraeli generally favoured the continuing support of the Ottoman Empire as a force for stability in the area, whereas Gladstone took up the Christian cause both in Bulgaria and Bosnia. He wrote a preface to Miss Irby's book and supported her work, and wrote a polemic calling for the Turks to be expelled from Europe as a result of their atrocities in Bulgaria, which had an enormous circulation. However, it was Disraeli who represented Great Britain at the conference of Berlin in 1878 which was intended to resolve the issues raised in the Great Eastern Uprising and make a sensible settlement at the end of the Russo-Turkish war. At this stage, Disraeli the imperial pragmatist was prepared to accept and endorse the changes to the Ottoman Empire which needed to take place; and the great powers proceeded to make those changes without consulting the minor powers involved.

As a result of the Treaty that followed the Congress of Berlin in 1878, which was held at least in part to make sure that Russia did not make disproportionate gains from its victory over Turkey in the previous year, Serbia and other countries gained their independence. Bosnia gained a new master: the dual monarchy, which was to administer the territory 'on behalf of the Sultan'. She thus passed straight from one imperial power to another.

Austro-Hungarian priorities

Since the expansion of the Ottoman Empire in the fifteenth century, Bosnia had been a Turkish domain. The Hapsburg empire had created the Military Frontier in an attempt to prevent further expansion of the Turkish empire into Croatia, which was an Hungarian possession; but by the mid-nineteenth century the Ottoman Empire was no longer a threat to its Hapsburg neighbour.

There was a strong case for absorbing Bosnia as a means to rationalise the boundaries of the empire in this area; to give wider access to the Adriatic; and to prevent other powers such as Germany or Russia from moving in. There was also a strong case for not doing so, mainly because it would upset the racial balance within the empire and lead to problems with the Hungarians, who would be jealous of a Slav influx.

What was the emperor to do? As a natural conservative, Franz Joseph favoured the *status quo*, although he considered the military option from time to time. When he finally acted in 1908, the risk of serious fighting seemed at its lowest, and the prospect of victory was almost a certainty. This expectation proved to be correct. Some local fighting took place as the Austrian troops advanced and occupied the towns, and losses occurred; but the forces of the dual monarchy were soon victorious. [14]

The Ottoman empire accepted a *fait accompli* which it was too weak to oppose; and the international community as a whole abided by the terms of the Treaty of Berlin. There was spontaneous opposition to what had happened in Belgrade, where the populace as a whole was disgusted at what had taken place; but the Serbian government took no action. Austria had succeeded, and the Emperor Joseph had finally won a war, if only a very small one. Bosnia faced a bright future as part of the dual monarchy—or so it seemed.

Acquisiton, Government and Administration

Austria promised Turkey that:
  i.   The fact of annexation would not prejudice the rights of sovereignty of His Imperial Majesty the Sultan;

ii.   Turkish money would continue to circulate;
iii. Bosnian revenues would be used locally;
iv.   The administration would employ Turkish officials and Bosnian natives;
v.   The Muslims would enjoy freedom of religion; and
vi.   The name of the Caliph-Sultan would continue to be recited in Friday prayers.

However, as Malcolm (1996) points out, only the last two promises were properly kept. Turkish money was excluded; Bosnia was brought within the Austro-Hungarian customs union; and its administration was largely taken over by non-Bosnian citizens who were mainly of German-Austrian origin. Occupation would clearly be followed by full annexation when the right moment came; and when the Austrian Emperor joined the Three Emperors' league with Russia and Germany in 1881, one of the confidential clauses stated that 'Austria-Hungary reserves the right to annexe the provinces at whatever moment she shall deem opportune.'

The Austrian invasion of Bosnia was unpopular with its Bosnian Serb population, especially as the defects of Turkish administration receded into distant memory; and the new imperial power needed to station a large number of troops in the province to deal with local insurgencies. However, the Hapsburgs were used to such a situation, and had such troops stationed throughout the empire. Those troops were not of local origin and had no local ties. Like the janissaries, their loyalty was to the emperor.

A military presence, however, was necessary but not sufficient to ensure a successful administration. How was Bosnia to be administered?

Dualism by design: The two governors of Bosnia

In order to avoid allocating it to either Austria or Hungary and thus upset the balance of power within the empire, Bosnia was designated as crown land. It was therefore administered by the Minister of Finance, one of the three joint ministries in the dual monarchy as established in the 1867 *ausgleich* (compromise). In effect, the Minister of Finance was Governor of Bosnia simply by virtue of his office. However, Bosnia also possessed a military governor, and the two potentates did not always agree.

To some extent, this reflected imperial dissension in Vienna, and especially the rivalry that developed between Franz Joseph and his nephew

Franz Ferdinand. In the early twentieth century, Franz Ferdinand, the heir apparent with what amounted to his own administration in waiting in Vienna, tended to favour the person and policies of the military governor, whereas the aged emperor inclined more towards the views of the civil administration; and we shall see the consequences of this dual responsibility for Bosnia as our story unfolds.

Gradualism

Austrian policy in Bosnia reflected general imperial policy, which was one of gradualism. The aim, at least of the civil governor, was that the new territory would gradually be absorbed and assimilated into the Hapsburg empire, to the point where the Bosnians would come to see themselves as unquestioningly owing their primary loyalty to that empire and its emperor. Habit, political realities, and economic incentives would combine to enable the Bosnians, or at least the more moderate ones, to perceive that they had a better future within the empire than outside it; and their loyalties would adjust accordingly.

Some imperialists went further. The governor Benjamin von Kallay (who was appointed as Minister of Finance in 1882, and who died in post in 1903) was a professional bureaucrat of Hungarian background who believed in the imperial ideal and thought that it would be possible to create a new sense of Bosnian-Austrian identity. His plans failed because of the rival pressures on Bosnia of Serb and Croat nationalism. They would have failed in any case, it may be presumed, because of the counter-productive policies of the military governors and their rigid repression of dissent.

Investment in Bosnia

According to Malcolm, who presents a generally positive view of the dual monarchy and its benefits, the scale of post 1878 public investment in Bosnia was colossal, and by 1907 the government had built thousands of kilometres of roads and railways and 121 bridges. Moreover, it had not neglected education, no doubt at least partly because a modern state needed a literate population. Austria built nearly two hundred primary schools, three high schools, one technical school and one teacher training college (which the conspirator Danilo Ilic later attended). Some of these investments, of course, could be of military use as well as benefiting the economy; but they were still investments. The major industrial development that took place created a new proletariat, which was to have political and social as well as economic consequences. Foreign (i.e. German, Czech, Pole and Ruthenian) settlers were encouraged to settle in Bosnia and to take land on favourable terms. Given that a large number of Moslems left Bosnia for the Ottoman Empire proper after annexation in 1878, this meant wholesale demographic changes.

Architecture

The visitor to Sarajevo after 1878 would notice many new buildings, some of which were of undoubted architectural merit and added to its cosmopolitan aspect. Sarajevo was now visibly Austrian as well as Balkan in appearance, and the new constructions—schools, museums, churches, theatres, factories, breweries, barracks, banks and the inevitable government offices—were of symbolic as well as functional importance.

The Town Hall [15] which Franz Ferdinand was to visit on 28 June 1914 in between the two attempts on his life which took place on that day, was built in the orientalist or neo-moorish style and is an impressive building [16]. Some of the other new buildings tended to be in the baroque style which had been in fashion in Vienna, although reduced in proportion and of less grandiosity.[17] Provinical capitals must not outdo the imperial capital in splendour, although they might be used for experiments. (Street electric lighting was tried out in Sarajevo before it was used in Vienna, allegedly so that its safety might be first established on a Slav testing site.)

At the same time, the older buildings remained: the Austrians did not tear down in order to rebuild, and Sarajevo is a pleasing mixture not only of the scared and the secular, but of central European and Byzantine architectural styles.

Mosques, minarets and medrassas:A traditon of religious tolerance

The visitor who walks in an easterly direction along the neat and tidy quay beside the river Miljacka to the point where Franz Ferdinand was assassinated, and then turns and walks northwards and away from the river, will find himself in the old Turkish bazaar, in the midst of which are to be found mosques, minarets and a medrassa—as well as a centre for Hebrew studies which dates back to when the Ottoman Turks accepted Sephardic Jewish refugees into Sarajevo, as they were being expelled from Christian

Europe. Saraejvo is rightly proud of its traditions of religious diversity and tolerance, which have survived many conflicts.

Religious policy under the dual monarchy

Like the Roman and Ottoman Turk imperialists before them, the dual monarchy favoured a policy of religious tolerance. Although the Hapsburgs themselves and the great majority of the imperial aristocracy were Roman Catholics, other faiths were also tolerated and indeed encouraged as a force for stability—although the emperor preferred, where possible, to appoint the head of the church himself. It is noteworthy that the Bosnian 'Parliament' or Sabor of 1910 was constituted on religious lines:

Sabor, 1910

37	Orthodox
29	Muslim
23	Roman Catholic
I	Jew
Total	90

The emperor Franz Joseph was a supporter of a multi-cultural and religious society, and was happy to respect faiths other than his own—a policy which his nephew, with his characteristic illiberalism, supported with less enthusiasm.

Bureaucracy

According to Glenny (Glenny, 1999, page 268), the number of administrators in Bosnia increased under Austrian rule from 120 Muslims in 1878, to 9533 persons of different faiths in 1908—some of whom were locals, and some of whom had been imported from elsewhere in the empire. It is to be assumed that many of the senior administrators were of Austrian-German origin, although this would certainly not have applied to all of them: the Austro-Hungarian empire was a genuinely multi-racial and multi-cultural society, and did not only promote or make use of Austrians of German background (as we have already seen with Kallay). Indeed, class was probably a more significant factor than race. Many if not most senior officials were of aristocratic origin, and identified themselves automatically with the emperor and the ruling elite, which protected their interests and shared their outlook on life.

Austria-Hungary was not a totalitarian state, and although the emperor Franz Joseph might have wished otherwise, he was not an absolute ruler. Although there was censorship, there was also a relatively free and healthy press. There were parliaments, not only in Vienna and Budapest, but also elsewhere; and there was a tolerated opposition, which was able to express its dissent to government policies without being locked up for its pains. The difference between reform and revolution was accepted, at least in theory; and although the emperor himself was a massively conservative figure, both Crown Prince Rudolf and later the Archduke Franz Ferdinand indicated their intentions for wholesale reforms of the empire, by means of which to ensure its survival.

However, Austria-Hungary was by no means a liberal democracy, and although it accepted the rule of law, it practised legalised repression. Especially in newly acquired territories such as Bosnia any sort of political expression was severely limited, and the government's stick was more in evidence than its carrot—as we shall see in considering the official treatment of 'Young Bosnia', in the next chapter.

In summary, from 1878 onwards Bosnia was occupied and administered by the dual monarchy as a crown land which was the direct responsibility of the Ministry of Finance, although security was in effect the responsibility of the military governor. There was a relatively straightforward policy of gradual modernisation which applied to everything but the ownership of land, where the Austrian authorities were reluctant to change the Turkish system which they had inherited, and thereby upset the Moslem landowners. Although some of the more obvious injustices of the old system were rectified, no radical reform took place. There was heavy investment in the economic and social infrastructure and a significant change of population. Bosnia, in essence, was being 'Germanised'; and not everyone was happy with this, although opposition was neither organised nor openly articulated.

The Hapsburgs believed that they could absorb a new and significant Slavic influx into the imperial population by a mixture of incentive and repression; and we would suggest that for the majority of the population this policy was likely to prove successful. The advantages of joining the empire should be persuasive to those who remembered the stagnation of

Ottoman rule, and had no strong nationalistic views; and the powers of repression available to the state were considerable.

Clearly, there was no intention to return Bosnia's administration to the Sublime Porte in Istanbul; and in 1908 Vienna made its position absolutely clear by formally annexing Bosnia, taking advantage of the international political situation to do so. Annexation made no practical difference to administrative practice, since a heavy investment policy was already in place, and it was not expected that the change would lead to any real difficulties. Both politicians and military were for once in agreement in Vienna, and the emperor and heir apparent managed to speak as one. They thought that they had been rather clever: but their optimism was misplaced.

The Archduke Franz Ferdinand was to visit Bosnia for himself, in 1914, arriving in a resort named Ilidze, just outside Sarajevo, on 25 June. There he was reunited with his wife Sophie, who had proceeded by a different route. For two days, the archducal couple pursued parallel duties. On 26 and 27 June, the Archduke inspected the summer manoeuvres of the 15th and 16th Army Corps, which were the culmination of their annual training programme. At the same time, the Duchess Sophie inspected schools, hospitals and places of worship as part of her own programme. On the evening of 27 June, they held a formal dinner to celebrate their hotel. Their formal visit to Sarajevo was due to take place on the following day. The day in question was 28 June 1914.

THE BULGARIAN ATROCITIES

A pamphlet that W E Gladstone published in 1876, *Bulgarian Horrors and the Questions of the East*, attacked the Disraeli government for its indifference to the violent repression of the Bulgarian rebellion in the Ottoman Empire (Known as the Bulgarian April uprising) and achieved a remarkable circulation. An often-quoted excerpt illustrates his formidable rhetorical powers:

'Let the Turks now carry away their abuses, in the only possible manner, namely, by carrying off themselves. Their Zaptiehs and their Mudirs, their Bimbashis and Yuzbashis, their Kaimakams and their Pashas, one and all, bag and baggage, shall, I hope, clear out from the province that they have desolated and profaned. This thorough riddance, this most blessed deliverance, is the only reparation we can make to those heaps and heaps of dead, the violated purity alike of matron and of maiden and of child; to the civilization which has been affronted and shamed; to the laws of God, or, if you like, of Allah; to the moral sense of mankind at large. There is not a criminal in a European jail, there is not a criminal in the South Sea Islands, whose indignation would not rise and over-boil at the recital of that which has been done, which has too late been examined, but which remains unavenged, which has left behind all the foul and all the fierce passions which produced it and which may again spring up in another murderous harvest from the soil soaked and reeking with blood and in the air tainted with every imaginable deed of crime and shame. That such things should be done once is a damning disgrace to the portion of our race which did them; that the door should be left open to their ever so barely possible repetition would spread that shame over the world!'

NOTES

[1] The other great powers were strongly interested in the result of the Russo-Turkish war, and did not wish to see Russian interests triumph, nor the Ottoman Empire completely vanquished. Hence, the settlement achieved at San Stefano was modified in Berlin, at which great power interests dominated the debate and the lesser powers were barely permitted to speak. Nevertheless, the war resulted in major change. Romania and Montenegro gained their independence from the Ottoman Empire, and the entirely new state of Bulgaria was set up. At the same time, the dual monarchy gained the right to 'administer' Bosnia on behalf of the Sultan.

[2] It is, however, a constant factor in Serbian geopolitics and may help to explain its close relationship with Montenegro—a smaller and poorer country which had gained access to the sea.

[3] Forces fighting against the Ottomans consisted of troops from Bulgaria, Montenegro, Greece and Serbia, and irregular soldiers as well. Serbia's cause was popular with Young Bosnia and many Bosnian Serbs, including Gavrilo Princip, volunteered for active service.

[4] The roots of the University of Belgrade go back to 1808 and it was formally constituted in 1905.

[5] From the economic point of view, Serbia might have done better to concentrate on developing its own economy and infrastructure, rather than lusting after Bosnia as a possible acquisition. On the other hand, politics is not always dominated by economic reasoning. The Falklands War (1981) between the United Kingdom and Argentina

was a disaster for the Argentinian dictator, General Galtieri and a triumph for the British Prime Minister, Mrs Thatcher. Was either party really motivated by economic reasoning, despite the potential value of the seas around the Falklands? We doubt it.

6 The movement of peoples is one of the more complex and contentious areas of social studies. Peoples are not always easy to identify, nor are their movements clear to the latter-day historian. They do not simply move in one direction. They may return, as well as travel away. They may fight, conquer, inter-marry, or be absorbed, to disappear almost without trace. And history is, in any case, not always a disinterested search for the truth. In many cases, the task of the historian is to find the 'evidence' for a political construction of reality. Thus in Afrikaner-ruled South Africa it was important for the Apartheid regime to be able to prove that the Dutch had arrived, before the Bantu tribes moved into the area.

7 Byzantium, renamed Constantinople, was to be the centre of the eastern Roman Empire for a millennium.

8 The Bogomil heresy deserves either a book of its own, or to be left alone as a variation of Christianity only to be found in the Balkans, which has disappeared almost without trace. We have chosen the second option. For a detailed account of the Bogomil church, we suggest the relevant chapter in Noel Malcolm's Bosnia: a short history (Malcolm, 1996). As the Lonely Planet guide to the Western Balkans points out, this short history is far from short.

9 Bosnia was officially conquered in 1463 and Herzegovina in 1482.

10 This would have had disadvantages for the Ottoman Empire, which taxed Christians much more heavily than its Moslem subjects.

11 The Janissaries adopted a variation of Islam that allowed alcohol and did not emphasize the prohibitions of Ramadan.

12 Miss Irby 'adopted' Bosnia and Herzegovina and remained resident in Sarajevo until her death. She was not the first Englishwoman to change her life in such a way, and the tradition continues. One of Sarajevo's main streets is still named after her.

13 The four were Turkey; Russia; Austria-Hungary; and finally Germany, which had strong commercial interests in the Balkans and beyond, and intended to build a railway from Berlin to Baghdad. The United Kingdom had no vital interest in the Balkans and was more concerned for regional stability.

14 Total Austrian losses came to 946 dead and 3980 wounded (Malcolm, 1996, page 135.)

15 In American English this would be called the City Hall (see Remak, *passim*.)

16 Regrettably, the building was shelled and extensively damaged by artillery fire during the war from 1992 to 1995. (It was no longer the Town Hall and had become the National Library and a priceless repository of documents.) Happily, it is now under reconstruction. Its main architect, Alexander Wittek (1852-1894), was a

remarkable product of the empire, who had visited Cairo in order to research the project, and was a world-rated chess player as well as an architect. He was to lose his reason and end his days in a lunatic asylum in Graz.

[17] Vienna's most grandiose construction, the Ringstrasse, was not completed until the 20th Century, when part of it was officially opened by Kaiser Wilhelm II of Germany—a diplomatic gesture intended to emphasize the close relationship between the two Germanic empires which had met in war in 1866. As C. Northcote Parkinson commented in Parkinson's Law (1957), an empire, whether military or commercial, usually celebrates its success architecturally long after its point of greatest achievement has been passed and it is on the downward slope.

CHAPTER THREE

The Politics of Extremism:
Anarchism, Socialism and Nationalism in the Balkans

The development of political awareness in Bosnia

Political expression of any kind came relatively late to Bosnia, which was a Turkish province until 1878, whereafter it became part of the Austro-Hungarian Empire—although full annexation was not declared until 1908.

Bosnia under Turkish rule was not noted for its political activity. The main reasons for this were the active repression by the Turks and their local agents of anything which might have seemed rebellious, and the lack of general political awareness of the Bosnian population at large. This was directly related to the very low level of education to be found in Bosnia, and the lack of any sort of process by which political debate might take place.

In a province that lacked schools, newspapers, roads, railways, industry and unions, and in which most people made a living from the land as they had always done, radical political debate was hardly to be looked for, either from the intelligentsia or the proletariat: for neither could be said to exist.

Under the Turkish administration, very few Bosnians went to school, and none or almost none to university—for which they would in any case have had to travel outside the Turkish Empire, to Vienna, Prague, or Zagreb, or even further afield, for Istanbul had no such institution. [1]

The bright boy might hope for some form of education with the church; but if he were successful in this endeavour, he was likely to become a monk or a priest, and was therefore unlikely to engage in political debate, for he had other items on his agenda.

After 1878, he might also try to join the military school, and obtain his education by that means; but that committed him to service in the imperial army, in which military officers, substantive or prospective, were expected to respect and uphold the *status quo* rather then engage in political debate; and in any case it was only an avenue of opportunity to a small minority.

The Hapsburg Empire recognised that education was important, but had to begin the process more or less from scratch, by building primary schools and training the teachers that they needed.

Such schools presented a problem in defining and promoting loyalty. The administration needed to decide what ought to be taught, and for what purpose. The authorities had no desire to create an educated class which would not be loyal to them. The curriculum offered within the new schools needed to be carefully controlled so as to ensure that an educated (and therefore more useful) population still knew its place.

However, no regime except the most totalitarian is entirely able to control what happens in the class-room, and perhaps more importantly, in the school environment in general; and the new secondary schools which were created in towns such as Mostar and Sarajevo became hotbeds of political intrigue.

The new generation of educated Bosnians began their education late— Gavrilo Princip first went to school at the age of nine—and were therefore ready for political intrigue at an age when in other circumstances they would be already at university, but in Bosnia they were still at school.

The situation was made worse in that the Austrian authorities banned any form of association in Bosnian schools, even sporting associations, for fear, presumably, that they would be a cover for nationalist activities. In banning such associations, they naturally made them much more popular: for which adolescent has never felt the urge to break the rules?

Since open associations were forbidden, secret societies sprang up overnight like mushrooms in the Bosnian forest, and the young Bosnians who might otherwise have been playing football, or in other ways diverting their energies into non-political activities, found an almost unnatural interest in politics, literature and national history—a situation which was to lead to conflict not only between the students and the authorities, but between the younger generation in Bosnia and their parents, who were generally conservative.

The policy of repressive authoritarianism by such die-hards as General Potiorek, military governor of Bosnia in 1914, fostered just the sort of rebelliousness which it sought to suppress. Bosnian students—it seems absurd to call them school-boys, for these were strapping young men who grew moustaches and affected fedoras as a fashion item—could not be repressed by authority, whose last resort was to close the schools. This meant even more political intrigue, since the students no longer had examinations to work for.

From this atmosphere emerged Young Bosnia, a revolutionary organisation dedicated to the emancipation of the homeland and its freedom from the *Schwabe*—a term of contempt used by the Bosnians for both Germans and Austrians.

Young Bosnia

As much as anyone else, the brilliant young student Vladimir Gacinovic founded Young Bosnia—for which he was inspired by the example of Young Italy. Young Bosnia was not a formal organisation, with a chairman, set of regulations, and subscription charge, but a loose federation of students and young people who shared revolutionary ideals. As we have seen, repression tended to foster what it sough to crush, and the secret societies founded at Mostar high school included a secret library, a secret literary society, and a society named Sloboda (Freedom), headed by a peasant's son named Bogdan Zerajic, which concerned itself with ethics and politics.

Vladimir Gacinovic was a prominent member of Sloboda, and wrote extensively on nationalism, socialism and revolution for the interest of his fellow students. He was an intense young man, and was described as carrying to extremes 'a tendency to feel the sufferings of the society in which he lived as though they were his own' (Dedijer, page 177)—a description which also applies to Gavrilo Princip. Both Zerajic and Gacinovic are to play an important part in our story.

A new morality

It might have been expected that Young Bosnia would concentrate its energies on the political agenda. However, their intentions went very much deeper: they wanted to see a new model of man, and a new relationship between the sexes, from which would flow political change. In forming their more general ideas, the Young Bosnians were very much influenced by what was happening in Russian revolutionary circles, which we shall go on to explore.

Talking to the Austrian psychiatrist Dr Martin Pappenheim in 1916, Princip defined the Young Bosnians as revolutionary in their intentions, rather than, like the older generation, seeking to resolve the situation in Bosnia by peaceful change. At the same time, political change was not enough: what was needed was a new morality and a new society. As Dedijer writes (page 208) :

'These Young Bosnians believed that society could be transformed only by the influence of morally strong and socially developed persons, who by their own examples would create a new, better type of man. In this attitude there was the influence of Chernyshevsky and other Russian populists, and of Mazzini, but particularly of the founder of Serbian socialism, Svetozar Markovic, whose socialist idealism Jovan Skelic has summed up: "Particularly in small countries, ideas are worth only as much as the men who advocate them."

'Princip and his friends upheld the morality of the simple life and the virtues of mutual aid, as expounded by Kropotkin; in their private lives they tended to adopt revolutionary asceticism and puritanism. They did not drink; an expression of love towards a girl was regarded as a violation of her dignity; physiological life had little meaning. Gacinovic wrote to Trotsky (who was working as a journalist in the Balkans in the 1900s, and became acquainted with revolutionary youth): "In our organization there is a rule of obligatory abstinence from love-making and drinking, and you must believe me when I tell you that all of us remain true to this rule."

'The hard core of the Young Bosnians kept to such standards. It was a personal reaction against the stark realities of Bosnia and Herzegovina, a wish to be different from their fathers, and a revival of the ethics of the idyllic days of the *zadruga*. Chastity was a strict rule among the Young Bosnians. The would-be assassin Bogdan Zerajic, although a man of 25, never had sexual intercourse, as the Sarajevo police reportedly established after his death; and Princip confessed his virtue to Dr Pappenheim.

'(T)he Young Bosnians... firmly believed that the Hapsburg authorities were deliberately fomenting the moral corruption of the population. They pointed, for instance, to the introduction of special military brothels, institutions unknown in the history of Bosnia and Herzegovina up to 1878...' Princip is reported to have said to a friend: "syphilis and clericalism are an unhappy inheritance from the Middle Ages which the present generation does not know how to cure."

Men and women

'Gacinovic ... criticised what he termed the exclusively materialistic outlook of the Bosnian students studying abroad, their physical, intellectual and moral degeneration evidenced by the empty hours they spent in cafes...' This reproach applied to female students just as much as to men.

'Svetozar Markovic ... influenced Gacinovic greatly on the question of the equality of men and women. This problem was particularly difficult in Bosnia and Herzegovina, where the patriarchalism of the kmets had been strengthened by the attitudes of the Turks. Gacinovic also followed the advice of Jovan Skerlic on the necessity of a struggle for women's rights.... In the spirit of Chernyshevsky, he wished that the emancipated women of Bosnia should play the role of social reformers—"Let them remember the enlightened apostolic mission of Russian, French, Spanish and Italian women, who died on the gallows with the cry for liberty and greetings to their country and their people." His idol was Sonya Perovskaya, one of the conspirators in the assassination of Tsar Alexander 11.'

We may note that Gacinovic was somewhat in awe of his Russian friends, and at the same time perhaps a little envious. He wrote to Trotsky, in another letter:

'You Russians know very little about us, much less than we know about you... We are, if you wish, your ideological colony. All colonies lag behind their metropolis.' (Dedijer, page 226.)

Gacinovic firmly believed that women could be of vital importance in the revolutionary struggle, and there were indeed women members of Young Bosnia. But none played an activist's role, and there was no equivalent of the Russians Sonya Perovskaya (who was hanged for her part in assassinating the Tsar in 1881) or Vera Zasulic (whom the jury found not guilty of shooting the governor of St Petersburg in 1878, although she

39

admitted to the crime). It is interesting to note when the young idealist actually met one of his idols, his ideas were firmly challenged. 'Gavrinovic personally had close spiritual relations with several girls in the Russian revolutionary movement (one of whom) criticized him strongly for his nationalist outlook and similar prejudices.' (Dedijer, page 210).

With its much larger population, Russia had a larger pool of potential revolutionaries of both sexes to choose from than any Balkan state or province[2,] and was at an advanced stage of social development compared with Bosnia or Serbia. Indeed, no Balkan state had developed the base of educated and emancipated women from which the revolutionaries would emerge. As Dedijer (page 176) points out, in 1902 there were only 30 Bosnians with a university education at all—and far from being revolutionaries, they tended to be conservative in their outlook, no doubt very contented with their position of comparative privilege. We do not know how many, if any of them were women. However, that situation was soon to alter, for even in the most remote province of the Austro-Hungarian empire, change was in the air.

Gavrilo Princip and emancipation

Dedijer writes that:

'Gavrilo Princip, less sentimental than Gavrinovic, and more reserved in the expression of his feelings, cherished a similar attitude towards women, believing that creative work is the primary goal of life. He was a friend of Nedjelko Cabrinovic's sister, Vukosava, who was three years younger than himself. When she was twelve years old, Gavrilo found her reading a cheap novel called *The Secrets of the Istanbul Palace*. He took the book from her hands, bringing her next time Oscar Wilde's stories and a novel by Uskokovic, a Serbian writer. They exchanged many letters afterward, and the girl once pawned her golden cross in order to send some money to her brother and Princip when they were in Belgrade in the winter of 1913-14. Vukosava remembered Princip as a "reserved boy, sometimes witty, almost sarcastic, with deep eyes, handsome teeth, and a very high forehead." He tried to widen the girl's intellectual horizons, sending her books and reproductions of well-known paintings. He also wrote her poems and many letters...' (Dedijer, page 211).

These were destroyed in the war, but one written by Gavrilo to

Vukosava on the eve of 28 June, was reconstructed as follows:

'I feel a deep, sincere pain reading your letter, as if I were looking at the grief of a girl abandoned by everyone and forgotten. Do not suffer and do not let bloodshot eyes reveal your sorrow. Think and work. One needs a lot of strength in order to live, and action creates this. Physical labour also strengthens the character and firmness of will. Be individualistic, never altruistic. My life is also full of bitterness and gall, my wreath has more thorns than others. I go from nothingness to nothingness, from day to day, and in me there is less and less of myself. Do read, you must read: this is the best way to forget the tragic side of reality...' (Dedijer, page 211.)

Young Bosnia and religion

The traditional Bosnian peasant was religious, or at least observed the religious formalities. Most were orthodox, some Roman Catholic, and some Moslem, although the Bosnian Serbs tended to be orthodox in their allegiance. Religion, for the Serbian orthodox believer, was a matter of unquestioning faith: Gavrilo Princip's father was noted for his piety, and his punctiliousness in observing the religious rites, although his mother was not religious. The young Bosnians were fiercely anti-clerical, and rejected the faith of their fathers as a matter of course. Trifko Grabez, the son of an orthodox priest, was asked at his trial how he had come to pursue assassination as a path of action, since this would certainly go against the teachings of his father. Grabez explained, with the conviction of youth, that he accepted part of his father's instruction, but not all:

'"Are you an atheist or a deist?"

"I am a believer!"

"How could you reconcile your religion with the murder of a man made by God? From the religious point of view this is a sin."

"My religion does not go so far."

"Your father is a priest. What sort of education did he give you? Did he try to evoke religious feelings in you?"

"He gave me an education in the spirit of the Gospel."

"Did you follow the advice of your father?"

"As a child I listened to him, but when one comes into contact with other boys, then other influences prevail."

"Have these young men no faith?" Finally asked the President.

"Not the faith you think; they have a national religion of a higher type," answered Grabez.'

(From the Sarajevo trial, as quoted in Dedijer, page 212.)

Revolution by persuasion or violence? The Russian influence

The paradox of the ideas of Young Bosnia was that whilst they advocated and attempted to practise the highest ideals of personal conduct, they were prepared to perpetrate violence in order to achieve political goals. To that extent, they resembled the youthful idealists who had formed *Land and Freedom*, a nineteenth century movement dedicated to social and political change in Russia, and which had moved from peaceful means to the reluctant acceptance of violence.

According to the Russian historian Geoffrey Hosking (Hosking, 2001) *Land and Freedom* had its origins in the influence of a novel by Nikolai Chernyshevsky entitled *What is to be Done?*, first published in 1862. 'It portrays an artel of seamstresses, young women who had broken away from patriarchal families dominated by husband or father in order to pool their resources and make clothes for sale. In the background, somewhat veiled (because of the censorship) but unmistakable, is a conspiratorial circle of young men, political activists preparing for a coming revolution. Rakhmetov, their leader, trains himself by an ascetic regime of theoretical study, body-building, moderate food, and abstention from sex.' (Hosking, page 307.)

The Russian revolutionary movement thus combined the aims of the need for political change and the emancipation of women. As Hosking points out, there were sociological grounds as well as ethical reasons for the latter. Tsar Alexander 11's reforms created tension in the traditional noble families, partly because he had reduced their income and partly because he had created new educational opportunities for their children. 'The generation conflict, serious enough between fathers and sons, became explosive when it took place between fathers and daughters. Many middle-aged men were outraged that their daughters were not content to seek security in a traditional marriage or to accept a life of dependence and service within their own family, but wanted to go into the big, bad city, sit unchaperoned in lecture halls or even anatomy theatres, then open their own bank accounts and set up their own businesses. So the question of self-realization was especially acute for women, and it became an important part of the socialists' ideal of self-emancipation within a more mutually supportive society. (Hosking, page 308.)

Another book, *Historical Letters*, published in 1869 by Petr Lavrov, 'was widely read and became a kind of Bible of the intelligentsia. He (Lavrov) preached that intellectuals, since they owed their education and culture to the sweat and toil of the masses, had a duty to repay the debt by going out to them and sharing the fruits of their learning. He believed that revolution would ultimately have to be the work of the people themselves, and rejected the anarchist Bakunin's idea that blind destruction would prove fruitful. Instead, he argued, the level of culture and consciousness of the peasants must first be raised, so that they could bring their own socialist potential to full fruition and not dissipate it in indiscriminate violence.' (Hosking, page 309).

Land and Freedom goes into action

In 1873, a group of young people felt that it was time to put idea into practice. They dressed simply, learned the necessary trades to make themselves useful, and went to the people, with the feeling that what they were doing was the equivalent of setting out as missionaries to darkest Africa.

The people in question, the Russian serfs[3], were originally reported to have rejected their self-appointed saviours with suspicion and contempt, and to have denounced them to the authorities; although Hosking reports more recent evidence showing that the peasants were prepared to listen to those members of *Land and Freedom* who could offer practical help, and talked to them in language that they could understand.

However, even if their efforts were not rejected out of hand, the representatives of *Land and Freedom* came to realise that they were not going to change Russia by going to the people, who were innately conservative and suspicious of change. Moreover, the movement had been penetrated by the police and show trials were held.

The People's Will

From within *Land and Freedom* emerged *The People's Will*, a group that embraced the need for assassination, and dedicated itself to the task of assassinating the Tsar Alexander 11 himself—a task it was able to achieve in 1881, but which had no effect in changing imperial Russia, save for an increase in repression and the creation of a more effective security police. Some revolutionaries would have welcomed this as the intended outcome of their act, for the more openly repressive the state, the more likelihood of a mass surge against it. Such was not, however, the outlook of *The People's Will,* which believed that the assassination of the Tsar would somehow promote immediate change—just as Princip and his colleagues later believed that the assassination of Franz Ferdinand would somehow serve Bosnia's ends.

An Anarchist ideal: The British text

Unlike the enthusiasts of *Land and Freedom,* Princip and his friends had no need to 'go to the people' as a voyage of discovery. They were already from the people, as the sons of peasants, shop-keepers, tradesmen and small artisans, with the occasional orthodox priest; and they could claim with some justification that they knew what life was like in the villages of rural Bosnia, as in the poorer parts of Sarajevo and Belgrade. They were not part of a social elite, and had not rejected a privileged position in life in order to change society—although their ideas on the need for change would have sounded just as odd to the ordinary Bosnian's ears, whether they came from fellow countrymen or not.

What appealed to Young Bosnia was the anarchist vision of an ideal society. That society consists of a series of interlocking communities, in which people work with their hands and provide for their own needs; in which craftsmanship and beauty are held in high esteem; and in which the relationship between the sexes is based upon equality and mutual respect— the sort of society, in fact, which was portrayed by the English anarchist, arts and crafts designer and political activist William Morris, whose Utopian idyll *'News from Nowhere'* was read with approval by Princip and his friends[4], and which describes a state of affairs which is as far removed from the reality of their experience of life, after the decline of the *zadruga* or traditional Serb communal organisation, as it is possible to imagine.

The brief life and death of (political) gradualism

The graduates of Mostar High School carried their ideals elsewhere in

Bosnia. Some went on to attend the universities of Vienna, Prague and Zagreb, where they were influenced by the writings of the philosopher (and later first President of the new republic of Czechoslovakia) Thomas Masaryk (1850-1937), who advocated revolution by cultural reawakening and rejected violence as a means to political change: a policy known as gradualism. However, the 1908 formal annexation of Bosnia and Herzegovina into the Austro-Hungarian Empire led the Young Bosnians to reject gradualism and re-embrace the need for a more active resistance movement.

Vladimir Gacinovic left Mostar in 1907 and joined a seminary in Reljevo, near Sarajevo, where, true to form, he set up a secret revolutionary society named Sava. Like his colleagues, including Bogdan Zerajic, he was for a while influenced by Masaryk's ideas. However, 1908 changed everything, and he fled to Montenegro and then Serbia to join the Serbian army as a volunteer.

Other Young Bosnians, including students at the University of Vienna, set up secret societies and formed links with Narodna Odbrana in Belgrade. (Narodna Odbrana was an open movement that had sprung up amongst patriotic Serbs to oppose the 1908 annexation. Its secret equivalent was *The Black Hand*, created in 1911—which adopted much the same badge and slogan as the Internal Macedonian Revolutionary Organisation).

So keen were the Young Bosnian students to take action against the hated Austrians that some of them volunteered to go to Serbia for guerrilla training. Their proposal was at first rejected, but later some did go on to receive training, and to become part of the secret intelligence network that the Serbs established in Bosnia.

Others still went further abroad, including another leading member of Young Bosnia who left for Russia in 1909 in order to 'contact Russian revolutionaries and learn their methods of secret work.' (Dedijer, page 180: the person in question is not identified). However, no military action on behalf of Bosnia was forthcoming in 1908.

Young Bosnia, 1908-1914

Gacinovic returned to his High School studies in Belgrade, graduating in 1910 at the age of twenty, which was not unusual for high school students who did not begin their education until they were nine. Gacinovic immediately enrolled at the University of Belgrade and began to attend courses on Serbo-Croat literature given by Professor Jovan Skerlic, who had a leading influence on the Young Bosnians. After one term Gacinovic transferred to the University of Vienna on a Serbian stipend.

Here, as Dedijer puts it, he found many of his friends from Mostar High School's secret societies. They continued their work, but in a more organised way. In 1911 Gacinovic, who had joined both the Black Hand and Narodna Odbrana, proved an active, almost hyperactive organiser, setting up secret intelligence cells amongst willing sympathizers in Sarajevo, Vienna, Zagreb and elsewhere. He communicated with them by means of the magazine *Zora*, which was ostensibly a literary review.

Gacinovic visited Switzerland for the first time in 1911, establishing links with Russian revolutionaries of all types who were living there or passing through, and entering a Swiss university in 1913. Gacinovic made friends with Serge Kibalchich, the son of Nikolai Kibalchich who had been executed for his role in the assassination of the Tsar Alexander 11 in 1881. When the First Balkan War broke out[5] Gacinovic joined up and took part as a Serbian irregular, serving at the siege of Skutari in Albania. There is no evidence that campaigning suited his temperament, and he was to take no part in any further military or paramilitary action.

Annexation and its consequences

The formal annexation of Bosnia and Herzegovina in 1908 by the Austrian authorities was a stimulus for student activism, and indeed 'direct action.' It discouraged (ended would be a stronger word) the conversion of the membership of Young Bosnia to a peaceful movement under the influence of thinkers such as Thomas Masaryk; and it severely weakened any possibility that an enlightened Austrian administration could develop a new spirit of subordinate nationalism that linked the three religions of Bosnia within the tolerant and comforting embrace of the Austro-Hungarian empire—as Count Stefan Burian, who became Joint Minister of Finance (and therefore de facto administrator in chief of Bosnia) after 1903, had hoped to achieve.

Annexation led to the creation of Narodna Odbrana in Belgrade, and thence The Black Hand. It radicalised a new generation of Bosnian students and workers and pushed them in the direction of seeking active support from Belgrade. Arguably, it led to the *attentat* of 28 June 1914, the invasion of Serbia by Austria-Hungary one month later, the Great War that followed, and the destruction of the entire Austro-Hungarian empire—although this may be to present too simple a causal chain.

On the other hand, what else could the Austrians have done? They could hardly leave the *status quo* intact for ever, by administering what was officially the Sultan's territory for an indefinite period.[6] Their best hope was, in fact, to attempt what they did attempt, only to do it better: to develop the new provinces of Bosnia and Herzegovina to a point where the great majority of the indigenous population could see the real advantages, in economic, social, and even political terms, of being part of a prosperous and well-administered, multi-racial empire based on the fundamental principles of religious toleration and the rule of law.

'Repressive tolerance'

Under such circumstances, student radicals could be isolated and contained: to be allowed a certain amount of intellectual freedom, perhaps, provided that they did not threaten the foundations of the state itself. (This was to be called 'repressive tolerance' by the philosopher Herbert Marcuse in an essay written in 1965. In 1908, the phrase had yet to be coined, but the practice was already in place—although the Austrian administration was more adept at practising repression than tolerance. The work of the Italian writer and activist, Antonio Gramsci (1891 to 1937), who was a near contemporary of Gavrilo Princip and his colleagues in Young Bosnia, is also relevant. However, the impact of his ideas came later.)

The importance of Young Bosnia

How significant was Young Bosnia, and to what extent did it articulate a clear political strategy? The Balkan historian Vladimir Dedijer, a Serb and then Yugoslav himself, takes them very seriously, whereas Malcolm (1996) is dismissive:

'Much has been written about the political philosophy of these young activists—perhaps too much, for there is a limit to the amount of philosophically interesting material to be found in the heads of a loose assortment of idealistic but ill-educated teenagers. They were fiercely anti-clerical; they wanted social revolution just as much as national liberation; they were especially keen on the writings of anarchists or anarcho-syndicalists such as Bakunin, Herzen and Kropotkin; and above all they wanted to be heroes.'

Malcolm continues by pointing to the tradition of heroic failure which had already been established in the Balkans before 1914:

'The first in a succession of hero-martyr-assassins was a depressive student from Herzegovina called Bogdan Zerajic, who went to the opening day of the new Bosnian parliament in 1910, fired five shots at the military governor (Marian Varesanin) as he left the ceremony, missed with every one of them and then used the sixth bullet to kill himself…'

He describes a different aspect to the character of the introverted and bookish Gavrilo Princip:

'In the summer of 1912 a Bosnian Croat, Luka Jukic, tried to assassinate the governor of Croatia in Zagreb. Earlier that year Jukic had helped to organise protest demonstrations of schoolboys in Sarajevo, together with Gavrilo Princip and several other youths who would later be involved in Princip's assassination plans in 1914. On this occasion, as one boy noted in his diary, "Princip went from class to class, threatening with his knuckle-duster all the boys who wavered in coming to the new demonstrations." '

(Malcolm, 2002, pages 153-4)

Futile as Zerajic's example may have appeared, he had at least broken new ground; and whether or not an attempt at assassination may be regarded as in some sense an indication of progress, it was a breakthrough in political consciousness in what had been until very recently a part of the Ottoman Empire.

Overall, Young Bosnia was a significant organisation. Firstly, it existed. This was an achievement in itself, in a province which was ruled first by one oppressive imperial regime and then another, neither of which tolerated political dissent—or indeed open political debate. Secondly, it radicalised a section of Bosnian youth. Thirdly, it provided an ideologist, in Vladimir Gacinovic. Fourthly, it provided a martyr, in Bogdan Zerajic. His example was to be an inspiration to Garvrilo Princip and his friends, who swore allegiance to his memory and ideals. Without Gacinovic, this would not have happened; for it was he who wrote the obituary of his friend, *Death of a Hero,* and created the legend. Without Zerajic, there was no basis for that legend.

Vladimir Gacinovic: his end and legacy

When the First World War began Gacinovic made himself unavailable for service in the Austro-Hungarian army by the simple expedient of moving to Paris, where he continued his friendship with Kibalchich, decided once and for all that his sympathies lay with the socialist revolutionaries rather than the social democrats, and met Trotsky once again, to argue furiously but in friendship about the necessary shape of the future revolution.

Surprisingly for someone with his background, and with so many connections, Gacinovic appears to have played no part in the events of 28 June 1914 and their aftermath. Indeed, from 1913 onwards his influence on his fellow revolutionaries seems to have declined. In Paris, he was still full of energy, and Trotsky, still at this stage working as a journalist, and someone who knew the Balkans well, described him as follows:

'In a corner of the café Rotonde, beside me, in a cloud of smoke which one cannot find anywhere else, is sitting a young Serb. Despite the very strong crowd, one's eyes must rest on him, even against one's will. He is one of these types that are bound to provoke a feeling of uneasiness among orderly people. Tall, thin but strong, with an expression of restlessness in his eyes and in the lines of his face, he watches everything and everybody with such intelligence, for greedy impressions of other people's lives, but still capable of saving himself from being drawn into them. This young man, barely out of his teens—he is hardly 23—has his goal. He is a Bosnian, an intimate friend of Princip and Ilic.' (Dedijer, page 182.)

Vladimir Gacinovic was well placed to play a leading role in Balkan revolutionary politics and to help to create the enlarged Serbia that eventually emerged. He had the right background, he was well educated— far more so than the average member of Young Bosnia—and he proved both a fluent propagandist and a political theorist who was prepared to change his approach in the light of changing circumstances. He was an active joiner and organiser who made the right friends; and he did not lack personal courage. Perhaps his problem was, as Trotsky said, that he made people feel uncomfortable about themselves; and perhaps in his life in exile he gradually lost his zeal for change.

Gacinovic withered away, unhallowed and unacknowledged: an obscure figure in a Swiss café, whose death in August 1917 remains unexplained. Was he poisoned by secret service agents from Vienna, as a final revenge for Sarajevo? Was he put out of business by the last remnants of the Black Hand, lest he still had secrets to betray? His death remains a mystery, as does his life; and the man who might have played a major role in the redefinition of the Balkan political landscape was never to do so.

The cult of martyrdom

Perhaps Gacinovic's epitaph should be that more than anyone else he had advocated the cult of martyrdom, which had inspired Bogdan Zeracic and in his turn Gavrilo Princip. For those who have not been seduced by its charms, the appeal of martyrdom is a mysterious one. Why kill oneself, as did Zeracic, when nothing was achieved? He did not even wait to verify that he had killed or at least injured his intended victim, Governor Varesanin, before turning his last bullet on himself; and as it happened, that was the only bullet to reach its target. Nevertheless, in the history of the world since 1912 the cult of the murderous martyr has been extraordinarily influential; and Vladimir Gacinovic played a significant part in feeding that cult.

The paths to revolutionary leadership are varied. If we consider simply the Russian example, the young revolutionary can make his reputation as an orator, like Trotsky—a source of excitement, a firebrand, a charismatic personality, whom people follow because they cannot imagine acting otherwise.

Or he can exercise a ruthless determination to lead his chosen group in his chosen direction, like Lenin with the Bolsheviks—at the same time, as with Lenin, producing a mass of written propaganda by means of which to explain and justify both his ideals and the measures he puts in place to achieve them.

Or like Stalin, he can find the path to power by manipulating its levers. Stalin, who was neither orator nor ideologist, became general secretary of the party, and was thus able to record its decisions. In that position, he was able to promote his supporters and do down his rivals, and by the ruthless manipulation of both terror and propaganda, to become the leader whom the people barely knew, and had certainly never voted for, but who nevertheless controlled their destiny.

We may note, however, that in all three cases the leaders descended into the arena and did battle. Young Bosnia talked about doing so, but under Gacinovic's influence it came dangerously close to worshipping at the shrine of heroic failure. Gavrilo Princip, however, was to change all that—and to start what was at first called the Third Balkan war by his efforts.

Russian and Balkan terrorism: A brief comparison

Nineteenth Century Russia was the home of applied terrorism, and Russian terrorists were capable of achieving spectacular results. In 1881 the Tsar Alexander 11 (ironically, the tsar who had emancipated the serfs) was killed by terrorists from an organisation called The People's Will. They wished to overthrow what they saw as a tyranny and saw no other means to achieving this objective—although accordingly at least to Albert Camus, they recognised that what they were doing was fundamentally immoral.

The People's Will was wiped out by the new Tsar's ever-vigilant security forces, but was succeeded by an organisation named Combat—the terrorist arm of the political party known as the SRs or socialist revolutionaries.

Combat SR

It might be claimed that Combat was the most successful terrorist organisation in pre-communist Russia, although statistics in this area are naturally far from reliable. It came into existence in the 1890s and by 1907 it had burnt itself out. During that short period, it was effective in carrying out the assassination of high officials, and it was highly successful in generating both fear and fatalism amongst the ruling classes. It was also far more effective in using terror than either the Bolsheviks or the Mensheviks, with both of whom it was in ideological disagreement.

Strategy and tactics

If we accept the distinction between strategy and tactics which derives from the meaning of those words in the original Greek, strategy is what happens before battle begins, and tactics describes what happens on the battlefield when the opposing forces are in physical contact. Combat's strategy was as follows:

(i)   To separate the political and terrorist elements of the Socialist Revolutionaries, so that the political element could legitimately deny all knowledge of terrorist activity, and would not be able to betray vital information if interrogated;

(ii)   To allow the terrorist organisation within the SRs, Combat, to plan and mount its own operations as an autonomous activity, without the knowledge and specific authority of their supposed political masters;

(iii)   As a natural development of the above, to practice the cell system of security within Combat, so that no-one could betray the whole organisation, nor any more than his immediate contacts of the four or five members of his cell, only one of whom had any links to another cell;

(iv)   In common with most terrorist organisations, to make Combat self-funding by its terrorist-allied activities, such as bank robbery, extortion, and the theft of weapons and explosives; and

(v)   To hunt out and punish any traitors or supposed traitors within the organisation with extreme vigour and ruthlessness. Dead people do not betray their comrades.

The key elements of SR strategy were therefore rigid separation, tight security and extreme ruthlessness, and these enabled it to become an effective organisation, although they also contained pitfalls which helped to bring about its demise.

Combat Tactics

Combat tactics had much in common with those practised by *The People's Will*. Both groups believed in proper reconnaissance and planning; in close contact with the enemy; in the use of effective explosives, which they were capable of developing themselves; and in self-sacrifice as and when necessary. They were aware of the public relations aspect to their actions, and tried to avoid killing women and children associated with the chosen target, since such deaths would have aroused public sympathy. (People who could be classified as supporting 'the system' by choice, such as Tsarist officials working for the chosen target, were fair game.)

Combat Ethics and Psychology

Combat attacks were chilling episodes, in which a chosen assassin would if necessary shadow his chosen victim for days, waiting for the right opportunity, before lobbing a bomb into his lap from as close a distance as possible—thereby demonstrating both that he was prepared to die himself as a result of the explosion, and that he was reckless, in effect, as to the death of anyone else who may have been in the vicinity, such as a coachman, guard, or adjutant to the military governor or senior official who was the primary target. The bombs used were sophisticated, nitro-glycerine being the preferred type, and appallingly destructive. They were designed by experts within the organisation, some of whom were scientists by training.

How did organisations like <u>Combat</u> manage to recruit, equip and train people for such acts, given that they were not out-and-out psychopaths? We begin with the work of the French philosopher Albert Camus. What follows was first published in his work *'The Rebel'* in 1950. A shortened version of this work, entitled *'The Fastidious Assassins',* was published in 2008.[7] Camus deals with both *Combat* and *The People's Will.*

Albert Camus (Camus, 2008) describes Combat as bringing together the most outstanding personalities of Russian terrorism (op. cit., page 56), and he proceeds to eulogise about their ethics and determination. According to Camus, the Russian assassins were men and women of honour, selfless, dedicated, and prepared to die for their convictions. They recognised the evil of what they were doing, and although they sought to make their operations as clinical as possible, and to kill or injure the chosen target and no-one else, they were still aware of the fundamental immorality of assassination. As Camus puts it, their actions were necessary but inexcusable; and the only way in which they could even partially atone for what they did was to accept their own death as a consequence.

At the same time, they built up a fantastic solidarity. They were isolated not only from the great mass of Russian people but even from their own families, both for reasons of security and because they had embraced a set of beliefs that were fundamentally alien to the majority of mankind. They lived in a sort of joyful austerity, and were ready and willing to embrace death. In his view it is the defining characteristic of Combat's leading members.

"'How can we speak of terrorist activity without taking part in it?' exclaims (sic) the student Kaliayev [who murdered the Grand Duke Sergei Alexandrovich in 1905].

'Almost all are atheists. 'I remember', wrote Boris Voinarovsky, who died in throwing a bomb at Admiral Dubassov, 'that, before even going to high-school, I preached atheism to one of my childhood friends. Only one question embarrasses me. Where did my ideas come from? For I had not the least conception of eternity.' Kaliayev, himself, believed in God. A few moments before an attempted assassination which failed, Savinkov saw him in the street, standing in front of an ikon, holding the bomb in one hand and making the sign of the cross with the other. But he repudiated religion. In his cell, before his execution, he refused its consolations.

'Secrecy compelled (the assassins) to live in solitude. They did not know, except perhaps in the abstract, the profound joy experienced by the man of action in contact with a large section of humanity. But the bond that unites them replaces every other attachment in their minds. 'Chivalry', writes Sazonov, 'our chivalry was permeated with such a degree of feeling that the word "brother" in no way conveyed, with sufficient clarity, the essence of our relations with one another.' From prison, Sazonov writes to his friends: 'For my part, the indispensable condition of happiness is to keep forever the knowledge of my perfect solidarity with you.' As for Voinarovsky, he confesses that he said, to a woman whom he loved and who wished to detain him, the following phrase which he recognizes as 'slightly comic' but which, according to him, proves his state of mind: 'I should hate you if I arrived late for my comrades.'

'This little group of men and women, lost among the Russian masses, bound only to one another, chose the role of executioner to which they were in no way destined. They lived in the same paradox, combining in themselves respect for human life in general and contempt for their own lives—to the point of nostalgia for the supreme sacrifice. For Dora Brilliant, the anarchist programme was of no importance—terrorist action was primarily embellished by the sacrifice it demanded from the terrorist. 'But', says Savinkov, 'terror weighed on her like a cross.' Kaliayev himself is ready to sacrifice his life at any moment. 'Even better than that, he passionately desired to make this sacrifice.' During the preparations for the attempt on Plehve, he stated his intention of throwing himself under the horses' hooves and perishing with the minister. With Voinarovsky also the desire for sacrifice coincides with the attraction of death. After his arrest, he writes to his parents: 'How many times during my adolescence the idea came to me to kill myself. ...'

'At the same time, these executioners who risked their own lives so completely, only made attempts on the lives of others after the most scrupulous examination of conscience. The first attempt on the Grand Duke Sergei failed because Kaliayev, with the full approval of his comrades, refused to kill the children who were riding in the Grand Duke's carriage. About Rachel Louriée, another terrorist, Savinkov writes: 'She had faith in Terrorist action, she considered it as honour and a duty to take part in it, but blood upset her no less than it did Dora.' Savinkov was opposed to an attempt on Admiral Dubassov in the Petersburg-Moscow express because: 'If there were the least mistake, the explosion could take place in the carriage and kill strangers.' Later Savinkov, 'in the name of terrorist conscience', will deny, with indignation, having made a child of sixteen take part in an attempted assassination. At the moment of escaping from a Czarist prison, he decided to shoot any officers who might attempt to prevent his flight, but to kill himself rather than turn his revolver on an ordinary soldier. It is the same with Voinarovsky, who does not hesitate to kill men but who confesses that he had never hunted in that he finds 'the occupation barbarous' and who declares in his turn: 'If Dubassov is accompanied by his wife, I shall not throw the bomb.'

'Such a degree of self-abnegation, accompanied by such profound consideration for the lives of others, allows the supposition that these fastidious assassins lived out the rebel destiny in its most contradictory form. It is possible to believe that they too, while recognizing the inevitability of violence, nevertheless admitted to themselves that it is unjustifiable. Necessary and inexcusable, that is how murder appeared to them. Mediocre minds, confronted with this terrible problem, can take refuge by ignoring one of the terms of the dilemma…

'But the extremists, with whom we are concerned, forgot nothing. From their earliest days they were incapable of justifying what they nevertheless found necessary and conceived the idea of offering themselves as a justification and of replying by personal sacrifice to the question they asked themselves. For them, as for all rebels before them, murder was identified with suicide…. '

In Camus' view, real rebellion is a creator of values.

Camus writes with conviction but his analysis is more philosophical than sociological, and we do not believe that it gives a balanced portrayal of Russian terrorism from 1861 to 1917. Indeed, in one sense it is obviously very far from balanced: whatever may have been their intentions, the activists of Combat SR killed and injured a very large number of innocent people in the attacks they mounted, and the charge of recklessness would apply on many occasions.

Anna Geifman (Geifman, 1993) provides a useful antidote to the sympathetic protrayal of terrorist motivation and activity offered by Camus. Her analysis, which makes extensive use of police records, shows that:

- Terrorism was practised by a very wide variety of extremist groups;
- Many terrrorists were psychologically disturbed;
- There was a considerable overlap between terrorism, criminality, and psychopathy;
- Children were exploited;
- Some terrorists recognised that their activities were contradictory to the Marxist doctrine which they officially espoused, but persisted anyway;
- The anarchists, as their name might suggest, were most prone to carry out random and spontaneous acts of terror against impromptu targets, some of which attacks did not assist the revolution in any way; and
- The authorities were in the end able to suppress terrorism, so that Combat was ineffective after its last two spectacular bombings of 1905. Despite concentrated efforts, they were unable to kill another leading figure, and ceased to be an effective force by 1907, by when the police were effective in guarding identified targets.

The Combat terrorists were professional revolutionaries, who had moved far beyond the self-sacrificial ideals of The People's Will. They were motivated by psychological needs as well as political aims, and amongst their number were the ordinary but far from decent criminals.[8]

Youthful assassins

Some of the points that Geifman makes are of particular significance when we consider terrorist activities in the Balkans. For example, consider age and circumstances. The three main assassins of the Archduke Franz Ferdinand were all very young men. None of them had reached his twentieth birthday, and none was even an undergraduate, let alone the product of a university. Cabrinovic was a jobbing printer who still tended to return home when he needed help, and Princip had not finished school. The court was not inclined to deal with them as adults, despite the seriousness of their crimes and the penalties they faced.

The same youthfulness was seen in Russia, where the participation of juveniles in terrorist activities was a significant problem, not only for the authorities but for older revolutionaries. 'Nearly 22 per cent of all SR terrorists were between 15 and 19, and another 45 per cent were between 20 and 24. In Belostock one combat unit formed in 1905 was composed entirely of school-children who belonged to the PSR... The participation of teenagers in radical politics in the borderlands was also widespread, and this led Leon Trotsky to assert in his biography of Stalin (presumably with disapproval) that the growing percentage of Russian terrorism's victims who had been merely wounded, as opposed to killed, indicated that the shooting was increasingly carried out 'by untrained amateurs, mostly by callow youngsters.'

Geifman put forward psychological as well as ideological reasons for what was going on.

'In considering motives for the widespread participation of minors in extremist activities, another factor of primary importance in the natural course of maturation should not be neglected, namely, the need to assert oneself as an individual with a unique identity, a developed set of values, and a well-defined world outlook. This process usually involves borrowing the values of others, thereby validating them. In the chaos and instability that reigned in 1905, in politics as well as in individual lives, many juveniles seemed to sense that the moment was extremely propitious for youthful rebellion...'. Other youthful rebels included children from bourgeois or aristocratic backgrounds rebelling against their parents; those who were destitute, or semi-destitute, and therefore had little or nothing to lose by embracing the terrorist cause; or criminals and drop-outs.

Geifman goes on to acknowledge the advantages of using young people in terrorist activities:

'Perceiving distinct advantages in selecting youths for combat duties, adult terrorists readily recruited minors for terrorist operations, motivated by psychological as much as practical considerations. They recognised how easy it was to exploit both the desire of the youngsters to assert themselves as heroes, and the fearlessness in the face of death typical of many adolescents, who talked with enthusiasm about dying in action, and not even for the sake of the revolutionary cause.'

Just as with the IRA later on, youthful rebels were used (and exploited) to gather information and spy out targets, carry out reconnaissance, make bombs, carry weapons and explosives to and from outrages, and also to carry out the terrorist acts themselves, for their older colleagues knew that they saw themselves as having less to lose than older revolutionaries; and were more likely not to be executed by the authorities.

In conclusion

What may be concluded from this brief historical comparison?

It is clear that the Bosnian assassins admired and learned from the Russian theory and practice of political violence, although their own activities were carried out on a very much smaller scale. (We have already noted Gacinovic's admiration for Russia, as expressed in a letter to Trotsky.) What happened in Bosnia was tiny by comparison with what was going on in Russia, where the veterans of Combat SR were able to gain a level of professionalism which was never available in the Balkans. Assassination, like any craft, improves with practice.

The Sarajevo assassins were more nationalist than revolutionary, despite the ideals of Young Bosnia.

The participation of Colonel Apis in assisting the Bosnian cause had no apparent equivalent in the Russian arena—although Russian terrorism was characterised by the active participation of *agents provocateur*, some of whom did a great deal of harm.

The membership of Young Bosnia and other proto-terrorist organisations in the Balkans, unlike that of *The People's Will* or other Russian terrorist groups, did not include members of the intelligentsia or the disaffected aristocracy, or indeed persons of Jewish origin. Jews, or persons of Jewish descent, were prominent in Russian revolutionary politics, Trotsky being a prominent example.

The Sarajevo conspiracy was a male affair, in which no woman played any significant part. Indeed, it is difficult to find any part played by a woman at all: a very obvious contrast with Russia, where there were some very well-known female revolutionaries, some of whom found their way to the scaffold. Cabrinovic's sister had plenty to say to the British journalist, Rebecca West, about her brother: but that was many years later, and she had played no part in any conspiracy, although Nedjelko Cabrinovic's whole family and their servants were arrested after his arrest.

The young Bosnians, and in particular the group to which Gavrilo Princip belonged, cannot easily be aligned with either the analysis of either Albert Camus or Anna Geifman. They had neither the single-minded determination of The People's Will nor the criminal associations and psychotic tendencies of at least some of the members of Combat. The young Bosnians were not only young but immature, or rather, adolescent; and their ideas about life itself (for example, on the relationship between the sexes) were based on theory rather than experience. The Sarajevo assassins, unlike some of their equivalents in anti-Tsarist Russia, were neither professional criminals nor psychopaths who obtained a pleasure from violence which their ordinary lives could not supply: and indeed their addiction to violence was highly selective. They were, however, very like The People's Will in one regard: they were perfectly prepared to die for their beliefs.

Their behaviour, as with all behaviour, arose from a mixture of motives and causes, and it would be a mistake to offer a singular explanation. Gavrilo Princip and his younger colleagues were clearly determined to resolve the adolescent challenge and to prove themselves as men. Princip bitterly resented being classified as too small and too weak to fight for Serbia in the First or Second Balkan wars; and his comrade Cabrinovic was thoroughly ashamed of the fact that his father was a police informer.

Both men saw an *attentat* as a chance to prove themselves in action, and it is clear from the trial notes that Cabrinovic was almost childishly proud of what he had done. However, their behaviour did not arise solely from feelings of inadequacy, and it would be a mistake to draw that conclusion. There is more to human nature than is dreamt of in the reductionist's philosophy; and not all behaviour leads back to a single reason or cause. How people account for their own behaviour may not tell us the whole story: but it is a part of it.

Anthropology was a popular discipline in the 19th century and had its practitioners in the Balkans. Professor Jovan Cvijic (Dedijer, page 256) 'spent several decades studying the social psychology and traditions of the Slavs in the Dinaric Highlands.' His work, which was first published in the early twentieth century and before the Sarajevo *attentat* took place, is supposedly empirical. However, the professor, working partly through assistants, tended to emphasize the negative characteristics of the rural Slav population who were encountered. He admitted their capacity for creative imagination, feelings for honour, desire for heroic deeds and readiness for martyrdom (all of which we may see in the young Gavrilo Princip.) But he believed that these characteristics could develop (or degenerate) into what the professor called the Violent Dinaric Type.

This type tended to work as a shepherd, which Cvijic saw as an occupation allowing for too much idleness, which in addition to the values as quoted above, generated the development of features such as 'egotism, obsessional egocentricity, unlimited ambition, and pretentiousness'. The type was likely to feel 'underestimated, not understood by society, and persecuted by it; in some cases the delirium of greatness and the complex of persecution appear(ed) side by side.

'Professor Cvijic believed that the positive characteristics of the violent type were derived from the same dispositions as the negative ones: both show(ed) a marked concentration of attention, will and activity... They (are) able to provoke events which could bring great practical consequences... They are people extremely sensitive to injustice, they rebel against it...' He further commented that this type was likely to take justice into his own hands, and could be both mystical and destructive.

In the Dinaric highlands, then, the hills were alive not so much with the sound of music as the rustle of Professor Cvijic's assistants, as they observed the shepherds supposedly dreaming of 'direct action.' However, we may set this aside as a helpful explanation for the emergence of political extremism in the Balkans, and indeed for the events of 28 June 1914. Overall, Professor Cvijic's assessment of the Violent Dinaric Type seems to have some face validity; and we may easily see some of the features of Gavrilo Princip in this category. On the other hand, the type is drawn so broadly as to be capable of a very wide application; and to this author, at least, there is a whiff of pretend-science or non-science about the 'Violent Dinaric Type', which suggests the enjoyments of popular astrology rather than the rigours of real science. The philosopher of science and analyst of the scientific method, Professor Karl Popper (1902-1994), classified both astrology and Freudian psycho-analysis as pseudo-sciences resting on unfalsifiable explanations.

Conclusion

Young Bosnia was a radical movement which was determined to liberate Bosnia from Austrian control, but was not so clear either as to how to do so, or what to put in its place.

The majority of Young Bosnians were of Serb 'ethnicity' and the movement had no great appeal either to Bosnian Croats or Bosnian Moslems, although the Bosnian Serbs did not set out to exclude them.

No-one was seriously arguing for an independent Bosnia, and its most likely future would be as part of a greater Serbia. However, the majority of Bosnians might have accepted a future as part of the Austro-Hungarian empire, had that remained a possibility for them: and that majority might have included a majority of Bosnian Serbs.

Gavrilo Princip represented one section of Bosnian Serb views, but his brother Jovo, the practical Princip who sought to build a better future for his family and himself, probably represented a much larger opinion: what was later to be named 'the silent majority.' Most Bosnians were probably not committed to an 'ism' of any sort, whether anarchism, socialism, communism, or anything else; and nationalism was not yet the force that it went on to become in the 20th Century. However, it was nationalism that was to change the face of the Balkans as both the Austro-Hungarian and Turkish empires disintegrated, and to create the consequences that are with us still.

NOTES

[1] No university existed in Istanbul until 1900. When founded, it came under close scrutiny from the secret police. The Osmanli Turks were a conservative people, and when the Sultan was seen travelling on a train, he was described as having become a Christian. This was not a favourable comment.

2 Political violence in the Balkans was not confined to Serbia or Bosnia. The Internal Macedonian Revolutionary Organisation (IMRO) was a highly destructive organisation which later doubled its destructiveness by splitting into competing factions (Glenny, 2000, page 185). Political violence needs to be distinguished from other kinds of violence in the Balkans, much of which, especially in Albania and Montenegro, was the result of perceived insults to family honour. In other ways, the Balkans were not especially troubled by crime, which in its 'organised' variety, i.e. drugs, prostitution and state-enhanced corruption, is a characteristic of the current era. (For an account of growing up in Montenegro in the 1890s, see Djilas, 1958—*Land Without Justice*.)

3 The serfs had officially been emancipated in 1861, and were therefore no longer serfs. However, the term remained in use.

4 According to Dedijer (page 201) 'a copy of that book has been preserved with the signatures of both young men.'

5 The First Balkan War began on 8 October 1912, when Montengro declared war on Turkey. Montenegro was soon joined by Serbia, Bulgaria and Greece, and although the war lasted only six weeks it was a remarkably bloody affair, in which the comparatively new weapon of the machine gun made its mark on the European battlefied. Turkey lost most of Turkey-in-Europe, and the Second Balkan War followed immediately as the victors quarrelled over the spoils.

6 Developments in Ottoman Turkey were another reason for Austrian action. The Young Turks staged a revolution in 1908 and overthrew the Sultan. Under a more democratic government, Turkey would have a more credible claim to re-establish its own administration in Bosnia.

7 We may note that Camus's experience of terrorism was not entirely theoretical, since he was a member of the French resistance to the Nazis during their occupation of Paris in the Second World War. After the war, Camus might have been expected to condemn the brutal French response to the uprising against their rule in Algeria. However, Camus who was himself a 'pied noir' or European Algerian by origin, refused either to support or condemn the uprising, and appears to have remained sympathetic to the French Algerians. Tthe plot of his most famous novel, The Outsider, concerns the murder of an Algerian Arab by a French Algerian—a murder for which the man accused refuses to make a conventional defence, and is executed.

8 An informal distinction was maintained in Northern Ireland during the recent troubles (1969 onwards), between terrorists and 'ordinary decent criminals' or ODCs. The use of the word 'decent', although ironic, implies a preference on the part of the security forces for dealing with the predictable and indeed unavoidable reality of ordinary crime, in which each side knows where it stands, accepts the 'rules of the game', and is dependent on the existence of the other—as Joseph Conrad pointed out in his novel '*The Secret Agent.*' As Conrad writes, policemen and criminals understand each other, and have more in common than perhaps either side would care

to admit. In this story, based on a true event, the head of the 'special crimes section', a certain Chief Inspector Heat, reflects that he would much prefer to deal with ODCs than with unstable and unpredictable fanatics like 'the professor', his main anarchist opponent, who is ready at any moment to blow himself and anyone else in his vicinity to smithereens.

9 Nationalist terrorists tend to be the young, as studies of ETA and the IRA have shown. Older men and women are more cynical and have other responsibilities: or they have already been killed. It is a moot point as to whether or not older men, the 'godfathers of terrorism', are directing operations from behind the scenes.

10 This type could be described as an early example of offender profiling, and was presumably influenced by the work of Cesare Lombroso (1835-1909) who was active in research and publication on 'criminal types' in the second half of the nineteenth century, and whose studies were to help found the discipline of criminology.

11 (Sir) Karl Popper was born in Vienna to a middle-class family of Jews who had converted to Protestantism Under threat of Nazi persecution, he emigrated to New Zealand in 1937 and moved on to London in 1946, where he published, amongst other famous texts, *The Open Society and its Enemies.* He was an associate of his fellow Viennese émigré, the Nobel prize winning economist Friedrich von Hayek (1889-1992), and was knighted under a conservative government. Von Hayek was distantly related to Ludwig Wittgenstein and showed a similar patriotism, serving as an artillery observer for the Austro-Hungarian armed forces during their 1917 Italian campaign.

CHAPTER FOUR

The good assassin: the background, character and ambitions of Gavrilo Princip

Thirteenth of July 1894 was a very hot day, even at such a high altitude as Grahovo Polje, a tiny hamlet 2,500 feet up in the highlands of western Bosnia, nestling beneath the craggy Mount Dinara (8,000 feet) and overlooking the hot and dry Dalmatian coast to the South. It is an underdeveloped region now. It was very much more primitive then.

Despite being heavily pregnant, Nana had been working all day long in the meadow, gathering newly cut grass and assembling it into heavy bundles. After this, she went back home and washed linen in the brook, milked a cow, felt her labour pains and rushed silently towards the house that she shared with her immediate family and most of their relatives. [Dedjier, page 187].

Nana's husband, Petar Princip, although not the towering giant of Serbian folklore, was the head of the *zadruga*, and in theory at least made the decisions for their small community, although in fact he was a reticent if not a bashful man, who would have been happier, one infers, to delegate this task to others. He was not present for the birth, but away on business as the village postman, a task he took very seriously: he was a conscientious if literal-minded man, sometimes subject to the ridicule of his fellow villagers; and he had a need to pursue a range of interests as his share of the *zadruga* was only about four acres, from which it was impossible to derive a living—especially as he still had to pay a tax to the local Moslem landlord or beg, despite the replacement of the Ottoman administration of Bosnia by that of Austria-Hungary in 1878.

The new administration had proceeded very cautiously indeed on land reform, a subject of immense controversy in Bosnia, and had in effect made no changes to the Turkish system, whereby a minority of Bosnian Moslems owned the land and extracted both money and labour from their predominantly Orthodox tenants. The Moslem landowners were not ethnic Turks, but were Bosnian Slavs who had converted to Islam during the long period of Turkish rule—a conversion which had major economic and other advantages. They formed a significant sub-class in Bosnian society, and their interests did not always coincide with those of their Turkish overlords. Thus the Bosnian Serb peasants who were at the bottom of the system had been accountable to two different sets of masters; the Begs, and the Turkish authorities at the caliphate as well. Austro-Hungarian administration after 1878 removed the latter imposition, but not the former.

Nana was not allowed to cry out because Serbian women, like their menfolk, were expected to be both stoical and taciturn, and not to complain of their lot. She reached the household and fell on the bare earthen floor by the open hearth. Within a very short time the baby was born, falling in its turn on the stones formed around the fireplace. Nana's mother-in-law ran into the house, bit the cord, washed the baby in cold water in a wooden bowl, and dried it with a coarse hempen cloth produced from within the resources of the *zadruga*.

She built up the fire which was always smouldering, even on the hottest of days; brought in a bale of barley straw for the mother to lie on in comfort; and began to serve the rough, intoxicating plum brandy which was at hand to the horde of relatives who had rapidly filled the house, once they sensed that something was up. Nana had had many babies before, and most of them had died. It was to be hoped that this new arrival would survive, especially as it was a boy, and could therefore be expected to help on the land. But it was a poor, sickly, weak-looking child and would be unlikely to survive the coming winter in the highlands, where comfort of any kind was difficult to find, and even to provide the bare necessities of life was a continuing struggle. Better christen it quickly, before it succumbed.

The new baby was to be called Gavrilo. Nana had wished to call him Spiro, after her dead brother, and Petar, the father, had expressed no view on the matter; but the parish priest decided the matter. Ilija Bilbija was a giant of a man, weighing 275 pounds, with a voice, according to Gavrilo Princip's Serb biographer, like the Archangel Michael. As the parish priest in a small Eastern Orthodox congregation where there were no dissenters, he had what Max Weber, the German sociologist, would describe as both legitimate and traditional authority. He also possessed charismatic authority, for he had led his parishioners in the agrarian uprising against the Turks which had begun in Herzegovina in 1875 and had lasted until the Austrian invasion of the formerly Turkish provinces of Bosnia and Herzegovina in 1878. Ilija had lived up to the finest traditions of the fighting priests of the Balkans, who led their communities in peace and war.

Arthur John Evans

In so doing, 'pope' Ilija had met and been admired by a young Oxford graduate named Arthur John Evans, who was travelling in Bosnia during the Great Eastern Uprising (1875-1878) and covering events for the *Manchester Guardian*, whose editor had appointed him their foreign correspondent in the Balkans. Evans' letters provide a remarkable picture of what life was actually like for the people during the Bosnian uprising,

The young, self-confident graduate was a ready and perceptive commentator, who was far from impressed by the qualities of many of the local priests whom he met on his travels, whether Eastern Orthodox or Roman Catholic; they were both ignorant and corrupt, and fleeced their parishioners unmercifully. However, Ilija was an exception.

Baptism and childhood

13 July was the name day of Saint Gabriel. The new baby would be baptized Gavrilo. There would be no argument. There was none, not even from Nana, who had wished to commemorate her dead brother, for the family knew better. The name Gavrilo Princip was accordingly written in the parish register on 13 July 1894, and later wrongly copied into the civil register for the preceding month, which would have made the new birth one month older. The scribe was a relative of the parish priest, a young man known to be careless in his work, and the consequences of this mistake were to be addressed by the highest officials of the Austro-Hungarian empire in twenty years time.

For the moment, however, all that lay in the unknowable future. The baby had been born. It would have a future, but none knew what. In the past, the young Gavrilo would have found employment as a serf, or possibly a gendarme, working for the Turks, or as a merchant or trader. Now other possibilities were beginning to present themselves, for even in this most remote and recently acquired province of the Austro-Hungarian empire; possibilities that may have been more apparent to Nana than to Petar.

Gavrilo survived his childhood, but never became the big, strapping peasant that his parents might have wished for. He soon showed himself to be the spitting image of his mother: he had her curly hair, her blue eyes, and her pointed chin. She was known to sing like an angel, but we do not know if he inherited this quality.

She must have been a very determined woman; and it would appear that Gavrilo took after his mother in character as well as appearance. In later life, she described him tersely as 'a quiet boy, but every blow he received he would return twofold. He read much and kept silent most of the time.' [Dedjier, page 190].

Interestingly, Gavrilo himself agreed with the first part of this description. When interviewed by a prison psychiatrist, a Dr Pappenheim from Vienna, in Theresienstadt fortress in Bohemia in 1916 (Princip had been moved thither because the war which he had caused was going badly for the Austrians, and they did not want this prize political prisoner to fall into enemy hands), he was asked about his childhood, and replied: 'I was always a quiet, sentimental child, always earnest, with books, pictures.' Gavrilo may not have wished to reveal very much to the psychiatrist, whom he had no especial reason to trust, and his training in Serbia would have inclined him towards concealment rather than revelation. Moreover, although he was a quiet young man, by all accounts, he was not necessarily given to introspection. Nevertheless, Dr Pappenheim's interview notes have a whiff of authenticity about them, and it is a great pity that they were never written up into a complete psychological profile.

A childhood friend stated that:

'In his early childhood Gavrilo showed exceptional signs of development. He started to walk very early, in his ninth month, and as a child was very alert and active. As a boy he did not like to play much with his mates: he preferred to tend the calves and to watch the kmets working in the fields.

Even before he went to school (which was not, in fact, until the age of nine), as he walked behind his calves, he liked to pretend that he was a schoolboy, carrying a bag on his back with some old books. When playing with children he was very rough, often striking boys stronger than he, especially if he felt that they were doing wrong to him or that the stronger ones were slighting him.'

Gavrilo was to retain these characteristics throughout his life. He was a solitary, introverted person, and yet capable of forming close friendships, at least with the same sex: he was very shy with girls. He was proud of himself, and did not suffer sleights; and there is an undertone of aggression in his behaviour, which Malcolm (Malcolm, 2002, page 154) picks up as he describes Princip's behaviour at secondary school in 1912, when he was encouraging his fellow school-mates to take part in a protest against Hapsburg authority:

'Princip went from class to class, threatening with his knuckle-duster all the boys who wavered in coming to the new demonstrations.'

Personality and inheritance

Overall, we would say that our subject shows the same psychological profile as someone brought up in very different circumstances, the Heir Apparent, Archduke Franz Ferdinand. They were both, we would infer, introverted intuitives; and we explore this classificatory system as an annexe to the next chapter.

Overall, Gavrilo seems to have inherited more of his mother's character than his father's. What, if anything, did he inherit from his father, and what are we to make of the relationship? According to Dedijer, Petar was in many ways an exceptional man for the Grahovo valley, and should have been an admirable member of the community. He never drank, never swore, and was a pious Christian. He made a hobby of planting trees around his house, in his hamlet, and even along the road to the next village. He took his duties as postman very seriously, and would carry the heavy load of mail himself if there were too much snow for the horses.

But he was not altogether esteemed by his fellow villagers, some of whom would make fun of him behind his back; and we may infer that Petar was someone who took life very seriously, and may not have had much sense of humour. He was not interested in politics, and unlike his wife had

Among his people:
The young Gavrilo listens to his elders

no special ambitions for his sons. Altogether, it seems doubtful that he had a major influence on his son Gavrilo; and part of the reason for that is that the son went on to acquire an education which his father had never possessed—and which had not been considered necessary for his older brother Jovo.

Finally, we may note that according to family tradition Petar Princip's father, Jovo Princip, was killed in 1881 by the Austrian head of the new local administration (Dedijer, page 67). If this was true it is curious that it was never mentioned at his grandson's trial for treason and murder as a partial explanation of his motivation.

The Older Brother

The eldest son of the family, Jovo, who was seven years older than Gavrilo, was describe by Gavro in prison as an 'ordinary person': by which we may take it to mean that he had no interest in politics. Jovo, however, was a young man of great determination, who was determined to make something of life for himself. He left the valley at fifteen to make his living where he could. He settled in the village of Hadzici near Sarajevo, where he became the assistant to a timber-merchant. He was clearly a very enterprising young man. 'He soon became his own boss; at the age of twenty-one he owned several pairs of horses and was thinking of starting a little saw-mill of his own. Yet he did not break away completely from his family. He sent money to his father and took care of the education of his brothers, Gavrilo and Nikola, who was two years younger. (Nikola, it would appear, also attended the village school, and went on to complete his education elsewhere, eventually becoming a doctor.) The old bonds of *zadruga* life had not disappeared completely.' (Dedijer, page 189).

Primary school

At the age of nine, Gavrilo was entered for the local school, and began his formal education. Petar would have kept him out of school, for he had never learned his lessons, and he needed Gavrilo to look after his sheep; but Nana insisted. Only three of her ten children had survived infancy, her three boys: and she wanted the best for them.

Gavrilo seems to have enjoyed his lessons, at least at this stage of his education. His first year was difficult, until he settled in, but 'from the

Bazaar and mosque, Sarajevo 1910

second to the fourth classes he had excellent marks and for his hard work he received from his teacher a collection of Serbian heroic folk poetry, which he read in his father's home to the assembled *kmets* at the evening parties called *selo.*' [Dedjier, page 190]. He was to describe to a friend the profound impression that the *selo* made on him, in his childhood:

'The wet logs on the open fire gave the only light to the closely packed *kmets* and their wives, wrapped in thick smoke. If I tried to penetrate the curtain of smoke, the most that I could see were the eyes of human beings, numerous, sad, and glaring with some sort of fluid light coming from nowhere. Some kind of reproach, even threat, radiated from them, and many times since they have awakened me from my dreams.' (Dedjier, page 190).

Serbian Folklore

All of this was to be of great significance in moulding the young Gavrilo's character and ambitions. The Serbs as a race have traditionally placed great emphasis on the role of poetry in building national awareness and solidarity, for an equivalent of which in British culture we should need to examine the poems of the Welsh or Irish bards, or the tales of death and destruction handed down by the Angles and Saxons which we know from such texts as Beowulf, and which are related to the Norse sagas. Poems of this sort are characterised by strong rhythm and are easily committed to memory. They fulfil three purposes, outside their pure aesthetic value. Firstly, they transmit a culture to a people who cannot read or write. Secondly, they create an image of a golden age which once existed. Thirdly, they create a sense of resentment, and an overwhelming desire to recreate what had once existed and has now been lost.

The myth of a past Utopia is common to many groups or tribes; but it is of especial significance to the Serbs. Why was that age taken away, and how may it be re-achieved? Who is to blame for the present state of affairs? In the case of Serbia, with its myth of the golden age shattered by Moslem invaders, the iconic enemy is obvious: the Turks. In the case of the Bosnian Serbs, there was a more immediate enemy at hand in 1894: the Austrians. They had invaded, conquered and occupied Bosnia and Herzegovina in 1878 and in effect added them to the Austro-Hungarian empire, although the annexation was not formally completed until 1908.

It is unlikely that this formalization of the *status quo* made any practical difference; the Austrians had already shown by their investment policy over the previous thirty years, that once they had occupied Bosnia and Herzegovina they intended to stay for ever. The Austrians provided a convenient focus for Bosnian resentment, particularly as the memory of Turkish oppression faded. It was to be an inherited grievance, as it were, that drove Gavrilo Princip to extreme action in 1914.

One year before the formal annexation, in 1907, Gavrilo had reached the age of thirteen, primary school finished, and there was no secondary school near-by. Unless something could be found Gavrilo would have to begin work as a labourer or farm-hand. His brother Jovo, the businessman in the making who accepted a degree of responsibility for his younger brother, read that the Military School in Sarajevo was accepting healthy boys of 14 as cadets, and that tuition, board and clothing was free. Perfect! Gavrilo could train to be an officer in the Austro-Hungarian army, at the Emperor's expense! Petar, who had no political views, easily accepted the idea, and set out for Sarajevo with his young son to enlist him in the military.

It was August 1907, and Gavrilo had never been away from home before. There is no evidence that he ever returned, or was to have any further

Would-be brides on show near Old Servian church: Easter Monday, Sarajevo

contact with his parents except by letter; although he was to remain in contact with his brother Jovo, on whom he depended for the financing of his education. It was a three day ride on horseback before they could catch a train, and when they arrived in Sarajevo both father and son must have been astonished by what they saw in this provincial capital. Gavrilo was so scared by the sight of men in Moslem dress in the first 'han' or inn that his father approached, that he fled in terror at the sight of the 'Turks' (In reality, they were far more likely to have been ethnic Serbs whose families had long previously converted to Islam) and his father had to seek lodgings elsewhere.

Sarajevo was the first town that Gavrilo encountered, and it was to have a major influence on him. He appears to have developed a love-hate relationship with this centre for trade and administration, where so much of his life was spent.

Sarajevo in 1907

Sarajevo in 1907 was a town of around 50,000 inhabitants and an important city to the Austrians who now administered Bosnia, just as it had been an important centre to the Turks who preceded them. Arthur Evans (Evans, 2005) had been horrified to note that in 1875 it did not possess a single bookshop, a factor he put down to oriental lethargy. However, his view of Sarajevo as culturally underdeveloped was unjustified.

Then as now, Sarajevo was a subtle blend of east and west. From its Ottoman past, it inherited its mosques, minarets, madrassas, palaces, hans or inns and public fountains, as well as the Casarsija or bazaar, in which the streets were each dedicated to a single trade. From the Austrians, it had acquired a swathe of new buildings, some of which would still have been under construction when the young highlander arrived with his father. There was no exclusively Austrian part of the city and the new builidngs were added amongst the old, which helps to give Sarajevo its unique multi-cultural inheritance. We may also note that the architects employed under Austria-Hungary did not simply seek to transport Viennese architectural ideas to a new setting but were influenced by local styles.

Sarajevo has a straightforward profile. It lies 500 metres above sea-level in a natural amphitheatre bisected by the river Miljacka, which flows from East to West along a valley surrounded by five high mountains. The main buildings are in the valley and there are clusters of houses on the slopes overlooking them. At the western end of the valley lies the little resort of Ilidze, which was developed by the Romans for its sulphurous springs. It was connected by railway to Sarajevo proper[1], and the city spreads naturally until it reaches the slopes of the mountains. The river Miljacka itself, which is the key locating feature in the assassination of 1914, is both short and generally shallow, although it has been known to flood.

Although Gavrilo Princip could not have been expected to remark it, the appearance of Sarajevo was being radically altered by the new imperial power, and the pace of change was impressive. Troops overcame local resistance in 1878, and a year later Sarajevo's first secondary school was opened in a large square near the Miljacka. In 1881 the first stone was laid for a Franciscan monastery, and in 1881 a brewery was opened, to be followed by the Hotel Europe in 1882. 1884 saw a Roman Catholic

Market-place on Easter Monday, Sarajevo

cathedral and hospital open for customers—and the bells of the cathedral
would have rung out as they had not been allowed to do under the Turks.
Eight years later, a synagogue for Ashkenazi Jews was opened. (Sephardic
Jews had been welcomed many centures before, under the Turks, who
were offically tolerant of all the peoples of the Book. The Sephardic
synagogue was in the old centre of town, almost next to a huge mosque and
Islamic study centre: for one of the most noticeable features of old Saraejvo
is that almost everything is side by side.)

In 1895, the streets of Saraejvo were lit by electricity; and in 1896 the
Town Hall was completed in the neomoorish style. There was no famous
Turkish bridge over the local river, as at Mostar, the capital of Herzegovina;
but the river Miljacka was crossed by a number of bridges, including the
Latin Bridge which had orginally been constructed by a Turkish merchant,
and the Imperial Bridge at which the Young Bosnian Zerajic attempted to
shoot dead the Governor Varesanin in 1910. The river had a long quay on
its northerly bank. To the north-east of the quay was the famous bazaar,

where the streets were devoted to traditional crafts, and there was a wide variety of 'oriental' goods on display—although some of them had been made in Austria, a phenomenon not unknown to empire.

There were cafes where tiny cups of Turkish coffeee could be savoured by passers-by who always had time to pause and gossip. Fittingly, the Austro-Hungarian governor's residence or Konak to the south side of the river was the former Turkish governor's place, completed in 1869—its three wooden predecessors had been destroyed by fire, a recurring problem in the city. There were orchards in the hills overlooking the town, where the plum trees blossomed and there was a strong sense of the countryside near-by, and there were also ruins, fortifications, and mosques to be seen; and except in winter, when the snow would have lain thick and heavy and made travel almost impossible, it must have been a very pleasant setting.

Another perspective

The perceptive observer and writer Rebecca West visited Yugoslavia in the late 1930s and met many people who had been present at the time of the assassination of Franz Ferdinand in 1914. She especially befriended one of the sisters of Nedjelko Cabrinovic, a conspirator with Gavrilo Princip. As a result, Rebecca West disapproved of what the Austrians had done to Sarajevo and took a very pro-Serbian view. In her judgment, which appears more an aesthetic than an economic one, the Austrians had done their best to spoil this beautiful city by 'Germanising' it. The Austrians had built breweries, rather than supporting the local wine business; although they had built roads, and bridges and factories, their motives had been exploitive; they had been concerned to develop their new province for the sake of Austria.

What, one might ask, did she expect? The Austrians <u>were</u> imperialists; but imperialism is not necessarily without economic and social benefits for those who have been colonised. Moreover, Austrian administration had replaced, not a golden age of independence, but Turkish rule. Bosnians, as any objective commentator would judge, were better off under the Austrians than under the Turks: an argument that the Serbia-favouring Mrs West does not explore.

Nevertheless, we may note that her anti-Austrian views were shared by the young Gavrilo Princip and his friends, and not simply because the Austrians or 'Schwabe' were an occupying power. Industrialisation and urbanisation under the Austrians had encouraged some of the other characteristics of the capitalist system, such as organised prostitution, of which the Young Bosnians wholly disapproved[2]—although at least some of their fellow-countrymen must have been seduced by this apparently new temptation, so alien to the values of the *zadruga*. Gavrilo Princip did not love commercialised Sarajevo, and was reported to have said on the eve of the assassination, that if it were a matchbox he would have crushed it.

Gavrilo changes tack

Gavrilo's brother took charge of his ward and set out to take him to the military school. On the way, he stopped to buy him some underwear at a shop run by another Bosnian Serb named Jovo Pesut, who knew the Princips. The two Jovos fell into conversation. Who was the boy, and what future had been planned for him? Jovo Princip described the plan, and Jovo said that to enroll his younger brother in the military school was a very bad idea. He would be brought up to be an Austrian, and not a Bosnian Serb. He would not necessarily serve in his own province: the Austrians, like most imperialists, practised a policy of divide and rule, and he might be stationed anywhere in the empire, unable to develop local loyalties, or to be near his kith and kin.

Like his father, Jovo Princip, a keen young businessman, was not politically minded. But he was persuaded by the arguments of the shop-keeper Jovo Pesut, which were, no doubt, advanced with some fervour, whereas his own views were half-hearted; it was the financial advantages of the military school which had appealed to him, after all, and not its imperial ethos. But if Gavrilo did not go to the military school, what was to be done with him? Jovo Princip could not afford to pay for his education; and he was a long way from home. Luckily, Jovo Pesut had the answer: the commercial school. Gavrilo would learn to become a merchant or trader, like his brother, and take advantage of what the new times had to offer, without sacrificing his identity. He could make a success of himself under Austrian administration, while remaining essentially a Serb. As Pesut put it (Dedjier, page 191): "If you want to listen to me as a friend, send him to the Merchants School. This school quicker than any other will bring him bread and profit, and what a profit!"

Jovo Princip was persuaded, and Gavrilo was enrolled in the Merchants' School on the same day. Jovo found lodgings for him with a respectable widow, Stoja Ilic, where the young Gavrilo was to share the room of her son Danilo, when he was at home. Danilo was some four years older than Gavrilo, but was to become a close friend, and their futures were to be bound together inexorably. For the time being, however, Gavrilo merely noted that his room-mate to be had a wonderful collection of books. Gavrilo was fascinated by books, and longed to meet their owner.

Gavrilo Princip spent three years at the Merchants School, from 1907 to 1910, studying as required and lodging with the widow Ilic in a street just off the bazaar. Jovo's business did not always go well, and when he could not afford the rent, Gavrilo would stay with his brother at Hadzici and commute to Sarajevo. In summer, like any peasant's boy, he was expected to help with the harvest. Gavrilo did not endear himself to his sister-in-law, and her mother. He had no interest in farming, or his brother's timber business, and was much more interested in reading: he was always to be found with his nose in a book, which they considered a useless activity that did not help the family business at all.

Gavrilo's character and education

What was the young Gavrilo Princip like, as a young teenager? His character seems to have been formed very early on, and to have remained much the same for the rest of his life: he was quiet, reserved, immensely determined, and very touchy about his lack of stature. A friend wrote of him:

"He did not like it, because of his small build, when his friends called him Gavrica; he longed to be nicknamed Gavroche, like Victor Hugo's boy hero in *Les Miserables*. He had a longish face, dark bushy hair, a wrinkled forehead, a very pointed chin, and his nose was a little twisted from an accident at school. His whole appearance radiated energy and determination, although his light-blue eyes softened the expression of his face. At first sight quiet and silent, in discussions he would sometimes become cynical and tough; stubborn but not pig-headed. I remember once when we were young schoolboys and we discussed the youth movement and youth leaders, I said about someone that he was a brave man; Princip retorted at once: 'We are all brave men, too.' [Princip was to use a phrase very like this at his trial].

He liked to make jokes and had a sense of humour. " (Dedjier, page 192)

Gavrilo Princip came to hate the merchants school, for it represented everything that the young, impressionable Bosnian did not wish to become. Evans, never a man to mince his words, had described the merchant class of Sarajevo in contemptuous terms thirty years before as money-grubbing peasants who had no interest in either culture or education, and were not prepared to do anything to assist even their own Bosnian Serb community to improve its situation; and there is no evidence that the situation had improved since then. Gavrilo discovered that he had no desire to become a merchant, and that their attitude to life was hateful to him. He would have to be careful in expressing this view, at least to his brother; but he was able to share it with the young Bosnians with whom he spent most of his time, and who shared his hatreds and burgeoning ideals.

What, then, was he to do? Gavrilo was able to persuade his brother, who was at first very understandably reluctant, that he should transfer to the classical high school. The long-suffering Jovo engaged a tutor in Latin and Greek, and Gavrilo was able to pass the examinations and to be accepted into the High School at Tuzla. He entered the fourth grade in the autumn of 1910, after three years in the Merchants School. Tuzla was about fifty miles from Sarajevo.

The new school was not a conspicuous success, for Gavrilo was no longer so quiet, studious, and withdrawn; and whilst we cannot describe him as a rebellious adolescent, he was beginning to behave more independently. He played an aggressive game of billiards; he took part in a protest about compulsory religious fasting; and he missed a large number of classes. He asked for a transfer to the high school in Sarajevo, to which he moved after one year in Tuzla. According to Dedijer (op. cit, page 193), 'Vaso Cubrilovic, himself a student at that time in Tuzla and one of the conspirators in the Sarajevo plot, described Gavrilo as a *stuha*, a slightly satiric description, signifying a restless spirit who could never settle down.'

By this time, Gavrilo was a young man of seventeen, deeply unsure as to what he wanted to do. Although deeply immersed in his books, he was not a brilliant scholar and was not likely to attract any scholarships. (This was in contrast to the Young Bosnia leader Gacinovic, whom Gavrilo Princip seems never to have met, although the two knew of each other.) If

Gavrilo were to go to university, that was still some distance away, and there was no guarantee that he would make it.

It was by now 1911. What was he to do? The answer was obvious. Gavrilo was a Serb, at least by identification. Serbia was at war, for the First Balkan War had just begun. He, Gavrilo Princip would fight for Serbia and prove himself a man.

The First Balkan War: An ambition frustrated

Unfortunately, his plans were frustrated, and perhaps the most significant decision in the young Bosnian Serb's life was made. Gavrilo Princip was able to make his way to Belgrade, to make contact with The Black Hand, and to join one of the training camps for comitadje or volunteer guerrilla fighters that had been set up to help the regular Serbian forces pursue the war. However, when he presented himself to Major Tankosic, the chief aide of Colonel Apis and fellow member of the Black Hand, the laconic irregular forces commander was not impressed. He took the merest glance at the willing young Bosnian Serb and dismissed him with a contemptuous gesture of his hand.

'You are too small and too weak', he said, and waved him away.[3] Whether the Major's peremptory assessment was correct or not (the comitadje were expected to be able to carry heavy packs, rifles and ammunition, to live rough and, in Tankosic's words, to sleep in the rain) this was a shattering blow to Gavrilo's pride, and was probably the major factor in his plans to take part in an assassination. If he could not impress his peers in one way, he would do so in another, by direct action: and the most radical form of direct action was to assassinate a leading figure who was publically associated with repression.

Assassination, however, could not be carried out alone. Whom should he assassinate, and with whose assistance? Clearly, a leading Austrian official must be the target. Bogdan Zerjaic had attempted to kill the military governor of Bosnia and Herzegovina, in 1910. General Varesanin had since retired, to be replaced by General Potiorek. Potiorek would do nicely; and the necessary assistance would be provided from the inner core of three young men who formed around Gavrilo Princip: Cabrinovic, Grabez and Ilic. All were Bosnian Serbs, and the backgrounds of all four had much in common.

Nedjelko Cabrinovic

Nedjelko Cabrinovic (1895-1916) was born in Sarajevo on 20 January 1895, the eldest of nine children. His father, a giant of a man, ran a second class café and was obliged to provide information to the police as part of his licence. The young Nedjelko and his father often quarrelled, sometimes violently, and the relationship between the two of them was a tempestuous one. Nedjelko was an impulsive boy whose life was ruled by his emotions, and might nowadays have been classified as hyperactive. He took a very early interest in revolutionary politics, which his father was the last person to understand: the elder Cabrinovic assumed that his son could simply be disciplined like a dog, and that was the worst treatment possible for a person of Nedjelko's character.

There is a fascinating portrait of the father in Rebecca West's account of her travels in Yugoslavia just before the Second World War, for the English actress, activist and writer became a great friend of Vukosava Cabrinovic, the elder of the late Nedjelko Cabrinovic's two sisters, who survived political imprisonment in the First World War, married and had children, and went on to qualify and practise as a dentist. (Before 28 June 1914 she had also become the friend of Gavrilo Princip.)

According to Vukosava's account, her father was not a bad man, but was an appallingly literal one. He had absolutely no insight into other peoples' emotions, and believed that he could rule his home with a rod of iron; in a curious way, even his rewards were punishments, for when he gave his daughter a new dress in which to play the piano at a public recital, it was made of something like sailcloth (so that it would last) and was impossible even to wear, let alone to serve as an appropriate item of apparel for a sensitive young girl.

Had they been characters in a Hollywood film, no doubt it would eventually have been revealed that the apparently hateful Mr Cabrinovic had a heart of gold beneath his brusque exterior, and simply needed the love of a beautiful daughter to bring it out; but Sarajevo was not Tinseltown, and he never realised the error of his ways. His embarrassment and shame at being identified as the father of a regicide can only be guessed at, although he was unlikely to have blamed himself in any way for what happened; and he was to take his own life in 1924.

Nedjelko attended the Merchants School in Sarajevo for one year, from 1907 to 1908, but failed to pass the end of year examination. His father promptly took him away from school, and the fourteen year old boy tried and failed at three trades before becoming a type-setter. Nedjelko was a natural rebel, and rapidly became involved in the union. He continued to live at home until he was fifteen, despite frequent quarrels with both his parents, and to continue his radical reading habits. Nedjelko had an active mind and should have been left at school to continue his education.

As it was, he was forced to choose what to read for himself, which did not give him a balanced education; and he was acutely aware, when he became involved in revolutionary activism, that unlike his colleagues he had left school at fourteen and could not be called a student. There was an element of academic snobbery, even in Young Bosnia; and even a youth such as Gavrilo Princip, who had remained in secondary education for four years after Nedjelko but failed to graduate from high school, clearly believed himself entitled, in some sense, to look down on his less educated colleague.

Nedjelko Cabrinovic left home at fifteen and lived and worked elsewhere, both in Bosnia and Croatia, and finally in Belgrade. He returned to Sarajevo in 1912, where his mother promptly burned his latest assembly of anarchist books, on which he had spent all his money. He found work as a printer, but was accused by the police of being a leading organiser of strikes, and was eventually banished from Sarajevo for five years. His father must have felt some responsibility for the welfare of his tumultuous son, for he was able, with the leader of the printers's union, to have the ban lifted; and Nedjelko came home once again.

Presence did not make the heart grow fonder, and the normal state of war was soon resumed between father and son. His father even ordered Nedjelko not to write to his sister, Vukosava, who was studying to be a teacher, in Croatia; but this ban was ignored. Nedjelko worked in Trieste and Belgrade once again, before returning home in June 1914.

Trifko Grabez

Trifko Grabez, like Vladimir Gacinovic, was the son of an orthodox priest of peasant origin. Trifko was born in 1895 in Pale, near Sarajevo, and was able to attend high school. In some ways, he seems to have been the most 'normal' of the inner group of three conspirators. Although he was committed to revolutionary activity, that was the norm for his associates; and outside his membership of Young Bosnia, which he joined as a school-boy, he appears to have been a normal young man with the normal appetites, neither as reserved as Princip nor as volatile as Cabrinovic. Grabez had a temper, for he was expelled from school and went to prison for a fortnight for having struck one of his teachers. (He did not return home at that stage, but found his way to Belgrade, where his studies were a success.) After his arrest in 1914 he defended himself vigourously in court, with the sharpness of youth, and was not ashamed to have taken part in the conspiracy.

At the same time, there is no indication that he wished to die. When the moment came for action, he did not take it; nor did he take his suicide pill; and when the police caught up with him near Pale, he was on his way back to Serbia and safety. He played an active part in the preparations for the *attentat*, and it was he who accompanied Princip on the 'mystic journey' from Belgrade to Sarajevo: they shared a mistrust of the babblesome Cabrinovic, who could not be relied upon the keep his eyes open and his mouth closed. If Cabrinovic was the martyr, always conscious of his slights, and Princip the sunken-eyed idealist whose company cannot always have been a cheerful experience, then Grabez was the normal young man.

Danilo Ilic

Danilo Ilic was the only son of a cobbler who died when he was five. His mother then made a living by taking in washing and by renting out a room to lodgers. Ilic graduated from the Merchants School in 1905 and worked as a prompter, labourer and porter before winning a scholarship to attend a teachers' training college from which he graduated in 1912. He worked as a teacher in Herzegovina, but suffered poor health and returned to Sarajevo, where he was able to find employment as a bank clerk. In June 1913 he visited Gacinovic in Switzerland and met some Russian social revolutionaries. When the Second Balkan war broke out he walked from Sarajevo to Serbia and served as a nurse, treating soldiers infected with cholera. He then returned to Sarajevo and worked as a proof-reader, editor and translator.

Ilic was a tall, quiet man who always wore a dark tie as a reminder of death, and was known as Hadji to his friends in Sarajevo, who regarded his travels in Switzerland and Serbia as the equivalent of the Moslem's visit to Mecca. He was to play a major and yet ambivalent role in the Sarajevo attentat, which we explore in depth in a later chapter.

These, then, were Gavrilo's closest friends; and it was with them that he was to make his mark in history. A better target than the military governor was soon to present itself: for Princip and his fellow-conspirators learned that the Heir Apparent himself was planning to visit Sarajevo. Fate had delivered him into their hands.

APPENDICES

Arthur John Evans (1851-1941) was an illustrious product of the Victorian era, whose interests and enthusiasm were infused with the optimism of an age in which nothing seemed impossible and progress was the norm.

Arthur graduated from Oxford in 1874 with first class honours in history, taking archaeology as a newly offered option. Small, short-sighted and highly energetic, Arthur was a fluent and vivid writer, who began to write for the press whilst travelling in the long vacation—a habit he was to continue.

In 1875, he visited Bosnia with his brother Lewis. There was a rural insurrection in progress, and despite their passes they were taken for Russian spies and briefly imprisoned by the Turkish authorities. On their release the two brothers travelled on to Sarajevo and then Mostar in Herzegovina, and then took a boat to Ragusa (now Dubrovnik).

Arthur Evans was both an adventurous and determined young man, and was certainly not to be deterred by the Turks in his ambition to find out what was going on. Evans was able to make contact with the Bosnian rebels, and came to admire them and to support their campaign against a corrupt and exploitative administration. Those rebels, as we have already remarked, were the immediate ancestors of Gavrilo Princip, who was born a generation after the insurrection ended, and tales of which would have influenced his childhood.

As Brown (Brown, 1993, page 19) records: 'On his return to Oxford, Evans found life extremely dull, but re-lived his travels when writing the informatively titled *Through Bosnia and Herzegovina on foot during the Insurrection, August and September 1875.* The book, published in 1876, was reviewed in the *Manchester Guardian*: "This is a most opportune contribution to the geography, customs and history of a country which has suddenly emerged from the dimmest obscurity into the full glare of European observation…" The book was a great success, extensively quoted in Parliament and indeed all over the country; a second edition appeared in the following year.'

Interest in the Great Eastern Uprising was sustained, and in 1877, Evans was appointed the Balkan correspondent of the *Manchester Guardian*. *Illyrian Letters* followed, in which the young correspondent continued to be deeply sympathetic to the insurgents and critical of the Turkish authorities.

In 1878, the Austrians replaced the Turks as the rulers of Bosnia, and at the same time Arthur Evans found a new interest. He met and fell in love with Margaret Freeman, the daughter of an Oxford professor who had been travelling in the Balkans. Professor Freeman's two daughters had been working for an English lady, Miss Irby, who had dedicated her considerable energies towards Bosnian famine relief. Miss Irby was an ngo founder and director before the term had been invented. Like many early ngo enthusiasts, Miss Irby was a friend of the great and the good—Gladstone, an enthusiast against imperial Turkey and its atrocities in Bulgaria, was to preface her book about the Balkans—and was to obtain the bemused respect of those whom she helped (as we mention elsewhere, a street in Sarajevo is named after her.)

Margaret and Arthur married and took up residence in Raguza. His newfound domestic bliss did not stop Arthur's investigative journalism, and in 1882 the Austrian authorities accused him of spying and placed him under arrest: the second regime to do so, in the same territory. Arthur Evans was banished from the Austro-Hungarian Empire, and that ended his career as a journalist.

From 1884 to 1908, Arthur Evans was the dynamic Keeper of the Ashmolean Museum in Oxford. In 1894 he first visited Crete, still in Turkish hands. He became a (controversial) expert and writer on Cretan ancient remains, to which he gave the name of the Minoan civilisation, after the Greek King Minos.

In 1911, Sir Arthur Evans was knighted for his services to archaeology, and in particular his work in Crete. Sadly, his wife and constant companion Margaret had died in 1893, and although building a substantial home for himself just outside Oxford on Boars Hill, he never re-married. He died in 1941.

Some further thoughts on Miss West

Miss West's book on the Balkans (West, 1939) is to be highly praised for the quality of its prose. However, much of what she records as fact is second-hand and would not stand up in court; and she does not check her facts. Let us consider, for example, two confident assertions that Rebecca West makes as a result of her visit to Sarajevo. They are to be found in West, 1939, pages 437 to 438.

One

Miss West argues that none of the three young men who took part in the assassination of Franz Ferdinand and who later died in prison showed any sign of tuberculosis before they went to prison; and that therefore they did not have tuberculosis beforehand. This opinion comes from her conversations with Nejelko Cabrinovic's surviving sister, a dentist married to a doctor whom Miss West and her husband befriended in their travels in Yugoslavia towards the end of the 1930s. The West view is unproven, and on the balance of probabilities, it is quite likely that the young men were already infected. Princip, Cabrinovic and Grabez had led irregular, impoverished, hand-to-mouth lives, whether as would-be students or itinerant workers; and tuberculosis was a widespread disease which struck both poor and rich alike—as we may note in the case of the Archduke Franz Ferdinand.

It may have suited Austrian propagandists to argue that the young assassins were infected with tuberculosis and knew it, and that therefore their mission was not quite so self-sacrificial as it appeared, since they were in any case doomed to die; but that assertion does not tell us whether or not they *were* infected.

Two

Miss West denies that Nedjelko Cabrinovic's father was a police spy. Again, her source for this assertion is the testimony of his daughter; and here we feel that she is on false ground. Why?

Firstly, it is generally asserted that Nedjelko's father <u>was</u> a police spy; and smoke is often the result of a fire.

Secondly, it seems highly likely that this was a condition of his employment as a licensed inn-keeper within a newly-acquired territory of the Austro-Hungarian empire, in which the empire wished to acquire as much information as possible at every level.

Thirdly, it would help to explain his son's embarrassment and desire to prove himself, which he showed on so many occasions.

Fourthly, it would explain why Nedjelko, a political activist and agitator with a known record as a supporter and organizer of strikes, was allowed to roam freely between Belgrade and Sarajevo, and indeed within Sarajevo itself, at the time of the imperial visit—and why the police failed to arrest him even when his presence was brought to their attention.

Finally, we may note the words of Nedjelko himself, at his trial. 'On another occasion, when a political opinion of his father was mentioned, Cabrinovic jumped to his feet and shouted to the presiding judge: "He was your spy!"'

(Dedijer, page 344.)

NOTES

[1] The railway has now been replaced by a tram and Ilidze has been absorbed into the suburbs of Sarajevo. The area around the tram and bus terminus is unlovely and in 2009 was in need of attention. Sarajevans visit Ilidze to walk, cyle, and visit the source of the springs. The hotel Bosna where Franz Ferdinand and his wife stayed in 1914 is still open for business.

[2] A commentator noted that the prostitutes of Sarajevo dressed as Muslims, even if they were Christian: presumably to offer a touch of the exotic East, or to lessen the shame on their own religion.

[3] Remak's account does not quite tally with this. According to his version, Princip followed the programme at the training camp, but was not then passed fit for active service. Remak presumes that it was already evident that he was tubercular.

CHAPTER FIVE

Stranger than fiction:
The Archduke Franz Ferdinand and his wife

"You think every man is an angel at the outset, and have unfortunate
experiences afterwards. I regard everyone whom I meet for the first
time as a scoundrel, and wait till he does somethng to justify a better
opinion in my eyes."
FRANZ FERDINAND

The birth of an archduke

The Archduke Franz Ferdinand was born in Graz, Austria on 18
December 1863. He was the first of three sons of the Archduke Karl
Ludwig and his second wife Maria Annunciata, who died of tuberculosis in
1871 at the age of 28. Franz Ferdinand's father then married for the third
time, as both his first and second wives had died young, and Franz
Ferdinand acquired a stepmother in 1873, Maria Theresa (1855-1944) who
was only eight years older than him.

He does not appear to have had a close relationship with his father Karl
Ludwig, who has left little impression on history except for the manner of
his death. However, the relationship between stepmother and son proved
an excellent one and Franz Ferdinand could always turn to her for support.
Franz Ferdinand, an aloof and apparently cold figure who was extremely
reluctant to confide in people, was able to confide in her; and he had need
of a confidante.

It seemed unlikely that the Archduke Franz Ferdinand would become emperor, for in between him and his eventual succession stood two other candidates: his first cousin, Crown Prince Rudolf, Franz Joseph's only son; and his father, the Archduke Karl Ludwig, the second of four brothers of whom the oldest was the reigning emperor.

Admittedly, his father was unlikely to succeed to the throne. In the first place, he was not very much younger than his older brother. Secondly, Karl Ludwig was unfitted by temperament for supreme power, and the Hapburg dynasty was sufficiently realistic to attempt to ensure that a suitable candidate came to the throne and not just the person who was next in line. The divine right to be king could show itself in various ways, and some aptitude for imperial power was needed if the Hapsburgs were to survive—which was always their fundamental priority.

Karl Ludwig was not hopelessly unsuitable, like his younger brother Ludwig, who had been spoiled by his mother, and who enjoyed dressing in women's clothing and spent his time 'cruising' Vienna looking for pretty young men. This in itself was not entirely a disqualification, for the Hapsburgs were surprisingly tolerant of sexual variation, provided that it was kept within bounds. Mistresses, discreet liaisons, and even the occasional orgy were part of the aristocratic way of life, to which Queen Victoria, with her strong belief in conventional morality, was to prove the exception rather than the rule; and her own son was to revert to type in taking mistresses and fathering bastards. Even the restrained emperor himself, Franz Joseph, was to take a mistress when his wife proved unwilling to satisfy his 'conjugal needs.'

Karl Ludwig had no sexual peccadilloes to retard or enhance his claim to the throne. He was a strongly pious man, described in Dedijer (Dedijer, page 89) as 'from early youth to the end of his days a docile pupil and tool of his religious teachers,' the Jesuits. He lacked the drive and determination to be an emperor and preferred private life, in which he fathered a total of six children by his second and third marriages. In any case, he removed himself from the equation in 1896, when he went on a pilgrimage to the Holy Land and drank water from the River Jordan, despite having been warned not to do so. He died of typhoid in May and removed another brother from the emperor.

Crown Prince Rudolf

From birth to untimely death, Crown Prince Rudolf was the official heir to the throne. Had he come to power he might have reformed his ramshackle empire for the better, for he did not lack intelligence and ideas, and he should have been able to appeal to a wide cross-section of the population—something which appeared to be beyond the power of the average Hapsburg. Hapsburgs tended to dwell behind the unbreachable walls of wealth, privilege and seclusion, and did not even read the newspapers—a weakness if they really wished to know what was going on.

Rudolf was born on 21 August 1858, the second child and only son of the Emperor Franz Joseph and his wife Elizabeth. As a male, he would succeed to the throne in place of his sisters, for such was the Hapsburg tradition. He had a better education than his first cousin Franz Ferdinand, for it was not left solely in the hands of a private tutor: and if his father was the unimaginative Franz Joseph, his mother was of a very different sort.

The Empress Elizabeth took a very great interest in his education, and subverted the machinations her powerful mother-in-law to do so. Elizabeth had great character; rather too much of it, in fact, and she was determined to see that Rudolf was not brought up to be the average Hapsburg.

Despite having married into the family, Elizabeth hated the Hapsburgs. She hated her mother-in-law, the power behind the throne who had placed her husband upon it, out of the line of succession. She hated the court. She hated the formality of imperial life in Vienna, with its parades, and speeches, and awards and endless ceremonies; and whilst she was prepared to take every advantage of being married to the endlessly patient Franz Joseph, she was never prepared to fulfill her part of the bargain, and provide a silent but visible support to his presence at centre stage.

Every marriage, it is said, is a mystery to those outside it. The most unhappy couples, who are constantly quarrelling and crticizing each other, remain united, whereas a superficial cordiality may conceal deep divisions. The marriage of Franz Joseph and Elizabeth was especially mysterious.

At first, it was a love match: she was an outstanding beauty, and he was a presentable young army officer and the emperor to boot. The normally restrained Franz Joseph fell in love with Elizabeth at first sight. They soon married, and when Elizabeth gave birth to her first baby, both parents were overjoyed. (They were to have four children: three girls and a boy.) However, the young mother was both headstrong and neurotic, and both characteristics were destined to become more prominent as she grew older. Unlike her husband, who was to spend a lifetime in compromising until his final and fatal decision to declare war on Serbia in 1914, Elizabeth was unable to compromise over anything. She was, it appeared, intensely able: she was certainly intense.

This unlikely marriage between the generally cautious autocrat and the headstrong neurotic seemed destined to fail, but in fact lasted until her death at the hands of an assassin in 1895—whereafter the emperor ruled as a widower, increasingly fond of his grand-children, but with only the company of Katharina Schratt, his long-term mistress, to provide the female element in which his life was so conspicuously lacking.

What did Elizabeth do for Franz Joseph? She provided him with four children, including a male heir. She took an interest in imperial affairs where she found them to be intrinisically interesting: she liked Hungary and the Hungarians, for example, and took the trouble to learn Magyar, a notoriously difficult language which bore no relationahip to any other European language apart from Finnish.[1] Elizabeth was able to converse with Hungarian officials as well as ordinary people, and to advise Franz Joseph on the internal doings of the other half of the joint empire.

If she failed to supply her husband with his conjugal rights, except so far as providing an heir was concerned, she made sure that those rights were satisfied elsewhere. The Empress Elizabeth took a keen interest in her husband's relationship with Katherina Schratt, the married Viennese actress whose profligate husband had deserted her, and far from disapproving of the adulterous relationship which developed between the middle-aged emperor and the younger actress, the empress encouraged it to the best of her ability, even befriending the actress herself.

But Elizabeth was not prepared to play her part on the imperial stage, and to act the part of the empress. A monarch does not have to be brilliant. She does not have to be witty, or charming, or even clever: monarchs build their reputation in other ways. But she does have to be there: and this Elizabeth, for all her good looks, expensive wardrobe, obsessive exercise and fanatical dieting, was unable to do. She would spend a week or two in

Vienna, probably staying away from the official imperial residence, and living elsewhere: and then she would leave again, to go hunting in England, or to stay in the villa that the besotted emperor had built for her in Corfu, despite the objection to its cost from the Viennese parliament; or to travel in Africa.

Meanwhile, the emperor rose at four a.m. each morning, washed in cold water in a basin held by a servant, ate a Spartan breakfast, and went to his office to complete another hard day's administration on work which might have been delegated to others, but from which he obtained the grim satisfaction of doing his duty.

These, then, were Rudolf's parents. He identified with his intelligent and beautiful mother, who could have done so much for the empire if she had put her mind to it, but was seldom in Vienna to do so. He had a more cautious and formal relationship with his father, who loved him but was unable to show it, and did not share his radical ideas—although he was aware of them from the reports of his secret police, for he kept his son under surveillance under the guise of protecting him.

The rebel within?

Naturally, Rudolf was commissioned into the imperial and royal army—the obvious training environment for the heir to the throne, and a good place for him to learn something about military affairs and sow his wild oats at the same time, since he would be able to rely on the discretion of his fellow officers who were also members of the higher aristocracy. Rudolf took to the military life, but was not wholly absorbed by it. He had wide interests, including a scientific curiosity; and he had a real interest in the future of the empire, towards the study of which he commissioned a 24 volume encyclopaedia. He was a good public speaker, capable of holding the attention of his audience; and he wrote radical articles in the press whose officially anonymous authorship was an open secret.

Rudolf, in other words, was a reformer from within. For a long time he retained a friendship with his cousin Franz Ferdinand, for both of them saw the empire as stultifying conservative and much in need of reform; but this friendship was discouraged by officialdom, including the church, and the two men gradually drifted apart.

Death of a crown prince

In many ways, Rudolf might have proved a competent ruler; but that was not to happen. His father failed to give his heir a significant command; and his military duties did not absorb him. In early 1886 he fell seriously ill, probably with a venereal infection, and from that time onwards he was a very sick man, drinking too much and heavily dependent on morphia (Van der Kiste, page 130). Since his fall from a tree in childhood he had been subject to severe headaches, and they became more frequent. Ill-health and self-indulgence were slowly destroying the potential of the crown prince, who was condemned, or at least allowed himself, to idle away his time and dissipate his talents during the reign of a father who appeared capable of going on for ever.

Rudolf removed himself from the line of succession by the simple if drastic expedient of killing his female companion and then shooting himself, at the imperial hunting lodge at Mayerling, near Vienna, during the evening and night of 29/30 January 1889—his official death being declared as on 30 January. This was the scandal to end all scandals, and had a shattering effect on the Hapsburg dynasty. Why did the Crown Prince, who had everything to live for, commit suicide? Other possibile explanations for his death were put forward, including murder by a person or persons unknown. But there is no evidence for such alternative accounts, and enough material to suggest, at least on the balance of probabilities if not beyond all reasonable doubt, that the Crown Prince Rudolf took his own life. Franz Joseph had no other sons; and Franz Ferdinand, his awkward and unbeloved nephew, became the heir apparent.

The education of an archduke

Franz Ferdinand was educated privately by a number of tutors, on such dry subjects as family history and constitutional law. An historian with a sense of humour, Joachim Remak commented on this (Remak, 1959): 'His education was private and of the sort that goes far towards explaining why there are so few ruling monarchs left in the world'—by which he meant that it was a very poor one. If the purpose of an education is to awaken a child's imagination, to give it some sense of belonging to humanity, and to teach it to think for itself, then the young Franz Ferdinand, like his uncle the Emperor, received nothing of this. Instead, he was encouraged or rather forced to learn by rote, and was given an unhealthy indoctrination into an extremely conservative view of the world, and the importance of the Hapsburgs to that world, by his very narrow-minded tutors, who rewrote European history for his benefit—and to one of whom, none the less, he formed a strong attachment.

With Karl Ludwig's strong approval Franz Ferdinand was steeped in the rituals and mysteries of the Roman Catholic church, which he was never to question. Unlike his brothers, he absorbed all of this and remained a practising and indeed enthusiastic Roman Catholic for the rest of his life. Roman Catholic, we might note, rather than a genuine follower of the life and teachings of Jesus Christ: for there was nothing very Christian about the Archduke Franz Ferdinand of Austria-Este. A sense of compassion, an instinct for charity and a belief in the fundamental goodness of humanity were not part of his make-up.

He did not master the languages which were highly desirable to a future emperor, if he were to be able to converse at least with his more important subjects; Franz Ferdinand's linguistic skills were confined to German, and he always found it impossible to master Hungarian, the second language of the empire. This may have partly accounted for his hatred of the Hungarians, whom he never trusted and for whom he never had a good word. We may note that there was nothing very exceptional for the time about Franz Ferdinand's education. Education within the Austro-Hungarian empire was a rigidly authoritarian process, and the writer Stefan Zweig describes its miseries in his autobiography, in which he claims that he learned almost nothing at school and could not wait to leave.

Franz Ferdinand grew into a strongly made man of medium height, who appears remarkably slim in earlier photographs, although he was to put on weight as he grew older. He had steel-grey eyes and a cold, hard, penetrating gaze, wore his hair en brosse, and cultivated what is called a cavalryman's moustache. In his photographs he usually looks stern, uncaring and unbending, although on rare occasions his face is transformed by a smile. In his portraits with his family, there is the ghost of another personality, and a hint of paternal pride. But those photographs are highly stylised, and the viewer is obliged to infer what lies behind that fixed gaze.

He enjoyed sports, especially hunting, and was an excellent shot with any weapon, including a revolver. His preferred method of shooting game was not to stalk the stag in its natural environment, like his uncle, but rather to organise a shoot in such a way that the game was driven towards the guns, and the eventual death-tally became quite horrifying. In his lifetime Franz Ferdinand shot over 5000 stags and an astonishing grand total of other animals. He was a quick and quick tempered shot and dangerous to be near, and his temper when shooting was liable to be explosive.

Franz Ferdinand had no interest in art or literature, except for an aversion to modern art, and cared little for the music for which Vienna was so famous: he is described by Stefan Zweig as sitting stone-faced at the opera and never smiling at or applauding what happened on stage.

In summary, the young Archduke was remarkably untypical of his class and period. He was not a man about town; he did not run a string of mistresses; he had no interest in art or culture; and he did not share the spirit of happy fatalism which characterised Vienna in the declining days of the Austro-Hungarian empire. The Archduke Franz Ferdinand did not believe that the empire was doomed, but he did believe that it was in need of drastic reform, both militarily and politically: and to this problem, he was to draft a radical solution.

Military service

The pattern for a young Archduke and potential successor to the throne was a predictable one. Firstly, he would be privately educated. Secondly, he would join the army. Franz Ferdinand joined the imperial army at the age of fourteen, in the cavalry. He was suited to the military life, although never popular with his fellow officers, as he was much too rigid and unsociable a personality for that. He particularly disliked, for both professional and personal reasons, those officers who insisted on speaking Hungarian. (German was the official language of the army, but not unnaturally, Hungarian regiments tended to use their native language on the parade ground, as well as off it.) His uncle, Franz Joseph, was aware of his nephew's unsociability and urged his nephew to cultivate a more human side: but the advice did not take effect.

Promotion came rapidly for the young Archduke. He was promoted to captain in 1885 at the age of 21; major in 1888, at 24; colonel in 1890, at 26; and general in 1896, at 32. Finally, in 1913 his uncle made him inspector general of the army.

All seemed to be going extremely well. He was the official heir apparent, after the deaths of both his father and his first cousin the Crown Prince Rudolf. His military career had proved reasonably successful, in so far as we can tell for someone who was never required to lead troops in battle; and he was poised to replace his uncle when the ageing Franz Joseph finally died. He had travelled to Italy, Germany, England and the Near East. He had made a world tour, from 1892 to 1893, travelling on the warship *Empress Elizabeth*, during which he was able to see something of the world far beyond the Austro-Hungarian empire, and, at least in theory, to broaden his mind and challenge his preconceptions. In practice it seems doubtful if this occurred, and the two volumes in which he records his travels do not contain any such revelation. Nevertheless, if narrow in his outlook, Franz Ferdinand had a highly developed practical intelligence. He was quick to weigh up both ideas and people, and to decide upon the advantages and disadvantages of a proposed course of action. Whatever else might be said against him, no-one could call the heir to the throne obtuse.

In 1913, Franz Ferdinand was full of ambition and ideas, and determined to reform an empire which was very much in need of it—just like his cousin Rudolf, and the two cousins had once been very close. The emperor may not have welcomed his nephew into his bosom, and did not share the secrets of state with him on a personal basis: but he did allow the heir apparent to prepare himself for supreme power by giving him access to the relevant information, and Franz Ferdinand had built up for himself a military chancellery in Vienna, staffed by highly intelligent yourg men—a sort of think-tank for the future ruler, in which information was sifted, possibilities were reviewed, options chosen or discarded, and policies formulated for future use. Everything was in his favour; or so it appeared.

Against this optimistic scenario, we may posit negative factors.

Firstly, Franz Ferdinand's health was a major problem, both because he was a victim of tuberculosis and for other reasons.

Secondly, he had made an unsuitable marriage, at least as far as Franz Joseph was concerned; and had estranged himself both from the emperor and his court.

Thirdly, it could be argued that he was quite unsuited both in character and personality for imperial power. If not mad, Franz Ferdinand was certainly unbalanced, with a ferocious temper and an inability to take a moderate view on almost any subject. He quarrelled with almost everyone, and rarely retained his followers for very long. Even if they were both loyal and competent he would become jealous of their abilities, and they would soon find themselves out of a job.

The exception to this was Colonel Alexander Brosch von Aarenhau, who proved a brilliant staff officer to the irascible heir apparent from 1905 to 1911, during which time he organised Franz Ferdinand's military chancellery so effectively that it became known, not entirely in jest, as the alternative government in Vienna: for most officials wished to keep themselves in good standing not only with the current emperor but his chosen successor.[2] Everyone liked the young colonel, and everyone could do business with him: what a contrast to his master! Colonel Brosch resigned in 1911, worn out, no doubt, by working for so demanding and unthankful a taskmaster. Like so many others, he was to die in battle in the service of the empire—in Brosch's case in 1914.

Overall, Franz Ferdinand's character was more suited to the role of a dictator in crisis than the management of a carefully-balanced, multi-cultural empire, in which one interest had always to be balanced against another; and his temper was only part of the problem.

The health of the heir apparent

Franz Ferdinand's mother, Maria Annunciata, had died of tuberculosis in 1872 at the age of 28. Tuberculosis in the nineteenth century was a major, if not the major, cause of premature death. Little was known about it, and there was no recognised and proven cure. Diagnosis with TB, which was especially prevalent in the poorest sections of sociey but could be found at any level, was almost a sentence of death, especially for the poorer classes. The patient would be isolated, encouraged to eat nourishing food and get plenty of rest and fresh air, if possible in a sanatorium in the mountains, where the air was clearer; and a recovery would be hoped for. The chances were not good.

Franz Ferdinand was diagnosed with tuberculosis in 1895, in both lungs. The news was a tremendous shock, and rapidly reached those who took care to know such things. Franz Ferdinand's opponents at court and elsewhere were delighted with the news that this extremely unpopular Archduke would apparently be out of the running in the race for emperor; and his younger brother Otto was treated as the unofficial heir apparent. Otto was everything that his older brother was not. Handsome, debonair and charming, he was an inveterate womaniser, which did his reputation no harm in Viennese society, where a 'man of the world' was very much preferred to the cold and withdrawn Franz Ferdinand.

The heir apparent did not do the decent thing and pass away quietly, but remained obstinately alive. Reluctantly but seriously, he applied himself to curing his disease, retreating to different climes, and retiring from public life as far as he could; and by the summer of 1897 he was pronounced out of danger. His younger brother had never been pronounced heir apparent in his place; and the unpopular archduke was back in business.[3]

The disease left its mark, for from then on the Archduke had to be careful of his health, and not to exert himself unduly: a considerable irritation for so active a man. Nevertheless, he was cured provided he were careful.

However, if tuberculosis were not enough, there were other concerns about the health of the heir apparent. We have already noted his appalling temper, and his propensity to fly into a rage on the smallest provocation. There was in-breeding in the Hapsburg family, which was exacerbated by the Haspburg Family Law, which forbade marriage outside a very limited strata, and which limited the gene pool. However, it usually showed itself as idiocy rather than paranoia; but there was something dangerously unstable about the Archduke. There was no official explanation for what may have been wrong with him, and none has emerged since. It is also entirely possible that the reports of his bad temper may have been exaggerated. He was not a popular man, and the press took every opportunity to smear his reputation.

Marriage

Time went by, and the Archduke Franz Ferdinand did not marry, despite a wealth of opportunities for so very eligible a bachelor: for in addition to his position as heir apparent, and plethora of titles as a leading Hapsburg, the Archduke Franz Ferdinand was extremely rich. He had with considerable private possessions in the way of estates, castles and commercial enterprises, which he ran very effectively; and a young Archduke in possession of a fortune must be in want of a wife.

He was expected and indeed obliged to marry not only someone from his own background, but someone of the same rank and status in the highest echelons of imperial society (or a foreign princess of equivalent status); and his marriage would need to be approved by the Emperor. Given his character and personality, however, Franz Ferdinand was determined to choose his bride for himself; and he was very much aware of the dangers of inbreeding. If he married, it would be for love; and not to impress the courtiers whom he hated and the public whom he despised, if he noted them at all. He said later, to his physician:

'When someone from our circle cares for a person, there is sure to be found some triviality in the family tree to make marriage impossible, and therefore, it happens that among us a man and his wife are always twenty times related to each other. The result is that half our children are idiots or epileptics.'

In 1895 Franz Ferdinand met the Countess Sophie Chotek von Chotkova und Wognin, at a ball in Prague. Whether or not it was love at first sight, we do not know; but the couple began seeing each other, and the relationship developed rapidly as they maintained a discreet contact thorughout his illness. A countess sounds sufficiently aristocratic, but it was not good enough for the imperial court. Sophie came from an impoverished branch of the aristocracy. She did not satisfy the requirements of the Hapsburg Family Law and could never be an empress. Their relationship became widely known in 1898, and the Archduke was urged to abandon it by his religious adviser, whose views he might have been expected to consider, and by the Emperor himself, who expressed his implacable disapproval. The Archduke Franz Ferdinand dug his heels in. He had fallen in love with the Countess Sophie, and she with him. They would marry, come what may; and he would retain his right to his inheritance.

Further pressure was applied, and the Archduke proved obdurate. This was Austria, and in the end a compromise was reached. He could, said the Emperor, marry his countess; but she would never become empress, and any children from the marriage would have no right of succession to the throne. In other words, it was to be a morganatic marriage. The Archduke was furious, but accepted a situation which left him little choice. On 28 June 1900, he swore an oath of renunciation in the Hofburg Palace in Vienna, in the presence of the Emperor, all the archdukes, and other dignitaries. His children would never succeed to the throne, and nor should his widow if he died before her. Sophie was promoted to princess, and then duchess: but she would never rank as an archduchess, nor obtain the rights and privileges that should have been accorded to the wife of the heir apparent. Three days later, they were married: he at 36 and she at 32. Franz Joseph did not attend the marriage, and nor did the bridegroom's brothers.[4] But Maria Theresa, who had pleaded on Franz Ferdinand's behalf with the emperor, was there.

The marriage of the Archduke Franz Ferdinand and his countess proved idyllic, and the Archduke was never happier than when at home with his wife and children, of whom there were three, Sophie, Max and Ernst. Marriage made him human, and he had married the right woman: Franz Ferdinand and his wife made a formidable team, with no chinks in their collective armour. Franz Ferdinand constantly praised his wife, and told his mother-in-law that marrying her was the best thing he had ever done. He wrote to her in 1904:

'The *most* intelligent thing I've ever done in my life has been the marriage to my Soph. She is everything to me: my wife, adviser, my doctor, my warner, in a word: my entire happiness. Now, after four years, we love each other as on our first year of marriage, and our happiness has not been marred for a single second.

And our children. They are my whole pride and delight. I sit with them and admire them the whole day because I love them so.'[5]

(Remak, 1959, page 25.)

They lived away from Vienna as much as possible, away from the Court and its stifling etiquette, where his wife was consistently humiliated. Franz Ferdinand and his wife maintained an official residence in Vienna, but spent as much of their time as possible at Artstetten, Chlumetz or Konopischt, privately owned castles in rural Austria and Bohemia. It was to Franz Ferdinand's advantage that he was a man of great wealth, owing to his Italian inheritance, and was never financially dependent on his uncle and the house of Hapsburg .

The Countess Sophie

Opinions vary about the character and personality of the wife of the heir apparent. She was a highly determined woman, both in appearance and personality. She was not loved by the people, for she had no gift for communicating with them, and was far from a legendary beauty like the Empress Elizabeth. Like her husband, she was strongly religious, and put the church before everything else; but her church was a dogmatic one. How ambitious was she? Was she prepared to accept the terms of the morganatic marriage, and would she never wish for her son to be crowned emperor? That seems doubtful: her husband and children were everything to her, and she would have done anything to see them succeed.

Despite the position of her husband, she had been consistently humiliated at court by a succession of petty-minded officials who seem to have been motivated by spite. The Emperor had accepted but never approved of the marriage; and he was the last person to flout tradition, overturn precedent and raise her status to an appropriate level. She loved her children: but was that for what they were, or the possibility that they presented? We must presume that her love combined the two. When would the time come when the tables could be turned, and her family achieve its rightful status?

Plans for the empire

What were Franz Ferdinand's ambitions for the empire, on the eve of his assassination? What would he have done if he had not been murdered in Sarajevo, and had instead succeeded his uncle in peace and not in war? His plans would have continued to evolve. We may be sure, however, that they would have involved radical change; they would have been highly controversial; and they would very probably have been unacceptable to the Magyar section of the dual monarchy, whom Franz Ferdinand regarded as incorrigibly disloyal.

The heir apparent planned to announce his plans as a manifesto on the day of his succession, and was prepared to deal ruthlessly with any opposition. How far did his plans go? Had he agreed a secret pact with the German Kaiser, Wilhelm 11, for a new Teutonic empire, to be ruled by the Kaiser, Franz Ferdinand and his son Ernst?[6] Although rumoured, this seems highly unlikely: for Franz Ferdinand was first and foremost an Austrian.

Franz Ferdinand was prepared for internal strife, but not for war. The emperor to be, as we have said before, was far from stupid. Moreover, as inspector general of the army he had a very good idea of its real strength, and he did not believe that the empire was ready to go to war. Indeed, a war with another major European power would have crushed it. The army was there as a unifying force, and to prevent or suppress revolution. Meanwhile, the empire's multi-racial and multi-cultural composition had to be re-balanced. How?

We must distinguish between Franz Ferdinand as an arch conservative on social matters and an outright bigot in some of his prejudices, and Franz Ferdinand as a shrewd political operator—although sometimes the distinction is hard to draw. In his attitude towards to the Jews, he was a bigot. In his view on the Hungarians, he recognised a genuine threat to imperial unity. His possible solution, although it was still under consideration at the time of his death, was to dilute or dissolve the Magyar threat and their achievements under the compromise of 1867, by replacing a dual balance of power between Austrians and Hungarians with a three-way balance of power between Austrians, Hungarians and Slavs—not dualism but trialism. The empire would henceforward bind together three major ethnic groups, held together by one army and owing allegiance to one emperor (who remained, in addition, apostolic king of Hungary).

Trialism and its disadvantages

Trialism sounded possible as a sort of federalist type solution to the problems of the dual monarchy, but would have presented major difficulties if put into practice. In attempting to solve one problem, the new emperor would have created a host of others, and he was too intelligent not to realise this. For a start, how would the Czechs, the Poles, and other ethnic groups react, if the South Slavs were given a special status within the empire? And in what way would this solution actually solve or at least dilute the Hungarian problem? If the empire was a cracked pot held together by wire, it was not a good idea to replace the wire.

Trialism seems to have been more a provocation than a seriously contemplated policy. After his lengthy period in waiting, the archduke was an experienced political operator, and quite capable of floating policy A in order to achieve effect B: in this case, to scare the Hungarians so much when they learned of his plans, that a less extreme policy might be accepted as an apparent compromise of his original position. However, the notion of trialism did lead to a strong reaction in a country which was not part of the Austro-Hungarian empire at all, and never had been: but saw trialism as a major threat to its own ambitions.

The threat to Serbia

Trialism was a distinct threat to Serbia and immediately perceived as such by its more astute political leaders. Since 1878, when Bosnia had ceased to be ruled by the Turks, and especially since 1908, when it had been formally absorbed into the dual monarchy as a crown land, the acquisition of Bosnia had been a clear and popular aim of Serbian foreign policy: for the Serbs believed that it was Serbia and not Austria-Hungary that shoud have absorbed Bosnia, and they did not see the 1908 annexation as irreversible.

Bosnian Serbs were Serbs, and were a significant part of the Bosnian population. Bosnian Croats were really Serbs, it could be argued, except that they had embraced Roman Catholicism; and Bosnian Moslems could easily be absorbed as a religious minority within a greater Serbia.

In other words, Bosnia should be part of Serbia. But the same logic could be used in another way. If trialism were adopted, the Bosnian Serbs would have a much stronger role to play in the Austro-Hungarian empire, which would be very much to their political, social and economic advantage. Rather than for Bosnia to join Serbia, it would be better for Serbia to join Bosnia, as the third element within the trialist solution. How ironic it would be, if the Archduke's plans to scare the Hungarians by promoting the idea of a policy of trialism which in reality he had no intention of implementing, were to lead to an adverse reaction in Belgrade—and a call for extreme if secret measures, against the Archduke in question!

Summary and assessment

Franz Ferdinand was one of the more complex personalities of history and aspects of his character and ambitions remain a mystery. Narrowly educated, socially isolated and yet fiercely intelligent and ambitious, Franz Ferdinand's outstanding talent would appear to have been for nursing a grudge: he made enemies easily and kept them for life. Indeed, there appears a fundamental insecurity in his make-up which he was never able to overcome, for a normal person would have put his grievances behind him, and Franz Ferdinand was unable to do so.[7]

On the other hand, we feel that this is a far from balanced picture of the heir to the throne. There is no evidence that he was mad, and his misdeeds, if misdeeds they were, were well within the accepted boundaries of aristocratic behaviour. Indeed, it could be argued that he was better behaved than his younger brother Otto, the Crown Prince Rudolf, and a host of other archdukes whose behaviour was self-indulgent at best, and was subject to constant investigation and rebuke in the press.

Franz Ferdinand blossomed on marriage and proved a devoted husband and father: a family united against the world. He did not make friends easily, although he was friendly with the German Kaiser; and he remained an isolated and lonely figure whose ambitions were for the empire and not for himself. As he became older he showed signs of sociability: he was a great cultivator of roses, for example, and in 1914 opened his gardens at Konopischt for the public to visit. An isolated example, perhaps: but hardly the behaviour of a self-absorbed monomaniac.

Franz Ferdinand was not an easily likeable or sociable person. He was never popular as an archduke, and the public far preferred his younger brother Otto, who would have been a more popular future emperor: for Otto was everything that Franz Ferdinand was not. Otto lived life to excess, whereas Franz Ferdinand did not appear, at least to the general public, to live life at all.[8]

If we had to summarise the character and personality of the future heir apparent in a phrase, we should say that he appeared to have been entirely lacking in what is now called emotional intelligence. The archduke Franz Ferdinand did not seem to care if he offended people, and it was almost as if he went out of his way to do so. He had no need to listen to the views of others: he was of the type who considers that he is right, and that everyone else is wrong. In military terms, he was the only one marching in step.

An introverted intuitive?

In the typology of Carl Gustav Jung, a psychologist of Swiss origin who was at first a follower of the Austro-Hungarian subject Sigmund Freud, Franz Ferdinand was an introverted intuitive—someone apparently guided by logic and rationality, who conceals his real and highly intuitive mental processes from all but his closest friends. As Jung's system was developed for American and later world usage the terminology was expanded, and one would need to classify him as an INTJ—an explanation of which can be found below in the appendix to this chapter.

APPENDIX

Personality

This appendix begins with the Myers Briggs Type Indicator or MBTI as adapted from the work of Carl Gustav Jung, and comments on its application to the character and personality of the Archduke Franz Ferdinand and others.

Jung divided personalities into eight types. Isobel Myers and Katherine Briggs, a mother and daughter combination who built on Jung's foundations, added another dimension to make sixteen. The INTJ is one of those sixteen types, and the initials stand for:

I   Introvert

N   Intuitive

T   Thinking

J   Judging

Their opposites are:

E   Extravert

S   Sensing

F   Feeling

P   Perceptual

Most of these words correspond to their everyday meaning. Sensing, however, should be understood as meaning something like 'practical', 'applied', or 'empirical' in everyday speech. The sensing person is the scientifically minded researcher, who tries to find things out by experiment, rather than presupposition. If his car stops, he opens the bonnet and looks underneath. He uses his practical senses, rather than his intuition. P and J will be explored later.

In our opinion both the Archduke Franz Ferdinand and his assassin, Gavrilo Princip, correspond in personality to the INTJ. What does this mean?

The INTJ is an introvert, and therefore tends to conceal his true self. Not necessarily unsociable, he draws his energy from within, and does not need the external stimulus of company to energize himself.

To the outside world, he tends to emphasize logic and rationality as his method of problem-solving. In reality, however, he tends to rely on his intuition in order to form opinions, evaluate others, decide options, and so on. He is an apparent rationalist: but below the surface is someone very different—someone who finds what he really believes in simply by intuition, but uses logic and rationality to justify his choices to others.

In Franz Ferdinand's case, he knew that he had to marry the Countess Sophie, and the opposition of others simply made him the more determined. That his passion was based upon intuition and not logic is indicated by his disapproval of his younger brother Karl's marriage. The younger archduke also wished to marry for love, rather than to satisfy the requirements of Hapsburg law: but his older brother saw no parallel between their two cases, and went out of his way to condemn Karl's romance.

The INTJ has feelings, but does not always show them. They are the weakest aspect of his personality, and he may often come across as a 'cold fish', wooden, unemotional and unfeeling—a judgement with which he finds it very hard to cope, since deep down he is a very feeling person. His problem is that he finds it very difficult to show his feelings. Since they cannot be suppressed altogether, they may express themselves in inappropriate or immoderate ways—such as in Franz Ferdinand's passion for slaughter[9] or indeed his obsession with collecting. Franz Ferdinand was never restrained in his pursuits.

As an introvert who suppresses his feelings, the INTJ is known as he really is to very few other people, who see a different side of him to that which is normally visible. Franz Ferdinand was able to reveal his true or inner self to very few people,[10] who appear to have included his mother-in-law, his wife, and his children. Franz Ferdinand's problems were compounded by his volcanic temper, his extraordinary sensitivity to criticism, and his intolerance for stupidity. A man of both high intelligence and instant judgement, he would usually believe himself to be right, and others wrong—even if this were not the case.

As for Gavrilo Princip, he revealed his feelings very clearly just once, during his trial—a disclosure all the more revealing for its rarity. His co-defendant, Nedjelko Cabrinovic (an almost exactly opposite type, and one we would characterise as ENFP, or extravert, intuitive, feeling and perceiving) was giving vent to his emotions once again in confronting his own feelings of guilt. Dedijer (page 345) records his words as follows:

'"I would like to add something else [said Cabrinovic]. Although Princip is playing the hero, and although we all wanted to appear as heroes, we still have profound regrets. In the first place, we did not know that the late Franz Ferdinand was a father. We were greatly touched by the words he addressed to his wife: "Sophie, stay alive for our children." We are anything you want, except criminals. In my name and the name of my comrades, I ask the children of the late successor to the throne to forgive us. As for you, punish us according to your understanding. We are not criminals. We are honest people, animated by noble sentiments; we are idealists; we wanted to do good; we have loved our people; and we shall die for our ideals."

'After this, as one of the lawyers recorded, Cabrinovic sat on the bench with his head bowed, barely controlling his feelings, while "Princip's giant nature, his enormous vitality, would not let him accept Cabrinovic's words unchallenged.... Princip jumped up and said briefly that Cabrinovic had not been authorised to speak in his name."

'The proceedings were interrupted for five minutes; one of the lawyers came up to Princip and asked him what he thought about Franz Ferdinand's words. Princip answered: "What do you think I am, an animal?"'

At the very end of the trial, Gavrilo's guard was firmly back in place, and he uttered his defence as follows: "In trying to insinuate that someone else has instigated the assassination, one strays from the truth. The idea arose in our own minds, and we ourselves executed it. We have loved the people. I have nothing to say in my defence."'

(Page 345.)

Finally, we may note that the extravert Cabrinovic described Princip to the investigating judge as 'a very reserved man.' Coming from Cabrinovic, this was not a compliment, but was more an expression of frustration. Cabrinovic did not so much disapprove of hiding his feelings as find it impossible to do so. He had also complained to Pfeffer that Princip was 'a real dictator and not honest with me'—because he had failed to trust him with information that Cabrinovic was bound to reveal at the wrong moment!

Judgement day

The fourth dimension of the MBTI typology is to divide people between P and J, or perceiving and judging. The judging person is not necessarily judgmental: J simply indicates someone who is never inclined to 'sit on the fence', and has no difficulty in making up his mind. Franz Ferdinand had no problem in making up his mind in any context, including in his judgement of modern art, to which he was violently opposed; and he was both judging and judgmental.

Jung, Freud and Dixon

Having characterised Franz Ferdinand as an INTJ, we must add that this categorisation is a description and not a constraint. It does not cover every aspect of his personality, and nor does it make him less than unique. Moreover, there is an aspect of his personality which indicates a strong contrast between him and his uncle, for example, but which does not immediately lend itself to a Jungian typology.

Franz Joseph was a conservative to the point of being a reactionary, although a very civilised one. He wished to pass on his empire exacly as it was, and would insist on considering even the most minor change before (normally) deciding against it—even if the issue was far too trivial for an emperor's attention, and should never have found its way to his office in the first place. (We might have called him an ESTJ, but are moving towards Freud.)

The authoritarian personality

In Professor Norman Dixon's terms (*On the Psychology of Military Incompetence*, Jonathan Cape, 1976) Franz Joseph, whose favourite occupation as a boy had been to play with his model soldiers, was the anal-obsessive type, who was especially obsessed by appearance and drill.[11] Dixon argues that his type of person, who shows aspects of the authoritarian personality, is unsuited to high command: and whilst we may note that Franz Joseph showed courage in battle, he was never the victor in any campaign.

Franz Ferdinand, on the other hand, we might best describe as a restless radical. He was always prepared to change things if he thought it would improve them, and appears to have had no respect for tradition or appearance for its own sake. Dixon describes this type as autocratic but not authoritarian, and attributes its characteristics to some of the world's most successful military leaders. They are confident in themselves, and have no need of 'bull-shit' to allay their anxieties. We do not infer from this that Franz Ferdinand would have made a great military leader; but we do note that his combination of flexibility and impatience, his limited attention-span, and the obvious fact that he would not have been deterred from pursuing a vital objective by the casualties incurred, did not necessarily unfit him for high command.

NOTES

[1] The Archduke Franz Ferdinand stated that the Hungarians had shown bad taste in choosing to remain in Europe at all. This showed that he had paid at least some attention to his history lessons as a boy, for the Magyars had indeed emerged from Asia; and that he was not entirely bereft of a sense of humour, even if it were often exercised at someone else's expense.

[2] Ironically, one issue on which both imperial interests in Vienna were agreed upon, was the desirability of the full annexation of Bosnia in 1908—an event which, it has been argued, was to lead to the collapse of the empire as a whole. The archduke was especially supportive, and urged all opposition to be crushed with an iron hand.

[3] Ironically, Archduke Otto was to die long before his older brother. Otto died in 1905 at 41, no doubt at least partly because of his life-style. Franz Ferdinand's sister, Margaretha Sophie, was by that time already dead: she had died in 1902, at 32. The only one of his full siblings to survive the heir apparent was thus the former Archduke Karl Ferdinand, who was forced to resign his honours and privileges in 1911, and became plain Karl Burg: he died of tuberculosis in 1915. Like his older brother, he had married for love; but neither brother supported the other in that enterprise.

[4] This aroused massive resentment in Franz Ferdinand, which he was later to take out on his youngest brother when Karl Ferdinand himself elected to marry a 'commoner'—in his case, Bertha Czuber, who was the daughter of a professor. Their marriage finally took place without approval and Karl Ferdinand went into exile. Franz Ferdinand might be accused of inconsistency in failing to support his brother's marital ambitions, in that both brothers had wished to marry for love. In reality, it appears that neither had supported the other's marital plans.

5 Of the main characters in this book, it is noteworthy that only Franz Ferdinand and Sophie sustained a happy marriage. None of the seven assassins was married, and nor was Colonel Apis. The emperor himself sustained an unhappy marriage with the help of his mistress, Katharina Schratt—in whose welfare his wife showed an uxorious concern.

6 This allegation, although of potential appeal to conspiracy theorists, is unconvincing. The Kaiser was a personal friend and a frequent visitor to Konopischt, the heir apparent's country estate in Bohemia; but that does not mean that the two men conspired together. Moreover, it is almost impossible to believe that the heir apparent would have planned to divide the empire and thereby place his eldest son in a position of power.

7 Normalcy in mental health, as elsewhere, is an assumption. George Bernard Shaw once described himself as one of the lucky few to have 'normal' eyesight.

8 There is a story that when some British diplomats were having dinner in an hotel in Vienna, a young Archduke Otto and some drunken associates burst into the room and danced naked on the table, before disappearing in the bemused silence that accompanied this memorable escapade. However, the Archduke Otto was not wholly naked. As a young officer in the army (and, no doubt, serving in the best of imperial and royal regiments) he very properly retained his hat.

9 His great-grandson very reasonably pointed out to me that hunting was a popular activity for the aristocracy, in Austria and elsewhere; that as a VIP, Franz Ferdinand would always be given the best position in which to shoot, and would therefore have a high score; that he was in any case acknowledged to be an excellent shot, who because of the fear of a recurrence of his tuberculosis had few other outlets for his energy; and that other hunters stuffed and mounted what they had shot, as well as Franz Ferdinand. Was the Archduke an enthusiastic hunter? Certainly. Did this prove that he was damagingly obsessive, violent, or even insane? Not at all. Is it an indication of his type? We think so.

10 The inner self is almost by definition hidden. The Johari window describes four aspects of our personality, open, hidden, visible to others and not ourselves ('blind') and unknown, and is another psychological chart of some use.

11 We may see another example of an anal-obsessive in General Potiorek, who failed to deploy his troops on the streets of Sarajevo to guard the Archduke Franz Ferdinand, *after* he had already been attacked, because 'they were wearing the wrong uniforms.'

CHAPTER SIX

The mysterious Colonel Apis and the 'Black Hand'

Colonel Apis[1] was a highly professional army officer, intelligent, sociable, well-educated and versed in his profession and with a considerable gift for leadership. To apply an overused word which is on this occasion wholly appropriate, he was charismatic. He exerted the magnetic force of his personality and charmed people into doing what he wanted: and he was usually able to persuade them that what he wanted was in the public interest. He was neither self-interested nor corrupt. He put the army and his country before himself, on every occasion, and acted for motives of the purest patriotism—as he interpreted the interests of his country.

And yet he was the prime force behind the conspiracy to assassinate the Archduke Franz Ferdinand, which resulted in disaster not only for Austria and its empire, and the population of Europe as a whole—but for Serbia itself, the country that Colonel Apis loved with a blind and unreasonable devotion, and for which he was ready to sacrifice his own life at any time.

Apis, whose military career up to a certain point was like a model for the curriculum vitae of the ideal Serbian army officer, was executed for treachery in 1917, together with his closest colleagues. The charges were based on fabricated evidence, but he was unable to defend himself. Indeed, he misread the situation altogether, and paid for his mistakes with his life.

How did all this happen? How influential was Colonel Apis, and was the Black Hand really the power behind the throne? What were his real motives in 1914, in sponsoring the assassination of the heir apparent of another state, Austria, with whom Serbia was not at war, and with whom she needed to maintain good relations?

In order to understand Colonel Apis, we need to begin at the beginning, and to recognise that the truth behind his life and times is less contradictory than one might have imagined: for the story of Apis is in essence a simple tale of a patriot who who went too far and should have been kept under control.

What's in a name?

In the first place, Colonel Apis was not Colonel Apis. His rank was genuine, the result of long military service by a brilliant and dedicated officer, but Apis was simply a nickname. Dragutin Dimitrijevic was born to an artisan family in Serbia in 1876 and joined the army as a cadet in 1891, at the age of sixteen. There are two versions of how the young army officer acquired his nickname, and each is equally plausible: indeed, perhaps each is true. Somehow that need not surprise us; for Apis (under either interpretation) was to spend most of his working life in Serbian military intelligence. Hence it was natural that he should have more than one aspect to his identity, and that there should be a systematic amibiguity even about his name: for in the world of intelligence, ambiguity and deception can become sufficient objectives in themselves.

Apis the bull

One version holds that Apis was nicknamed Apis after the Egyptian bull-god on account of his extraordinary physical strength. Apis was the God of Fertility; but his namesake died a bachelor and left his few possessions to a nephew. The word Apis had many associations in both Egyptian and Greek mythology. Apis-Atum was somehow connected to another Egyptian deity, Osiris, the God of the Dead.

Apis the bee

Another interpretation holds that Dragutin Dimitryevich was nicknamed Apis because of his extraordinary energy, after the Greek word for a bee (hence apiary.) Both descriptions are apt, and either or both could be true. Apis was a man of both extraordinary strength and energy, and he was usually at the centre of a plot.

Apis was a part of the Serbian military establishment, and did not therefore need a revolutionary name like Stalin, Trotsky or indeed that of his later compatriot Tito[2] in order to enhance his image and project a heightened identity. Or did he? There was something, if not revolutionary, then deeply unsettling about the highly patriotic army officer. He was a man to have as one's friend, and not as one's enemy. For if, unlike the Archduke Franz Ferdinand, the young Serbian general staff officer did not tend to bear a grudge, nor act from personal emnity, he was still profoundly dangerous.

A new army for a new state

The army which the young Dimitrijevic joined in 1891 was the new product of a new state. The Serbs, as we explored in Chapter Two, had their own territory in the Balkans and had once been ruled by their own king. But they had been conquered by the Ottoman Turks and absorbed into the Ottoman empire for 400 years, and it was only in the nineteenth century that they were able to establish first a form of local autonomy and then national independence from the decaying Turkish empire. Serbia had to struggle for its independence for a very long time, and, as with Greece, the process was not a straightforward one; but the outcome was the international recognition of the new state of Serbia at the Congress of Berlin in 1878, first as a principality and then in 1882, under the same ruler, as a monarchy.

The prince and new king of Serbia, Milan Obrenovic, changed his allegiance from being a Russophile and allied himself with Austria-Hungary. This policy, at first an entirely secret one, became both widely known and widely unpopular, especially in military circles. The new army that had been created to serve the new state was a radical one, and did not observe that distinction between political and military affairs which is generally considered essential to a healthy democracy (or indeed, a constitutional monarchy, as Serbia was intended to be.)

In order to expand his hitherto highly conservative army, which had up to that point been officered by the richest classes of society, Milan increased the number of regiments fourfold, and found that he needed a large number of new officers to command them. Training at the Belgrade Military Academy was reduced to a two year programme, and a large number of young men became officers who would not otherwise have been considered.

They included the brilliant young Dragutin Dimitrejevic, who showed such promise as an officer cadet that he was commissioned straight onto the General Staff: an achievement which would have been impossible in almost any other army, then or now, and shows not only the talents that he must have displayed, by Serbia's desperate need to modernise its armed forces.

A general staff was a new phenomenon—the staff college in Great Britain had only been set up in 1858, for before that the small number of officers who took their profession seriously had been content to gather and talk tactics in a room over a public house in Camberley, Surrey.[3] But the Serbian army needed trained leaders, and trained staff officers, and new tactics, and new artillery, and new everything, in fact—and the main problem was in how to pay for it. Taxes were going up heavily, and the peasantry that formed the bulk of the Serbian population was desperately unhappy with the regime in power. What was to be done?

1 April 1893—The First Coup d'Etat

King Milan Obrenovic, the first monarch of the new Serbia, had ruled the country from when full independence was established under the Treaty of Berlin in 1878, until he abdicated in 1893 and took himself off to lead the good life in Paris and Monaco for a few years. In his absence, a regency was established until his son Alexander Obrenovic (1876-1903; then aged 13) should reach his majority and be crowned king.

Alexander Obrenovic was not prepared to wait for his legal majority. On I April 1893, he took advantage of the popular unrest and staged a successful coup d'etat against the regency which included his own father—with whom he quarrelled and who was forced into exile, to seek refuge with none other than the Austrian Emperor, Franz Ferdinand.

A change for the better? Unfortunately, no. The new king rapidly made himself extremely unpopular. He lacked judgement, and acted far too rapidly, without taking either the people or any significant power base in the country with him. Alexander was young, impulsive in his actions, and reckless as to their consequences: a bad combination for a ruler in the Balkans, where there was no long-established tradition of constitutional monarchy to stay his hand. Alexander behaved as an extremist, abolishing the constitution and ruling despotically. And as if that were not enough, there was the whore Draga.

The royal whore

The whore Draga was the public's contemptuous description for the the Queen whom King Alexander married in 1900.[4] She was the widow of an engineer, and some years older than her second husband. Was she a lady of loose morals? She was certainly believed to be so. She was a proven liar, for she had claimed to be pregnant after marriage, and this was found to be untrue. Was the nickname deserved? Probably not; but it was in use in the more significant sections of society, such as among the young captains, majors and colonels who had been given a power base by King Milan's reforms, and who proceeded to exploit that base mercilessly.

The critics of the new royal family, who proceeded to put their words into action by slaughtering them in an act of brutality that stunned Europe, did not come from a traditional land-owning background: they did not feel an ancestral loyalty to the man in power, since he had seized it; and they had been radicalised by the spirit of the times. The Radical Party was the strongest party in contemporary Serbia, and it had its followers in the military. Young army officers in countries such as Egypt and Turkey were demonstrating that they could make a difference in politics, and their Serb counter-parts followed suit. (The Young Turks were to overthrow the Sultan himself in 1908).

Amongst the Serbian army officers who wished to make a difference was the young Apis, who had made such an impression on his contemporaries and showed an aptitude for leadership. Apis wished to remain an army officer, and not to become a politician himself. He had no desire to make speeches or stride the public stage.[5] But he knew how to win friends and influence people, in Dale Carnegie's telling phrase; and he did it best from behind the scenes.

Apis joined his radical colleagues in opposing the new regime, and as he was Apis, a natural leader and someone who did not believe in half-measures, he became the chief organiser of the plot to overthrow King Alexander. What would be the international reaction to such an episode, and how it would rebound upon Serbia's long-term interests, does not seem to have been a significant item on the agenda, which was devoted to how, more than why. In fact, the reasons for the assassination were twofold, and both were felt passionately. Firstly, the young radicals (who were at the same time extremely conservative) felt that King Alexander had brought his country into disgrace by marrying a manipulative and evil seductress, who had already lied about being pregnant and had been exposed in her deception. Secondly, if the couple did not have children, then it was rumoured that Draga's brother Nikodije, an unpopular member of the officer corps, would be declared the official heir to the throne. That possibility was wholly unacceptable, and needed to be prevented. But how?

Apis may have been a natural conspirator, but he does not appear to have been a natural assassin. His plots tended to be clumsy, ill-thought out, and unnecessarily complicated, and many of them failed. In this case, the assassins were successful in killing the royal couple, but had not prepared for the aftermath. What was the plan, and what happened?

11 June 1903—the second coup d'etat

A large number of conspirators joined the plot. They bound themselves together with a degree of ruthlessness which was later to characterise the Black Hand, and declared that they were prepared to kill anyone suspected of betraying them. Poison was considered, and assassination at a ball or at the theatre. But time was passing, and action was necessary before the conspiracy came to light, despite their vow of secrecy. On 11 June 1903, 28 military conspirators went into action. Led by the gigantic figure of Apis, they blew apart the gates of the royal palace in Belgrade, stormed inside, and opened fire on King Alexander's personal bodguards where they hid. Apis was seriously wounded in the process—the only bullet wounds he was to sustain in his distinguished military career, until he was executed by firing-squad in 1917—but continued to direct operations while he lay wounded and bleeding in the palace gardens, his revolver to hand. (He was prepared to shoot himself if the plan failed).

No-one knew where the king was actually to be found, as no servants had been engaged in the conspiracy, and no real operational plan prepared. The conspirators desperately searched the palace until finally they found Alexander and Draga hiding in a concealed clothes closet. They were called upon to come out, and guaranteed their lives. The royal couple made the fatal mistake of accepting this guarantee, for the blood of the conspirators was up and they were determined on slaughter. As the king and his wife emerged—the Queen, according to Dedijer, was dressed only in a petticoat, white silk stays, and one yellow silk stocking, and tried to protect Alexander with her body—the conspirators fell upon them both in a frenzy and hacked them to pieces, cutting off limbs and disembowelling them. Finally, the dismembered bodies were thrown through the window into the courtyard below, to the exultant cheers of the enraged killers.

On the next day, Petar Karageorgovic was declared King.[6] Since the coup had succeeded, no conspirator was brought to justice; indeed, they were congratulated in the Serbian Parliament, and some were to play an active political role from then on. As the bloody details of the coup receded into legend, so did its activists: they were the men who had overthrown the tyrant (and forced the rest of Europe to pay attention to Serbia, where royal misrule was not to be tolerated). Colonel Apis consolidated his reputation as a brave, resourceful and successful leader (he was to carry three bullets in his body for the rest of his life) and a force to be reckoned with in contemporary Serbia, in army circles and beyond.

He was appointed as professor of tactics at the military academy, a task to be taken on in addition to his duties on the general staff. He visited both Russia and Germany on military liaison duties: he was most impressed by Prussian military organisation, and recommended its adoption on his return. Apis, it seemed, was the coming man.

During the first and second Balkan wars Apis distinguished himself as an organiser, and carried out secret military missions on behalf of his government in liaising with Albanian tribesmen whose allegiance was needed. As a result of this he became horribly ill with Maltese fever, which caused his legs to swell enormously, and for which he was eventually compelled to seek treatment in Germany.

By 1913, Apis was no longer the man he had been. His legs were heavily bandaged and he was unable to take exercise by riding, so that he put on a great deal of weight. At the same time, he lost his hair and became completely bald. But he kept his charisma; he remained the *eminence grise* in Serbian politics; and he had become the director of military intelligence.

Colonel Apis as an intelligence officer

Colonel Apis's career and activities as director of military intelligence, a post to which he was appointed in 1911, were sufficiently improbable to be the stuff of a spy novel – except that they were true. As director, his tasks would have included both intelligence and security. Much of this information needed, both to protect Serbia from the plans of others and to further its own plans, was in the public domain; for part of the task of a good intelligence service is to collect, collate and analyse the raw data which is already available. Some of the information needed, however, was secret. In order to explore the secret domain, Colonel Apis needed to cultivate informants already in place, and to position his own secret agents in gathering intelligence. [7]

He was adept in both activities, and was able to establish a very wide network of sources of information, reporting to him personally, and prepared to act on his orders as necessary. They included military personnel, border guards, customs agents, and other employees of the state bureaucracy, as well as private individuals operating both within and outside Serbian borders. Some of Apis's contacts were members of Narodna Odbrana, or the Black Hand, or both, and some were not: membership of a secret and indeed illegal society increased Apis's hold over his operatives, and allowed him to mount secret surveillance on them. It was a gigantic spider's web; and at its centre was Apis.

He was described as:

'Gifted and cultured, honourable, a convincing speaker, a sincere patriot, personally courageous, filled with ambition, energy and the capacity for work... He had the characteristics which cast a spell on men. His arguments were always striking and convincing. He could represent the most intractable matters as mere trifles, the most hazardous enterprises as innocent and harmless. Withal he was in every respect a remarkable organiser. He kept all the threads in his own hand and even his most intimate friends only knew what was their immediate concern...

'It was for him to plan, organise and command, for others to obey and carry out his orders without questioning...

'Friends for Apis were at the same time very dear and very cheap. His friendship had a dangerous quality; but this made his personality very attractive. When he wanted to draw his friends into a conspiracy or some other adventure he behaved like a seducer.'

Naturally, all or almost all of his work was secret, and unaccounted for. Secret intelligence work required secret funds, and the only real guarantee of the probity of the enterprise was the personality and integrity of its director, Colonel Apis. As we have already declared, the colonel was not corrupt—unless the addiction to power be declared a form of corruption. He had few vices, and those were mainly concerned with eating and drinking, which could not be used against him as blackmail. He was a bachelor, and his sex life, if he had one, was a discreet affair of no concern to anyone but himself. Colonel Apis lived for his work; but he could not address it alone.

Major Tankosic

Colonel Apis's right hand man and most trusted aide was a Major Vosin Tankosic, who appears to have followed his master with a blind and utter devotion. Both were regular army officers, and both were members of the Black Hand, as members six and seven of its central committee. Major Tankosic acted as a sort of cut-off point for his senior officer, as we shall see in regard to the planning of the Sarajevo *attentat*. It was he who had face-to-face contact with the Bosnian assassins, he who supplied the materiel needed from various sources, and he who sorted out their training. There was no need for any assassins to meet Colonel Apis in person, and the less they knew about him, the less they could reveal under interrogation.

Major Tankosic, small, dark, intense, and a born soldier, distinguished himself during the first and second Balkan wars in organising and leading the Komitaje, irregular soldiers who volunteered for active service in support of the regular army, and were used for both direct combat and sabotage. Their contribution was extremley helpful; and he was determined that only the right people should serve. Motivation was not enough: proper soldierly qualities were needed.

Rade Malobabic

Rade Malobabic, according to his master's later account, was Colonel Apis's most trusted secret agent, and his main operator in Austria-Hungary. It may be that the colonel's judgement was at fault here, and that his Austrian-born agent was in fact working for both sides: Serbia *and* the dual monarchy. This is an issue which cannot be resolved in the absence of conclusive evidence: and it seems unlikely that such evidence should appear. If Malobabic did have multiple loyalties, they did not serve him well once the Great War began: he was imprisoned and tortured by the Austrians, escaped their custody in his bare (and large) feet, sought refuge with the Serbian authorities, and was imprisoned once again.

He was finally rescued by Colonel Apis, who gave his personal guarantee that this wandering intelligence agent should be trusted. None of this is conclusive evidence of anything other than Colonel Apis's capacity to trust his own man, who might have been 'allowed' to escape by the Austrians in the first place. Whatever the truth of the matter, Apis remained faithful to his agent, and they were executed side by side in Salonika in 1917.

Colonel Redl

Colonel Redl was not an agent of Serbian military intelligence, but his story is highly illustrative of the world in which such agents operated: a world too improbable for a spy story, but a world which was nevertheless true.

Alfred Redl was born a Ruthenian in Austrian Poland in 1864, and although of humble origin was successful in obtaining a commission in the imperial and royal army because of his extraordinary abilities. His rise was rapid and he showed an especial facility for intelligence work, becoming chief of counter-intelligence in 1900 and chief of intelligence in 1907—a post he held until 1912. Unfortunately for Austria's military secrets, he also became a Russian agent in 1902. He may have been blackmailed into this because of his homosexuality, which would have led to his professional disgrace and imprisonment or suicide if exposed. He was also a man of extravagant tastes, living well beyond his income—something which his colleagues should have noticed and investigated, but did not. Colonel Redl was in a position to do extraordinary damage to the Austrian state, and did so.

Firstly, he was able to betray, wholesale, Austria's military plans to the Russian general staff—who were then able to pass them on in their turn to their allies in Serbia and elsewhere. This would have meant, had Redl not been exposed, that when the First World War began both Russia and Serbia would have had invaluable knowledge about Austria's dispositions and intentions. However, it could also be argued that the damage was already done, despite his exposure, for much of the information that he passed on was of strategic value, and the plans based upon it could not easily be changed. The options open were limited, and the resources available to the Austrian army were a fixed item.

Secondly, Colonel Redl was able to distort, play down, and minimise the Russian threat to Austria-Hungary, since his Russian masters would have made sure that he was enabled to reveal only that which they wished the Austrians to know.

Thirdly, by manipulating his position as the confidante of both sides, Colonel Redl was able to appear almost omniscient to his Austrian masters: for his Russian handlers made sure that this was so. In fact, the high-living Colonel Redl enhanced his reputation in Austria as an intelligence officer of an extraordinary guile and subtlety, who appeared to be aware of what the Russian were actually thinking.

It was all too good, or bad, to last; and it did not do so. Colonel Redl was promoted to other duties, and his successor was able to discover his treachery more or less by chance: pride, as usual, had come before a fall. Colonel Redl had been working for the Russians for years! The unthinkable had happened, and it was entirely possible that he had betrayed the empire's entire war plans to their most likely and most threatening enemy. What was to be done?

It is clear what was not to be done: and that was what in fact occurred. Colonel Redl was an officer, and therefore a gentleman: and a gentleman did the right thing when disgraced. He accepted the pregnant revolver and the empty hotel room, and the single shot rang out. The emperor did not approve, for suicide was both a sin and a crime. The heir apparent was incandescent with rage, for now no-one would ever know what secrets the colonel had betrayed (and the possibility of running him as a triple agent was lost.) The result was a disaster for one colonel in military intelligence and his empire, but not for another: for it is reasonable to assume that the Russians, whom Colonel Apis cultivated so carefully in Belgrade, gave him some idea of what they had learned from the errant Ruthenian. Intelligence work is partly a matter of trading, and nothing is offered for nothing; but Apis, the *de facto* controller of the Black Hand as well as the head of Serbian military intelligence, would have had plenty to trade with his Russian counterparts, and may therefore have learned something of what they had gained from Colonel Redl.

The annexation of Bosnia in 1908: Norodna Odbrana and the Black Hand

The formal annexation of Bosnia by the Austrian Empire in 1908 created enormous popular outrage in Serbia, and especially in the capital, Belgrade, where there were days of protests and demonstrations, and where it almost looked as if the Serbian government would be forced into some sort of retaliatory action against Austria, on the strength of the popular will alone. In the end, however, popular protest died down, and it was believed that nothing could be done: Austria was too large, too powerful, and too economically dominant. Bosnia should have been joined to Serbia and not Austria: but the opportunity was gone. The situation was hopeless. Or was it? The Serbian people did not think so, and on 6 October 1908 formed a society (nowadays it might have been called a pressure group) to lobby for their cause. It was called Narodna Odbrana.

Narodna Odbrana

The new society was spontaneous, open in both its aims and tactics, and an expression of the popular will. It rapidly attracted a very large membership, and dedicated itself to the 'respectable' side of the campaign to incorporate Bosnia into Serbia by means of cultural awareness-raising and political lobbying. Nevertheless, Austria did not approve: and Austria, despite the failure of the so-called pig war of 1906 to 1908, was in a position to exert tremendous leverage on its much smaller neighbour— especially now that the dual monarchy was establishing a better relationship with the real Teutonic power in Europe, which was Germany. Both Austria-Hungary and Germany shared an economic interest in the Balkans, which included the extension of a cross-continental railway line to Salonika, in Greece: and finally the fulfilment of the Kaiser's dream, a railway from Berlin to Baghdad, which would need to run through Serbia, and to which that state had already agreed. She did not have much choice in the matter, on either issue.

Narodna Odbrana was disbanded—to live on in the less than fully informed imagination of the Austrian government and secret service, which was to blame it for the assassination of the Archduke Franz Ferdinand. Serbia, however, did not abandon its interest in Bosnia, but took it underground.

Gavrilo swears his oath of allegiance to the Black Hand in Belgrade

If Narodna Odbrana was Sinn Fein, in Irish terms, then the Black Hand was the Irish Republican Army—a very different kettle of fish, although there was some dual membership between the two.

The Black Hand was the cognomen for the Serbian secret society Udenijenje ili Smrt (Unification or Death) which was formed to bring about the unification of Serbia and Bosnia by any means, including murder. It was formed on 10 June 1910, and its constitution stated:

'**Article 1:** This organisation is formed in order to achieve the ideal of the unfication of Serbdom; all Serbs, regardless of sex, religion or place of birth, can become members, and anyone else who is prepared to serve this ideal faithfully.

Article 2: This organisation chooses revolutionary action rather than cultural, and is, therefore, kept secret from the general public.'

Its membership was enormous and penetrated every level of society, including top government officials and army officers. Its oath of allegiance was blood-curdling and its intentions were equally deadly. Its dedication was legendary. Its path to victory was certain. Its director, in fact if not in name, was the regicide, Colonel Apis. All these things were claimed for the Black Hand, whose legend lives on even to-day, if only for the suggestiveness of its name;[8] and there is an element of truth at least in some of them.

The Black Hand did attract a wide membership, although the exact number is a matter of conjecture. It might have been in the thousands. Its active membership would have been very much smaller. It was highly influential, if only for a limited period, until Prime Minister Pasic got the better of it; and it did provide the means for the assassination of Franz Ferdinand. That was achievement enough, if it be called an achievement. Finally, it seems reasonably clear that the Black Hand was not simply the plaything of Colonel Apis, whatever the power of his personality. There were others involved; and they did express other views. Unfortunately, as far as the assassination of Franz Ferdinand was concerned, although the majority of the central committee were reported to be opposed to the carrying out of this plan, they were unable to prevent it. Colonel Apis, like Comrade Stalin in Russia in a few years' time, had secured the levers of power for his own use.

Gavrilo and his associates conspire in a café in Sarajevo

The inner core consisted of a central committee, whose number six was Colonel Apis. He had not formed the Black Hand, although as a natural conspirator he would very soon have joined it. Because of his background and personality, he soon became its *de facto* director. Those who joined the Black Hand—the process itself was a terrifying one, in which we can see the influence of Colonel Apis, the plotter and regicide—were sworn to secrecy or death, but even then the organisation did its best to make sure that they had little or nothing to betray. Members joined a cell, and only the leader of the cell knew the identity of any member of another cell, so that communications were limited by design. The practice was based upon revolutionary cells in Russia, where a long tradition of active opposition to the Tsar and the machinations of his highly vigilant secret police had forced the revolutionaries to learn to be security conscious. We may also trace its origins to the secret societies in Italy, the Carbonari, which had been formed to achieve independence from Austria.

The Black Hand, and not Narodna Odbrana, was the organisation that promoted the assassination of the Archduke Franz Ferdinand in 1914, and provoked the first world war; and the Black Hand was in effect under the direction of Colonel Apis.

The situation in 1913

Serbia was in a strong position, having done well from the first and second Balkan wars, and having Russia as an ally. Nevertheless, she had been incensed by the annexation of Bosnia by Austria in 1908, and had protested vigorously about this. Rightly, she saw the Austro-Hungarian Empire as a threat to her ambitions in the Balkans, and even her continued existence: for what was to stop the Austrian army from occupying Belgrade, on one trumped-up pretext or another? And if she did so, would Russia really act to protect her fellow Slavs and little brothers—or would she side with her fellow imperial power? Under these circumstances, it behoved the Serbians to be extremely cautious: but this was not a conclusion that appealed to Colonel Apis.

The path to assassination and war

Apis the regicide clearly saw it as part of his duty to extend his attentions to other dynasties, and planned the assassination of several monarchs, including the apostolic king of Hungary, Franz Joseph. However, none of his plots was successful, and it is to be doubted how seriously he took them.

The Sarajevo Attentat

It has been suggested that Colonel Apis, using his subordinates, planned the whole assassination of Franz Ferdinand, and that the young Bosnians who actually carried out the deed were little more than his pawns (Remak, 1959, argues this interpretation, whilst at the same time giving full credit to the energy and determination of Gavrilo Princip.) Alternatively, Apis may have been a sleeping partner in the affair, content to supply the necessary materiel, but by no means playing a leading role. Did he approach the conspirators, or did they approach him? Was it his idea, or theirs? Even at this distance in time, when we might have expected that the whole truth would have emerged, there are many things about the assassination which are still uncertain. Let us consider the positions of the leading conspirators from early 1914 onwards, and see what we learn from the interactions that took place.

Gavrilo Princip

At the beginning of 1914 Princip had made his way to Belgrade from Grahovo, where he had made what was to be his last visit to his family, and his mother found him even more silent than usual. The official reason for his visit to Belgrade was to complete his high school examinations there, and he registered with the police on 13 March 1914. For once, he took his academic work seriously: he did not want it said that he had turned to assassination because he was a failed student.

His contacts in Belgrade were impoverished students like himself, and former *komite* members who were now dwelling on their past glories and scratching for a living. (Owing to Princip's actions, they were soon to find one as soldiers.) Many of the exiled Bosnian students lived together in one house, including Princip, Trifko Grabez and others. They spent much of their time in dingy cafes, indulging in political debate. Many of them were at least apparently committed to violent action against the Austro-Hungarian empire and its representatives, including the emperor himself, his heir apparent, and General Potiorek, the military governor of Bosnia.

Princip, as always, tended to keep himself to himself. However, he agreed in confidence with Nedjelko Cabrinovic to assassinate the Archduke Franz Ferdinand during his impending visit to Sarajevo, which was widely announced in the press, and appeared to offer the perfect opportunity for a blow for freedom; and the two youths soon admitted Trifko Grabez to the plot.

There is no evidence that Gavrilo Princip joined the Black Hand, and no reason to suppose that he would have been required to do so. He certainly protected its existence at his trial; but he did not have to be a member in order to do so. Gavrilo Princip was a very principled young man, utterly dedicated to the secrecy of his mission.

Despite his reticence, he was the natural leader of the potential assassins; and when it came to the time to talk details with the Black Hand, their most likely source of support, he was the obvious choice to make contact with the 'front man' for Colonel Apis—his subordinate, Major Tankosic.

However, Gavrilo Princip had already met the Major, and it had not been an enjoyable encounter. Princip, the would-be guerrilla fighter, had been personally rejected for service in the first Balkan war because he was too small and too weak. It was an assessment he bitterly resented. It was also a judgment, we would suggest, that was entirely reasonable under the circumstances. The man who had rejected him was Major Tankosic, who selected, trained and led the *komite* in 1912. Given his past rejection, Princip refused to meet with Major Tankosic once again, and instead put forward his associate, Trifko Grabez, for the meeting—a meeting in which he was nevertheless to take a guiding interest.

Nedjelko Cabrinovic

Cabrinovic, Princip's alter ego, had made his own way to Belgrade, where he found printing work, and we assume, hung around on the fringes of the revolutionary conspiracy. He was not fully trusted, both because his father was believed to be a police spy and because of his inability to keep his mouth shut, but he was an apparently willing conspirator.

Cabrinovic could not be trusted with secrets, and hence they were not confided in him; and nor was he chosen to meet Major Tankosic. The young Bosnian printer was a highly emotional person, who often acted without thinking; and the anticipation of his colleagues that he would not prove fully trustworthy was to prove correct. When he did become involved in the conspiracy, he sent postcards to his friends hinting at what he was about to do; he returned home and made peace with his father; he paid off his debts; and finally he had his photograph taken on the morning of the assassination, with instructions for copies to be sent on to friends. As preparation for his probable death (he fully intended to commit suicide after the deed, but nothing could be certain with Cabrinovic) this was thoughtful work. As a concealment against any possible police investigation, it was disastrous. He could hardly declared his intentions more clearly, if he had written and printed a prospective obituary in the local newspaper. Cabrinovic was to join his comrades Princip and Grabez on the 'underground railway' or 'tunnel' in travelling to Sarajevo, about which we shall say more later.

Trifko Grabez

Trifko Grabez was in Belgrade for the same reason as his colleagues: it was the natural location for a patriotic Bosnian Serb, and he also had examinations to complete, for which, as he later blandly explained at his trial, he preferred the Serbian educational system with its lesser emphasis on Greek and Latin. He met with Major Tankosic, of the Black Hand, and an agreement was reached between the experienced soldier and the young son of the priest. The Black Hand would finance, equip, and train the three young assassins, and assist in their movement to Sarajevo. Grabez reported back to Princip, who approved. Wheels were in motion.

Milan Ciganovic

Major Tanskosic withdrew into the background, and an intermediary named Milan Ciganovic was appointed to take things on. Ciganovic was then, apparently, in his early twenties, although if he is in fact the person who was photographed in Belgrade with Grabz and Princip at this time and tentatively identified as Ciganovic, he looks very much older. He had been a *komite* and personal bodyguard to Major Tankosic, and had found himself at a loose end after the war: he was glad to be of service.

The photograph shows Ciganovic as the old contender, sitting on a park bench in a park in a quiet and peaceful Belgrade between the younger revolutionaries Grabez and Princip, as if they were his trainers for a come-back which he would be ill-advised to undertake. To the modern observer, it is remarkable how young-looking are both Grabez and Princip, and how respectably dressed. Ciganovic looks rather more battered, and with far more experience of life. He had been a guerrilla fighter, and it shows.

There may have been another reason for the world-weariness to be seen in his eyes. According to some accounts, Ciganovic was working as an informer for the Serbian Prime Minister, Nikola Pasic, who needed his own and private source of information on the activities of the director of the Serbian intelligence service, Colonel Apis.

If Ciganovic were in fact working for Prime Minister Pasic, then there is circumstantial evidence to support this claim. According to Remak's account (Remak, 1959, page 247):

'In 1917, Prime Minister Pasic furnished him with some money and a false passport and sent him to the United States, where he waited out the war. In 1919, he returned to Serbia, received a small grant of land from the government, married, and settled down. He died in 1927, the only one among the principal plotters to die of natural causes outside prison. The price Ciganovic had to pay for this survival, however, was the open betrayal of Dimitrijevic.'

Whatever his real allegiance, Ciganovic knew his task. He received four pistols, six bombs, and some phials of cyanide. Training with the pistols took place in a park in Begrade. Gavrilo Princip proved the best shot. No training could take place with the bombs, which resembled a rectangular cake of soap and had a cap on the top of the detonator. This had to be snapped off and the detonator then struck. The delay before explosion was approximately twelve seconds.

The state-manufactured bombs may have been suited for an assassination because they were relatively small, and did not look like bombs; but the delay was far too long and their destructive power was uncertain. The conspirators might have done better to obtain the nitro-glycerine explosives used by their Russian contemporaries in assassination, which exploded on impact and whose destructive power was enormous. However, the bomber who equipped himself with nitro-glycerine was committing himself to a method of killing which was up close and personal and virtually certain to result in his own destruction. The Sarajevo assassins may have equipped themselves with suicide pills: but they lacked the experienced professionalism of the Russian socialist revolutionaries.

Danilo Ilic

Danilo Ilic had visited Belgrade at the end of the previous year, in 1913. He was a well-known leader of Mlada Bosna, and was reported to be a personal acquaintance of Colonel Apis. By January 1914 he had returned to Sarajevo to lodge with his mother once again. There he received an allegorical letter from Gavrilo Princip, telling him of the plot and asking him to recruit some local volunteers, so that it would not appear a Serbian conspiracy but a home-grown expression of discontent. Ilic did as he was asked, and that this stage appears to have been in full support of what was going on. His two local recruits were Vaso Cubrilovic, aged 17, the younger brother of Veljko Cubrilovic who was also involved in the conspiracy; and Cvetko Popovic, aged 16, a trainee teacher. Both Bosnian Serbs were very young, and neither can really have known what he was letting himself in for. Popovic described his feelings as follows:

'After I gave my word to join the plot I spent the whole night thinking and dreaming about the assassination. In the morning I was quite a different man. Convinced that I had only until June 28 to live, Vidovdan—St. Vitus Day—I looked upon everything from a new angle. I left my school-books, I hardly glanced at the newspapers which up to that day I read with interest. I almost failed to react to the jokes of my friends at which the day before I would have exploded. I tried to make jokes. Only one thought tormented me: that we might not succeed and thus make fools of ourselves.'

Muhamed Mehmedbasic

The third recruit was a Bosnian Moslem, Muhamed Mehmedbasic, aged 27. He was known to both Ilic and Gacinovic and had already had experience in this area, but not the sort of experience that would necessarily recommend him for further action.

When the conspiracy was hatched, Muhamed Mehmedbasic was away from both Belgrade and Sarajevo, residing in the countryside in Stolac in Herzegovina. The son of an impoverished Moslem feudal lord, who had trained as a carpenter, Mehmedbasic was older than the other conspirators and the only Moslem, which was a major reason for his choice.

He seems to have had a remarkable facility for being close to the action, but never quite following through. In January 1914, he had been sent to kill Governor Potiorek in Sarajevo, armed with a dagger and a bottle of poison for its tip. However, the expedition was a fiasco. According to his own acccount:

'From Toulouse I went to Marseilles and there embarked for Ragusa (Dubrovnik). At Ragusa I took the train, but noticed that the gendarmes were searching the compartments for something. Fearing I was the man they wanted I threw away the dagger and the poison in the lavatory. I afterwards found it was a petty thief they were after. When I reached Stolac I wrote (to) Gacinovic and, pending his reply, did nothing more about carrying out the outrage.'

(Dedijer, page 283)

This account of an apparent plan to kill General Potiorek (of which there are other versions) raises more questions than it offers answers. Was Mehmedbasic to carry out this attempt entirely on his own? How was he to get close enough to his target to carry out the murder, and how was he to escape afterwards? Was the Black Hand aware of this plan, and did they approve of it?

On the last point, we may note that this assassination attempt, if attempt it were, seems to have had nothng to do with Colonel Apis. Rather, it was organised at a conference of Young Bosnia in exile, held at Toulouse and directed by Vladimir Gacinovic. Gacinovic, a prominent member of Mlada Bosna (Young Bosnia), had a penchant for secret societies and conspiracies of any kind. He took no part in the Sarajevo *attentat*, although he was described as personally knowledgeable about it by no less a revolutionary than Trotsky. However, at the time of its execution he was resident in Switzerland.

Resumé

By May 1914, an assassination plan was in existence, the result of a combination of the efforts of the three members of the Black Hand, Apis, Tankosic, and Ciganovic, and the three Bosnian Serbs Princip, Cabrinovic and Grabez. They had plotted together in Belgrade to kill the archduke. Danilo Ilic had been informed of the conspiracy by letter to Sarajevo, and had recruited two local Bosnian Serbs and a Bosnian Moslem to make a full assassination party of seven men. Weapons and suicide capsules had been procured, and all that was now needed was to transport the three young Bosnian Serbs and their weapons from Belgrade to Sarajevo. Colonel Apis had covered his tracks and there was nothing to indicate a clear link from the Serbian authorities to the assassination of the future head of state of a friendly power.

There were, however, a number of questions that still remained unresolved. They included the following:

- How committed was Colonel Apis, to the plot? Did he really intend it to succeed? Did he really attempt to stop it, when he agreed to do so?
- Was Rade Malobabic involved, as Apis was later to claim at his own trial? Did he travel to Sarajevo to witness, direct, or even to stop the attentat altogether, under orders from the colonel? If so, what did he do when in Sarajevo, where he appears to have played no role at all?
- How concerned was Prime Minister Pasic, who was reported to know of the plot from various sources? If he was really concerned that the plot existed and had gone into action, and that a friendly head of state to be would be assassinated and the murder linked to his own government, why did he not take effective measures to stop it—for example, by warning the authorities in Sarajevo?
- What are we to make of the story that Pasic did attempt to warn the Austrian authorities, but in such a way that the message did not get through?
- How are we to assess the character and intentions of Danilo Ilic, whose behaviour became increasingly bizarre as the fatal day approached, and who appears to have been in two minds about the whole episode? Was he approached by Rade Malobabic at the last minute and told to abort the mission, or did his hesitations arise for other reasons? Putting it more simply, did he not have the bottle for the job?

We believe that the remainder of our text will give our readers the information needed to resolve these issues for themselves, using their own judgement. Our own assessment (and it can be nothing more) is that Apis favoured the assassination and did *not* send Malobabic to stop it, and that what he later said at his own trial cannot be relied upon; that the naturally devious Pasic did what *he* thought would be effective to prevent the murder; and that Ilic quite simply lost his nerve.

The mystic journey

'If I keep a secret, it is my slave. If I reveal it, it is my master.'

(This quotation was transcribed into a book kept by Gavrilo Princip, translated into Serbo-Croat from the original German.)

On Thursday 28 May 1914, Princip, Cabrinovic and Grabez left Belgrade together, on a boat for Sabac, a small border post facing Austria.

They made contact with Colonel Apis's contacts in the border guards, and proceeded to Loznica by railway.

They spent the night of Friday 29 May at Loznica, and quarrelled over security.

On the morning of Saturday 30 May the three men separated. Cabrinovic was to make his own way to Tuzla, using Grabez's passport and travel documents. The two young men looked similar, and Cabrinovic was well known to the police. He would try to enter Bosnia under a false identity, whereas the other two would attempt to return to their homeland without attracting official attention at all.

Cabrinovic travelled to Mali Zvornik in Serbia, arriving on 30 May, and made local contact. He walked across the border and spent the night in Zwornik in Bosnia, without the slightest difficulty. On the bext morning, he caught the mail coach to Tuzla, a small town 25 miles east of Zwornik, for the rendezvous with his colleagues. He had crossed the border without fuss and without weapons, and had not aroused suspicion. The journey of his comrades proved rather more problematic.

The Journey of Princip and Grabez

On Saturday, Princip and Grabez proceeded north to Ljesnica, where they thought that they intended to cross the border on foot, undetected and without passports. They slept in the Ljesnica border guards' barracks, and the next morning a border guard ferried them across the river Drina to an island much used by smugglers, where they awaited their next guide at an inn. The river could be crossed on foot at this point, and whilst they were still on Serbian territory, the area was so remote that they were unlikely to be caught by Bosnian border guards. The way to Sarajevo should be free.

From now on, an extraordinarily large number of local people were unwittingly involved in the plot to transport the two young assassins to

Saraejvo, and were to suffer the consequences when the Austrian authorities finally arrested them. The account offered here is a summary of the very detailed account offered by Remak (Remak, 1959). The journey may have demonstrated that there was a sympathy for what the young men intended to do, or at least a certain solidarity amongst Bosnian Serbs; but it also serves to illustrate that the three young men would have acted more wisely not to separate, and to have chosen a simpler way of returning to Sarajevo.[9] It also calls into question the judgement of Colonel Apis, who appears to have had a penchant for doing things conspiratorially when it was not necessary, and did not appear to shave with Occam's razor.

The following were next involved in helping the two young conspirators to travel on Bosnian soil:

- Mico Micic, a young farmer;
- Jakov Milovic, a smuggler and minor reprobate, who led Princip and Grabez from the island in the river Drina into Bosnia, and gave them shelter for the night;
- Obren Milosevic, who 'played the role of the simple-minded Balkan peasant to the hilt', according to Remak's account, and 'thought they (the two young men) were government officials;' and
- Veljko Cubrilovic, a young school-teacher, who met with Milosevic and the two 'government officials' outside the small town of Priboj, and took them on to the house of a prosperous old farmer named Mitar Kerovic.

At Kerovic's house, Grabez went to bed, exhausted. Princip now behaved quite out of character. No doubt exhausted by the journey so far, egged on by Veljko Cubrilovic, and with the feeling that he was amongst friends whom he could trust, he encouraged a massive inidscretion, and allowed the whole plot to be betrayed to his hosts, Mitar Kerovic and his three sons. According to Remak, Cubrilovic began the damage.

'The school teacher was now drinking glass after glass of plum brandy now, and feeling boastful.

"Do you know who these people are?" He asked the (four) Kerovices. They're going to Sarajevo to throw bombs and kill the Archduke who is going to come there."'

This was an admission of which Nedjelko Cabrinovic might have felt ashamed, but things rapidly worsened.

'Crossing over to the bed where he had placed his (horse's) saddlebag, Cubrilovic took out a bomb and displayed it to his hosts. Princip joined him, and demonstrated how to unscrew and throw the bomb. For good measure, he also brought out a revolver for the company to admire.'[10]

Comment is superfluous.

Later that night, June 2, about eleven o'clock, Princip, Grabez, Nedjo Kerovic and a friend got into a cart and left the Korevic household to its fate. The two assassins arrived on the outskirts of Tuzla early next morning, filthy and exhausted, and washed in the river. They had breakfast in a café, where they pretended not to know each other. Their drivers, Nedjo and his friend, had meanwhile gone on into Tuzla with the weapons to see Misko Jovanovic, a prominent local citizen and Serb enthusiast who managed the local cinema. Reluctantly, he accepted custody of the weapons for the time being: an action which was later to see him hanged.

The three young conspirators reunited and took the train to Sarajevo together, without any weapons but still with their cyanide capsules. On the train, the naturally gregarious Nedjelko Cabrinovic made casual conversation with a policeman, who obliged him with the dates on which Franz Ferdinand would visit the city. They arrived in Sarajevo without further incident on the evening of 3 June 1914. There were still 25 days to go before the assassination.

The weapons

The reader will recall that the assassins' weapons had been left with a reluctant custodian in Tuzla, on the pretext that it would be unsafe for three known political activists to take them further. Danilo Ilic took responsibility for their collection, and went by train to Tuzla on Sunday 14 June. He made contact with Misko Jovanovic, and asked if he would very much mind bundling the weapons in a harmless-looking package, and taking them on from Tuzla to Doboj, where Ilic would pick them up from him on the next day.

Jovanovic did mind, but had little choice in the matter. On the next day he took the weapons to Doboj, where there was no sign of Ilic at the railway station. Jovanovic left his package with a tailor whom he knew, and went off to do other business in town. Ilic arrived by a later train. The two men met at the station and went together to the tailor's, where the package was still being watched over by a young apprenctice. Ilic took the package on the next express to Sarajevo, changed outside the city to a local train, and completed his journey by street-car. At home with his mother once again, he hid the weapons under a couch in his room.

By 15 June 1914, therefore, both men and weapons were ready:. There were still 13 days to go until 28 June 1914, the chosen day for execution.

Waiting

The assassins intended to spend the time quietly before the *attentat*, and not to draw attention to themselves.

Trifko Grabez went home to Pale, where he spent time with a local girl.

Nedjelko Cabrinovic rejoined his family in town, where he made friends with his father before quarrelling once again.

Gavrilo Princip took up his lodgings once again with Danilo Ilic, and registered his address as there with the police on 15 June. He pretended to be slightly more extraverted than was his natural inclination, and was even seen to have a glass or two of wine with his friends: amiable young Gavro, who had not a care in the world.

Danilo Ilic himself was in a stew, because of fear, or because of a conflict of orders, or because he simply could not decide what was the best thing to do. Young Bosnia was moving towards the view that it should not be carrying individual assassinations, but working towards political action.[11] Ilic was sympathetic to this, as was his mentor, Vladimir Gacinovic, from his position of safety in Switzerland. Gavrilo Princip, however, was committed to action.

Muhamed Mehmedbasic remained at home, to come to Sarajevo on 26 June.

On the same day, the *Bosniche Post* anounced the route to be taken by the royal party on 28 June, for the benefit of patriotic citizens who wished to witness the event: they were urged to display the black and gold Austrian flag from their balconies to honour the occasion. The procession would drive along the Appel Quay in the centre of town, beside the river Miljacka, where there were a number of bridges and they would be forced to proceed slowly. From Ilic's point of view, it would make the ideal spot for an assassination: an assassination that would not be linked to Colonel Apis.

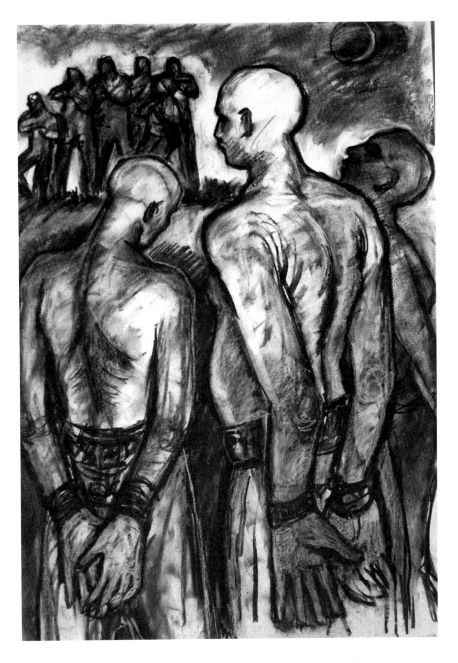

Colonel Apis faces the firing squad in Salonika in 1917

Nikola Pasic had no reason to love the Black Hand, and when he learned of its plot to assassinate Franz Ferdinand, he should have done his utmost to stop so reckless a plan. He did make some attempt: but it was not enough.

Firstly, the central organising committee of the Black Hand (on which Pasic would have had his own agent) debated what was in effect Colonel Apis's plot, which they had neither discussed nor agreed, and ordered him to stop it. Apis promised to do so: but the three young assassins had already been despatched on their mission.

Secondly, Pasic, whose devious character was not wholly dissimilar to that of Colonel Apis, and who would never take the short route when a diversion offered itself, made an attempt to communicate with the imperial minister of finance for Austria-Hungary, Count Leo von Bilinski. This was pitching things at the right level. Bilinksi was on one of the three ministers with responsibility for the whole Austro-Hungarian empire, and Bosnia as a crown land was his specific responsibility. Surely a word in his ear would be enough: but would it be the right word?

According to accounts of this period which still remain controversial, Pasic chose to brief a diplomat to pass on the message. The official chosen was Jovan Jovanovic, the Serbian ambassador to Vienna; and the message that this practised official gave to Leon von Bilinski proved a masterpiece of diplomacy, but not of common sense. He is reported to have said, that if it were true that the Archduke Franz Ferdinand would be visiting Bosnia in connexion with military manoeuvres at the time of Vidovan, then:

"I can assure Your Excellency that this will cause much discontent among the Serbs, who will consider it to be a provocative gesture. Maneuvers, under such circumstances are a dangerous thing. Some young Serb might put a live rather than a blank cartridge in his gun, and fire it. That bullet might hit the man who provoked him. Therefore it might be good and reasonable if Archduke Franz Ferdinand were not to go to Sarajevo."

Not surpisingly, Bilinski failed to see the hidden agenda behind this Balkan whisper, and no warning was issued, or reassessment of the risk of the visit made. Indeed, there was little that Bilinski might have done with such a message, even if he had attached more importance to it; for the security of the heir apparent lay in other hands. The official in charge of security for the Archduke's visit to Sarajevo was General Potiorek, the military governor of the province; and General Potiorek was not alert to the nuances of Balkan politics. As far as the general was concerned, the Archduke would be visiting Bosnia as the military guest of the military authorities, and sufficient precautions would be taken to ensure his security. The attempt to assassinate the general's predecessor in 1910 had been a miserable failure, or so it could be claimed, and General von Burian had survived the encounter entirely unscathed.[12] The emperor himself had visited Sarajevo in 1910, and had been received by respectful crowds. There was no real threat to the Archduke Franz Ferdinand; and if trouble arose, the military would deal with it. Subtle and coded messages would have had no impact on the general, even if they had been brought to his attention. Other officials connected with the royal visit which went so disastrously wrong were later to apologize for their negligence, and to regret what more they might have done. Not so General Potiorek, who was to blame others for what could not have been his own error.

The End of the Black Hand

The First World War was a disaster for Serbia. After some initial setbacks, Austro-Hungarian troops were able to overrun the country, and to occupy its capital: and in 1915 the government of Serbia was forced to flee. Their flight through the mountains of Albania was a desperate one, and there were many losses. They were eventually to find refuge in Salonika (now Thessaloniki in Greece) where they formed a government in exile in what had once been a major trading port of the Ottoman empire.

Whilst in Salonika, Prime Minister Pasic decided upon the final destruction of his old enemy, the Black Hand. The reasons why he took this decision at this time are not entirely clear, but the result was wholly conclusive. Pasic may have wished to make a separate peace treaty with the Austro-Hungarian administration under its new emperor Karl, and to have destroyed any evidence that the Serbians had once plotted to kill his predecessor as heir apparent. He may have wished to obliterate an unsavoury feature of Serbia's past, and to make sure that there was no threat from any military conspiracy to its future plans. Or he may simply have wished to avenge himself on Colonel Apis and his associates, who were no longer a threat to his authority but had done him such damage in the past.

Pasic may have been aided in his plans by the Serbian Prince Regent, Alexander, who would have shared his wish to extirpate the Black Hand and its regicides.

Whatever the reasons, and they were very probably a combination of the above, a 'show' trial was organised and Colonel Apis, together with Rade Malobabic, Muhamed Mehmedbasic and others, were charged with the attempted murder of the Serbian Prince Regent in September 1916. The trial was to take place before a military court in Salonika, and the normal rules of evidence were not applied.

The secondary purpose of the trial was to indicate to the wider world that Colonel Apis had indeed been responsible for the murders of Franz Ferdinand and his wife at Sarajevo, and that the Serbian government bore no responsibility. However, that event was forbidden to be discussed in court.

The star witness against the accused, according to Remak's account, was Milan Ciganovic.

There was much with which Apis might have been charged, but the attempted murder of the Prince Regent, organised by himself and to be carried out by Malobabic and Mehmedbasic, was entirely fictitious. Apis would have had no reason for such an action, and there is no evidence that it ever happened.

Apis, however, had been presented with a problem that he could not resolve. He was accused of conspiring against the nation that he loved, and to whose service he had devoted his entire adult life. The charges against him were false, and he could have opposed them to the best of his ability, no matter where the trial might lead. However, Apis might best serve his country by accepting the verdict of the trial, and thus acting the role of the scapegoat for Sarajevo. After all, what penalty would he really face? He remained a decorated senior officer, who still retained many friends in its military: and he simply could not believe that the Serbian authorities would sentence him to a severe penalty, or that if they did, any such sentence would actually be carried out. Rather, if he had to be convicted for the good of his country, he would be allowed a discreet retreat to a dignified exile. Apis misunderstood the situation, and it was a mistake that was to cost him his life.

The trial itself was a travesty of justice and its outcome was entirely predictable. On 23 May 1917 Apis and others were sentenced to death. (After his conviction, and presumably when he was in a very disturbed state or mind, Apis made a sort of confession of his role in the murder of the Archduke Franz Ferdinand which is a curious mixture of truth and untruth and does not resolve any of the remaining quandaries associated with that event, but instead leaves a document for rival interpretation.) The conviction of Colonel Dimitryevich did, however, give the Serbian authorities the opportunity to blame any Serbian participation in the assassination of 1914 on a renegade army officer who had since been executed.

As with Danilo Ilic after a previous trial, no deal was forthcoming, and the sentences passed by the court were carried out two days later. On 25 June, the blind-folded Colonel Apis was executed in a ditch near Salonika, with Rade Malobabic and an army officer named Lubomir Vulovic by his side. He remained both stoical and courageous to the end, and attempted to encourage his colleagues to face death with dignity. His last words were: Long live Serbia! Long live Yugoslavia!

The three men had asked for the shooting to be delayed until dawn, so that the firing squad might shoot straight. Nevertheless, it seems to have been a fairly haphazard affair, in which at least forty bullets were fired, none striking any victim in the head.

Perhaps some soldiers fired to miss. Perhaps some were simply poor shots, although the distance cannot have been very great, and by that stage in the war any infantryman should have had plenty of practice with his personal weapon.

Perhaps, like everything else about the murder of Franz Ferdinand, there was an element of improvisation even about the execution of its main planner, and a whiff of uncertainty about what was really going on.

The death of an obscure colonel in the middle of a world war did not attract international attention; and there is no monument anywhere in existence to Colonel Dragutin Dimitrijevic, known as 'Apis', the sixth member of the central organising committee of the once legendary Black Hand.

He was guilty of regicide in 1903, but so were many others who remained unpunished. He had played a leading role in the organisation of the murder of Franz Ferdinand; but it seems clear that Nikola Pasic knew of this plan, and did very little to try and stop it. It was not, in any case, the reason for his execution, which was that of political expediency rather than justice.

If Apis himself were not awarded a fair trial, he was not the sort of person who went out of his way to confer that benefit on others: and his approach to life and death shows an extreme ruthlessness which makes this author, at least, not entirely sympathetic to his sufferings. Colonel Apis died as he lived: on the edge. His actions over Sarajevo were reckless in the extreme and his involvement in national politics was wholly improper. Colonel Apis's patriotism may not have been a front for his ego, and it might nowadays fall under the description of noble cause corruption; but corruption is corruption, whatever the motive. Instead of devising more and more extravagant oaths of loyalty for murderous conspiracies, Colonel Apis should have paid more attention to the oath he took as an army officer, and practised a proper allegiance to the state.

APPENDIX

'Amongst all the things of this world information is the hardest to guard, for it can be stolen without removing it.' Erving Goffman

The Principles of Intelligence

The principles of any intelligence system, as laid down by NATO, are as follows:

1. Centralised control
2. Timeliness
3. Systematic exploitation
4. Objectivity
5. Accessibility
6. Responsiveness
7. Source protection
8. Continuous review
9. Security

Comments

To these nine princples we should add legality, which the original NATO doctrine did not include.[13]

Principles may clash. For example, intelligence needs to be both accessible and secure. The job of the director of intelligence is to ensure a working balance between the two, as with other clashes.

Classifying Intelligence

The following system, once common to NATO and other international alliances, is still in widespread use.

Source

A   Wholly reliable
B   Probably reliable
C   Possibly reliable
D   Doubtfully reliable
E   Not usually reliable
F   Reliability cannot be judged

Information

1   Confirmed by another source (true)
2   Probably true
3   Possibly true
4   Doubtfully true
5   Improbably true (probably false)
6   Truth cannot be assessed

The two systems combine, so that a report may be evaluated as B2, F6, or any other combination. Many reports which may be of great significance can or should only be graded as F6. A director of intelligence faces a real challenge when a report is received which could have catastrophic consequences, but may be graded as D4 or E5. What resources should be directed towards averting a threat which is probably false, but which, if true, would have a devastating effect? Further numbers may then be allocated in a risk assessment exercise, but in the end a judgment must be made.

1 Apis was not promoted colonel until the Great War had begun. Nevertheless, he has always been known by that rank, and it would be pedantic to describe him otherwise. Colonel, he became: and as a colonel he shall be known.

2 With a Croat father and a Slovene mother, the long-term communist Josip Broz assumed the nickname Tito to avoid identification and arrest in Royalist Yugoslavia between the wars. The name allegedly means 'here, there' in Serbo-Croat: but we may be sure that it has more than one interpretation.

3 As I wrote in 'A History of the Police Staff College' [Villiers, 1998) some would have considered that a very reasonable alternative.

4 In the same year as Franz Ferdinand married his beloved Sophie. This was another betrothal which some, including the emperor, saw as unfortunate, although the heir apparent naturally believed the opposite, and his marriage was a great success.

5 Should we compare Apis to the young army officer who takes a major interest in politics, decides he can do a better job than those actually in change, without the necessity for an election to replace them; and uses or misuses his military powers to become ruler in their place? Was he the Colonel Gaddafi or Chavez of his day? Far from it. Firstly, he did not put himself in power, and secondly, he would have had no political agenda had he done so. Apis was a natural conspirator, but not a natural politician; and in the end, those who were more adept in the political arena were able to defeat him. His career contrasts strongly with the one-time Colonel Mustapha Kemal, the Young Turk who went on to revolutionize Turkey and to make it into a modern, secular republic, under the name of Ataturk.

6 His family was to rule Serbia and then Yugoslavia until it became a republic; and his descendant Prince Alexander of Yugoslavia, born in Claridges, an hotel in London which was declared Yugoslav territory for the occasion, resides in Belgrade to-day.

7 The intelligence cycle as used by NATO is summarised as an appendix to this chapter, together with the principles of intelligence. There is noting secret about this frame-work, and nothing that would not have been understood by Colonel Apis in 1914. Information technology may have changed, but not the principles of intelligence.

8 The hand is a symbol of violence as well as of labour and love, and, to pursue the Irish comparison, it is interesting to note that the icon of an independent Ulster is a red or bloody hand. Legend has it that an Ulster chieftain cut off his hand and threw it ahead of his rival, in order to win a boat-race.

9 Remak's account of the attentat states that Ilic travelled from Sarajevo to Belgrade, presumably by train, in the week before the murder, in order to receive his final orders from Colonel Apis, whom he knew personally as a fellow member of the Black Hand. Remak states that it is not known what took place at this meeting. Our comment here is on the breach of security involved if such a meeting really occured.

As a leading member of Mlada Bosna, and a long-term political activist, Danilo Ilic must have been well-known to the authorities in both Bosnia and Serbia, and any movement on his part would have aroused curiosity and probably suspicion; and yet there was no secrecy about this journey. What was really going on? Did Apis wish him to cancel the assassination, and if so, why did Ilic not do so?

10 Remak refers to the pistols carried indifferently as revolvers or automatics. In fact, they were automatics. Automatics have the advantage over revolvers in that they can carry more bullets, the container which holds the bullets can easily be exchanged for another, and a safety catch may be used. On the other hand, a revolver has a simpler mechanism and is less likely to snag or jam.

11 This ideological controversy was not uncommon in terrorist organisations, and was replicated, for example, in the split between the 'Provisional' and the 'Official' IRA in 1972, when at a conference in Dublin the 'Provisional' IRA decided to continue with violence and the 'Official' IRA turned against it. Despite its provisionality, PIRA remained in action for another 30 years and is now represented in the government of Northern Ireland, a province which it had sworn never to recognise, under the Belfast or Good Friday agreement.

Splits in revolutionary or terrorist organisations may provide an excellent opportunity for the security forces to do damage to both wings, since in an general atmosphere of mistrust and fear the authorship of atrocities cannot be certain, and the use of agents provocateur is likely. The Russian secret service exploited just such a situation in the early 1900s, when the director of the active service unit of the socialist revolutionaries was in fact an agent of the Okhrana.

12 In fact, the general had been extremely lucky to escape the five shots fired.

13 We are indebted to Lt. Col. Raymond Bell, formerly of the directing staff of the police staff college at Bramshill, for this suggestion.

CHAPTER SEVEN

The Fatal Day: 28 June 1914

Archduke Franz Ferdinand von Osterreich-Este, heir apparent to the Austro-Hungarian Empire, wakes early. He is the guest of honour at the hotel Bosna, in the little resort town of Ilidze just outside Sarajevo. He has been dreaming about the Romans, who discovered the sulphurous springs there and built a camp. The Archduke admires the Romans. They knew what it takes to build and maintain an empire.

His wife Sophie lies beside him. He will become emperor, but she will not be his empress. The archduke was forced to agree to a morganatic marriage. His wife does not share his status, and their three children are excluded from succession.

The Archduke has come to Bosnia to inspect the manoeuvres of the southern army groups of the imperial army, of which he is inspector general. The manoeuvres were a success. He has congratulated the soldiers concerned, and reported the results to the emperor. That part of his task is complete.

Secondly, he wishes to find out for himself the state of affairs in Bosnia, which was only officially absorbed into the Austro-Hungarian empire in 1908, a mere six years before. So far, he is impressed with the reception that has been offered and the apparent loyalty of the local population: but his visit has yet to be concluded.

In making a formal visit to Sarajevo, he will take the opportunity to demonstrate that Sophie is not only his wife but also his consort, an equal companion for the man who is to be the next emperor of Austria and apostolic king of Hungary.

To-day is Sunday, 28 June. It is Vojvodan: the anniversary of the battle of Kosovo, when the Serbs were defeated by the Turks in 1389, and from which they date their occupation and subjection by the Ottoman Turks for the next 400 years. The date means nothing to Franz Ferdinand. The Serbs are not a race whom he admires—he once described their king as looking like a bad copy of a gypsy—and their history is of no interest to him. However, they do present a significant problem for his empire, for they are known to have designs on Bosnia—which includes a substantial Bosnian Serb element in its population.

The Archduke is a Hapsburg, and the Hapsburg tradition of government is one of intelligent autocracy. Sensible Bosnians, of any origin, will achieve peace and prosperity within the empire. Extremists, revolutionaries and nationalists, who are all the same in the Archduke's book, will be crushed.

The heir apparent takes Mass with his wife—both are lifelong Roman Catholics, and the hotel has dedicated a room for the ceremony—sends a telegram to his children, and is on his way as soon as possible. Franz Ferdinand is an impatient man. He has an empire to inherit, if his uncle ever dies. In his view, it is in poor shape, and there is much to be done.

Dr Edmund Gerde is the chief of police in Sarajevo. This morning he wishes he were not. He has a VIP on his door-step, and his strongest desire is that the day were over and the Archduke Franz Ferdinand were already on his way back to Vienna. Dr Gerde neither suggested nor welcomed his visit, and has not the resources to deal with it as he would like. The military authorities are officially in charge of security: but there is very little to suggest that they have approached that task with any intelligence, whether of the general or military variety.

General Potiorek is the military governor who officially invited the heir apparent to visit the province. General Potiorek is a law unto himself, who neither consults nor informs anyone else of his plans: and least of all a civilian. Gerde and Potiorek have not reviewed security for the visit together, and have no joint plans. Dr Gerde can only hope that what has been done will prove enough, and that he will be able to shift the blame to the military authorities in case of a disaster. Dr Gerde is a survivor. He knows that it is not what happens that counts, but where the blame ends; and he is determined that it will not end on his desk.

The way to prevent an assassination is simple enough. A good start would include a carefully planned route, to minimise danger; lots of troops and policemen on the streets, to act as a visible deterrent; and some good detective work behind the scenes, including the precautionary arrest of the usual suspects, and the penetration of any secret societies by the appropriate organisation, in order to prevent any more sophisticated attempt at assassination.

Finally, the potential target himself should be encouraged, if at all possible, to minimize the risk—a tall order with many leaders, who are determined to see and be seen, which means to travel on foot or in an open car, to mingle with the crowd where and when possible, and even to take charge should any emergency occur—whereas they should put safety first, and not make the situation worse for the experts like Dr Gerde.

In regard to his own safety, the Heir Apparent is likely to prove a challenge. He is widely known to be an impatient man, with a very quick temper, who is quite likely to disagree with the security arrangements and to act as he chooses on the spur of the moment. On the other hand, there is another side to the Archduke's character. He is a highly intelligent person, who understands that other people have a job to do; and he is also a sort of religious fatalist, who recognises that his fate is in the hands of God and not of his fellow men. In other words, if he is not prepared to take excessive security precautions, he is quite likely to be sensible—or so hopes the commissioner of police. If not, there is nothing that a lower order official can do about it, anyway: and so perhaps he had better practise a little fatalism himself.

In 1910, when the emperor Franz Josef himself came to town, over 200 suspects were placed under house arrest, and a number of others were told not to leave their houses; moreover, a very large number of troops lined the streets.

In 1914, however, preparations have been slack. There are less than 120 policemen on duty and there are no soldiers on view at all. Only 35 precautionary arrests have been made, which must be far too few. Have they detained the right people? The commissioner hopes so, but he cannot be sure. His organisation, by his own decision, has already made one culpable error: it has failed to detain Nedjelko Cabrinovic, a known agitator who would be much better behind bars for the day. But his father is a police supporter, who has been very useful in supplying information; and the police have made the wrong assessment of the risk posed by his son.

*

Franz Ferdinand, his wife, and his entourage walk to the Ilidze railway station in the bright morning sunshine and embark upon the very brief railway journey to Sarajevo. They disembark at the Philipovic army camp, where Franz Ferdinand carries out a short inspection. From now on, the journey is to be by motor car. Some vehicles have been borrowed for the occasion, and Count Franz von Harrach, a reserve army officer, will have the honour of conveying the archducal couple in his own Graef und Stift, an open tourer with the roof folded back.

The royal convoy leaves the Philipovic army camp in six vehicles. In the first car sit the (Moslem) Mayor of Sarajevo, Effendi Fehim Curcic, and the Commissioner of Police, Dr Edmund Gerde. The second contains the archducal couple, Franz Ferdinand and Sophie; General Potiorek, the military governor of Bosnia; Count von Harrach, the owner of the vehicle; and the driver. The third, fourth and five cars contain officials and the sixth car is in reserve. Some reports say that specially assigned detectives should have been part of the escort party, travelling with the convoy: but if there were such a plan, it has failed and they have been left behind at the railway station.

The driver of the second car is a Czech named Leopold Lofka, who is not familiar with Sarajevo. Count Harrach sits beside the driver, and the heir apparent and his wife occupy the back seat, with the hood folded down behind them. General Potiorek sits on an extra seat facing the royal couple, so that he is facing away from the direction of travel and unable to see what is coming unless he cricks his neck. In his stiff military uniform this would be a far from easy manoeuvre, even if he were inclined to do so.

His attention is focused on the royal couple who sit just opposite him, like passengers in a London taxi-cab which has somehow lost its roof. The two men wear full uniform with feathered helmets, while the Countess Sophie wears a white silk dress with a sash and a veiled picture hat surmounts her luxuriant hair. If Potiorek had possessed a sense of humour, he might have found it all slightly comic. But the possession of a sense of humour is a charge that has never been laid against him.

*

Gavrilo Princip rises early and leaves the little, white-washed cottage in Sarajevo in which he has lodged, one and off, since he was eleven years old. It has not been redecorated in his honour, and nor has it been reserved for his exclusive use. As an (Orthodox) non-believer, he does not attend mass; and nor does he have breakfast. Gavrilo Princip almost never has breakfast. He almost never has any money, and if he has, he is more likely to spend it on books than food. Besides, to-day he has other things on his mind.

It is eight o'clock on a bright, sunny morning, and there is an air of expectation in the town. Flags are flying cheerfully. Oriental rugs are on display on the balconies of the town, together with unsmiling official portraits of the heir apparent. Policemen are on duty, but not in overwhelming numbers. Plain clothes detectives will soon be mingling with the crowd, if they are not already doing so. The crowd is happy, excited, and growing: especially along the Appel Quay in the centre of town, along which it is known that the Archduke will travel.

Gavrilo stands in the street and talks to two acquaintances about to-day's event. The visit of an Austrian archduke means very little to the young Bosnian, it appears: he is no longer interested in politics, for he has to concentrate on his impending examinations. His acqaintances, who include the son of the state prosecutor, would like to spend more time with him, but he has other plans. He leaves them to take up his post at the Latin Bridge. He has an appointment with destiny.

*

Nedjelko Cabrinovic is a highly emotional young man on almost any morning, and on 28 June his feelings are running so high as to be almost uncontrollable.

He rises early and takes leave of his family, giving 20 crowns to his grandmother and five crowns to his sister. He is going on a long journey, he tells her, from which he will never return. Is he going to emigrate to America? He smiles. Maybe. She is used to his fantasies, and does not take him too seriously. Nevertheless, she is concerned. He does not seem his usual self this morning, and he has been very subdued in the last few days. Is he sickening for something? His health has never been robust.

152

Take care, she says. I will, he replies, and kisses her good-bye.

He would like to speak to his father, but cannot bring himself to do so. They would be bound to have a row, and Nedjelko cannot face a row to-day, his last morning on earth. His father, huge, red-faced, and shaking with rage, will thrust his face into that of his son, and demand to know that Nedjelko will do his patriotic duty and welcome the archduke, whose flag he has already displayed. Nedjelko has other other loyalities, and other plans; but they are not plans he wishes to share with his father.

Shortly after nine o'clock he leaves the house on his final mission. Bathetically, he finds that he has been accompanied by the family dog, and has to return it; the thought of a dog distracting his attention on this morning of all mornings is too much to be born. He checks in at the cake shop where he has arranged to meet Grabez, Ilic and Princip, who gives him his bomb and his cyanide. Cabrinovic leaves the shop and goes to a photographer in order 'to leave a memory behind.' He is photogaphed in a dark suit, unsmiling, his bomb just detectable as a bulge in his pocket. He orders six prints for family and friends. His friend Tomo Vucinovic is entrusted with dealing with the photographs, for Cabrinovic expects that he will be dead by the time that they have been developed. Does Tomo know what is in his friend's mind? We may be sure that he does.

Cabrinovic says good-bye to Vukinovic and walks to his post on the Quay, where he awaits the convoy. Although it is a hot day, he has buttoned up his coat tightly, so as not to drop his bomb. He has encouraged a local boy to join him, since he thinks it would seem suspicious if he were on his own. His companion is a deaf mute, who spends much of his time on the streets, and is very well known in the area. People will remember that he and Cabrinovic were together.

Whilst he is waiting, the young anarchist strikes up a conversation with a policeman nearby. In which car will the Archduke be travelling? He asks. The policeman obligingly tells him. He will be in the second car, an open tourer, a magnificent vehicle. He will be easily identified: he is a tall man, in full general's uniform, with feathers in his hat. Thank you, says the anarchist, who is also a socialist, and whose political ideas are really quite confused—and waits.

*

28 June is Vojvodina day. It is also Trifko Grabez's birthday. He is nineteen. How will he celebrate? He knows how. He will become a hero, together with his friends Princip and Cabrinovic. They have already discussed the plan, and Gavrilo and he have reached an informal agreement to act together. He takes up his official position, but he cannot see Princip, and is too impatient and too jumpy to stay in one place for long. He roams between the Latin and the Kaiser Bridges, looking for Princip, but cannot find him. Perhaps he has been arrested? He sees Danilo Ilic in the distance: but the older man is in no condition to reassure him.

*

Danilo Ilic is in a state of confusion. A few weeks ago, it was all so clear. They had plotted to kill the Archduke, and he had recruited the extra men. Then, according to a mixture of sources, he met either with Colonel Apis himself, or with his special representative for Bosnia, Rade Malobabic; and what happened at that meeting remains a mystery. Was he told to stop? Or to carry on? Or, most bizarrely of all, to make sure that if an attempt were made, it was not successful?

Ilic appears to have been in a double confusion as to how to what to do, as he is plagued by ideological doubts. Gacinovic is turning against the tactic of assassination, in favour of political work; and Gacinovic is his mentor. What is Ilic to do? [1]

*

Muhamed Mehmedbasic, the only Moslem in the assassination group, has taken up his position as the first assassin. He has a bomb, but no pistol, of which there were only four. That does not matter. If he does his job properly, the other assassins will not be needed.

*

The plan is very simple. The six assassins will line up along the Appel Quay, and attack the convoy when it is within striking distance, using both bombs and pistols. If one attack fails, there are still others to follow. Ilic is the seventh man. He has neither fixed position nor weapon, and will act as a roving co-ordinator.

There has been some suggestion that the assassins will attack in pairs: but this has not been worked out.

The plan is seriously flawed; so seriously, in fact, as to be almost impracticable.

The assassins have been placed on both sides of the street, thus contradicting the first law of planning an ambush, which is that the ambushing party should not fire on each other.

There is no look-out, to give a warning that the convoy is coming. (Given the topography of a narrow river running from east to west under various bridges in a very gentle convex curve, a look-out could have been posted on the other or south side of the river. His signal would still have been clearly visible, he would have been less likely to attract police attention, and he would have had a longer view of the approaching cavalcade than if he had been stationed on the north side, then called the Appel Quay.)

The assassins have no robust means by which they can communicate with each other.

The weapons are problematic. Pistols are of use only at close quarters, and none of the assassins is an expert shot. The bombs have a twelve second delay, whereas a bomb which explodes on impact would be far more suitable for this *attentat*.

There is no guarantee against civilian casualties.

There has been no proper briefing.

There has been no rehearsal or 'dry run.'

There has been no team-building. Only Ilic knows the full team, who have never met as a group. This may be good security, but it is bad for group morale and dynamics.

There is no plan for what to do after the event; and that reflects the fact that there has been no real appreciation made for the *attentat* as a whole. Will the plan succeed in killing the Archduke? It can only be assessed as possible but unlikely.

*

About 1015, Muhamed Mehmedbasic hears the convoy, and sees it go past.

He does nothing.

According to his own account (which, judging by his previous actions, cannot be taken as reliable), he fears that he is under observation by the police; and, that if he were to throw his bomb, he would injure innocent people who have gathered in large numbers. This is nonsense, or at best self-deception. Muhamed has either lost his nerve, or never had it in the first place.

One down: five to play.

*

Second in line is Cabrinovic, who has only a bomb: he has not been trusted with a pistol. Just after 1015, Cabrinovic hears the convoy. He has succeeded, for once, in not drawing attention to himself, and he has not been arrested or moved on: although a doctor standing across the street has noticed the tall, dark figure, wrapped in an overcoat and standing in the hot sun, and has wondered why he did not move into the shade.

Cabrinovic draws out his bomb, strikes the percussion cap against a lamp-post—the noise is quite distinct, and is mistaken for a pistol-shot by some listeners who later give evidence—takes careful aim, and throws it straight at the Archduke in the second car. The feathers in his hat make him unmistakable.

The driver sees the bomb in the air, and accelerates.

The bomb misses the person for whom it is intended. It bounces off the folded hood behind him and falls in the street, between the second and third cars.[2]

The bomb explodes, at street level, with a loud noise that can be heard as far away as the Town Hall. A number of spectators are injured, together with two of the officials in the third car: Colonel Merizzi receives a severe wound to the scalp that bleeds profusely, all over the lap of the lady-in-waiting sitting beside him. The convoy stops, except for its lead vehicle: Curcic and Gerde do not realise what has happened, and carry on to the Town Hall.

In flat contradiction of any policy on security, and exactly as a proper army officer might be expected to do, Franz Ferdinand wants to find out what has happened. Stop the car, he says: and they stop.

Cabrinovic swallows his suicide pill, which does not work, and jumps over the parapet into the river a few feet below. The Miljacka is only a few inches deep at this time of the year, and he is followed by four men, a barber, a shopkeeper, a policeman and a detective, who seize him. The barber draws a gun—it would appear that the private possession of fire-arms is not illegal in Sarajevo in 1914—and is stopped from shooting Cabrinovic there and then by the policeman, who points out that the young terrorist will need to be interrogated first.

Coughing badly from the effect of the poison, which has burned his throat and made him nauseous but is otherwise wholly ineffective, Cabrinovic is bundled up the river bank, thrust back onto the Quay, arrested and taken into custody.

He is ecstatic. Where the others had frozen, he acted: and if the archduke is not dead, that is not because of his inaction.

*

Franz Ferdinand sums up the situation. A bomb has been thrown by a madman. Its results are manageable. There is no sign of any other terrorist activity. The plan will continue. He orders the convoy to continue to the Town Hall, where he later decides to make a sardonic joke of it, telling his aides that 'those idiots in Vienna will probably put up a monument' to his attacker. 'Those idiots' are the court officials who have blocked his reforms and ridiculed his wife, as well as the radical press which has dared to criticise the monarchy. Their time will come.

*

Gavrilo hears the explosion. He is overjoyed. The plot has succeeded! He runs towards the spot, and in the smoke and confusion he sees Cabrinovic under arrest, and the convoy starting up again.

They have failed.

There is nothing he can do.

He considers shooting Cabrinovic and then himself, to hide all trace of the plot, and then has a better idea. The archducal party is due to return from the TownHall along the same route, later in the day. He will wait. Perhaps he will have another chance. What else is he to do?

*

Trifko Grabez hears the explosion, and dares to hope. He sees the cars pass, and sees that the Archduke is still alive and intact. He does nothing. Is the crowd too tight for him to pull out his bomb? He would like to think so, but he knows it is not the truth. When the moment came to act, as he later tells the court, he lacked the necessary fortitude. Trifko Grabez is an honest young man.

Vaso Cubrilovic and Cvetko Popovic are the last two members of the group, apart from Ilic himself: and he has no weapon. Neither has been properly inducted into the conspiracy, nor made any real 'investment' in it. Both fail to act, for which they offer different reasons. Cubrilovic claims that he did not wish to injure the duchess. Popovic says simply that he lost courage. It is not all he is to lose.

*

At the Town Hall, Franz Ferdinand has finally reacted to what happened, and is in a state of rage. The Mayor stands on the steps, preparing to make an effusive speech of welcome to his distinguished visitors, which will be entirely inappropriate in the light of what has happened, and which the Mayor is perfectly incapable of modifying. He begins. Franz Ferdinand thinks of what has happened, and how his beloved Sophie was so nearly killed. What is this nonsense? He loses his temper and lashes out.

"Mr Mayor," he says, "one comes here for a visit and is received with bombs! It is outrageous!"

Sophie calms him down, as she has done so often before. The Mayor stutters through the remainder of his effusive welcome, and the Archduke adds a comment in his reply, on the failure of the attempt at assassination. His final words and carefully coached words are in Serbo-Croat as he attempts to save the occasion.

Inside the Town Hall—an ornate building in orientalist style which has only recently been completed—Franz Ferdinand telegraphs the emperor to tell him that his life has been saved and to give his own account of what has happened before the Vienna press distorts it. Sophie goes upstairs to receive a delegation of Moslem ladies, who are prepared to unveil only in her presence. She is very quiet at first, but then happy to talk about her children.

Meanwhile, the visitors and officials confer downstairs. What is to be done? The original plan called for a visit to the National Museum, followed by a farewell lunch at the Governor's Residence and then some sight-seeing. However, that would mean driving through the crowded and narrow streets of the old city. Should the plan be modified, or even abandoned altogether?

The answer to this rests on the answer to another question. Was the bombing an isolated episode, or does the threat remain? Dr Gerde thinks there will not be another attack, and so does General Potiorek. Indeed, the general is quite certain about it, as he is about everything else:

"Do you think that Sarajevo is full of assassins?" He snaps to an anxious aide, who has asked a perfectly reasonable question. But the general's life is not ruled by reason. Moreover, he is in shock: he has just been nearly killed by a bomb, and although he is a military man, he is not used to the experience.

The discussion continues, with other options being suggested. Colonel Bardolff suggests that extra security measures be taken. Why not line the streets with soldiers? They could also provide a military escort, to guard the Archduke on his way to safety. Potiorek says, no. He is not prepared to line the streets with soldiers from the garrison, although there are men available: they are wearing the wrong uniforms. Potiorek is not by nature a stupid man, but he is a very obstinate one. At the moment, the difference is indetectable.

The Archduke decides. They will conclude the visit to the Town Hall, and then he must visit Colonel Merizzi in hospital, even though they have already learned by telephone that his injuries are not as serious as was at first thought. Can they do so, without driving through the narrow and crowded streets of the old city, where who knows what may be awaiting them? Yes, they can, says the general, who for once is right: all they have to do is to race back along the Appel Quay, the way they came. Then that is what they will do, says the Archduke. The archducal couple, however, will need to separate. As soon as her reception has finished, Sophie will return to Ilidze by the most direct route, with an armed escort. His wife must not be put at any further risk.

Baron Morsey goes upstairs to tell the Duchess Sophie of the change of plan. As the Moslem ladies have unveiled themselves, no man may enter. He must wait. The meeting concludes and the plan is presented to the duchess. Sophie says, no. She is calm now, and has got over her shock. She knows what she must do.

"As long as the Archduke shows himself in public to-day, I will not leave him."

Baron Morsey bows. She walks downstairs, and reiterates her decision to her husband:

'Wherever you go to-day, Franz, I will be by your side.'

In the middle of his actions, he is touched, and accepts her decision. It is her epitaph.

*

The party is about to leave. Colonel Bardolff attempts to check on the arrangements, but finds that no-one wishes to do so: they are all much too nervous. Has anyone briefed the drivers on the new route? No answer is offered. Gerde brushes off his very sensible questions. He is beside himself with fear and anxiety. They must go! Would that the day were over! It soon will be.

The party leaves the Town Hall, much as before. Count Harrach takes up his stance on the left running board, as if to protect the Archduke from further attack with his body. The Archduke laughs, but the soldier remains. As Remak says, it is a wonderfully Austrian gesture: kind, impulsive, brave, chivalrous and ineffectual.

Gavrilo Princip is waiting, on the quay, in the sunshine. The crowd is still discussing the bombing, but he does not talk to anyone. He does not know what to do; but he knows that he must do something. He crosses the road and takes up a new position outside Schiller's food shop, a well-known meeting place at the beginning of Franz Joseph Street. It is in the shade. There are fewer people. Perhaps he will have another chance from there. Does he go into the café, and order a sandwich? It seems unlikely. The young Bosnian Serb has other things on his mind.

The Mayor's car, is again leading the convoy which should now be taking the safest and most direct route to the hospital. It turns right and wrongly off the Appel Quay and into Franz Joseph Street, to go through the old town. The second car, driven by a chauffeur who has not been briefed, naturally and equally wrongly follows the car in front. General Potiorek intervenes. As usual on this fateful day, his decision is the wrong one. On this occasion, it is fatal.

"What is this?" He turns and shouts to the driver. "This is the wrong way! We're supposed to take the Appel Quay!"

The driver stops the car and puts her into gear to reverse. Gavrilo Princip, who has heard the cars approaching and is this time ready for action, sees his chance.[3] He takes out his Browning, runs forward and fires two shots. It is a distance of a few feet, and he has a sitting target. The gallant Count Harrach is on the other running board and can be of no use to the

*Gavrilo shoots the Arch-duke Franz Ferdinand and his wife
in Sarajevo on 28 June 1914*

heir apparent. A by-stander, an actor named Mihailjo Pusara, kicks a policeman who is attempting to intervene. General Potiorek, who is staring the assassin in the face, does nothing: all he succeeds in noticing is that the pistol-shot is very quiet.

The assassin has succeeded. Or has he? Gavrilo has decided to use his pistol, for the place is too crowded for a bomb. Circumstances are with him, in that no-one has stopped his attack. However, someone strikes him on the arm, so that his second shot misses its target: it was probably meant for the general, but that gentleman is unharmed.[4] So, apparently, is everyone else in the car. The heir apparent sits upright, with no expression on his face. Sophie has fallen sideways, and is leaning on his shoulder. Perhaps she has fainted. Two attacks, in one morning! It is too much.

The other cars have stopped, and their occupants crowd around. They agree with the general's immediate assessment: there has been a miraculous escape. Nevertheless, a doctor is sought for, and the driver, shaken but unharmed, is ordered to drive to the Governor's Residence, so that the Archduke and his wife may be examined. General Potiorek is determined that nothing else will go wrong.

*

It very soon becomes apparent that things have already gone wrong, and disastrously so. Princip's first bullet has pierced Franz Ferdinand's neck, and his second has gone downwards into Sophie's abdomen. Both are already dying, although no-one has yet realised. Blood gushes from the Archduke's mouth. His wife leans forward.

"For Heaven's sake! What happened to you?" She gasps, and leans forward, her head between his knees. Franz Ferdinand turns to her.

"Sophie dear! Sophie dear! Don't die! Stay alive for the sake of our children!"[5]

He sags forward. Count Harrach seizes him by the collar, and asks if he is suffering very badly.

'It is nothing,' says the Archduke several times, his voice gradually fading. They are his last words.

PLANNING AN ASSASSINATION

"No plan survives contact with the enemy"
CLAUSEWITZ

Any military-style operation should be planned, since, as the old soldier's axiom has it, failing to plan is planning to fail. The plan should be as simple as is possible under the circumstances; clear to everyone involved; and capable of being modified on the ground as events unfold and unforseen challenges present themselves. (Readers will recall that when Apis and his fellow regicides finally burst into the Royal Palace in Belgrade in search of King Alexander and his wife, they were unable to find the royal couple. Farce was swiftly followed by tragedy. One account has it that the conspirators called out the names of their intended victims, and promised the distraught king and his wife safety if they would reveal themselves—a promise that was spectacularly discarded).

The most important part of any plan is the aim or mission. What needs to be achieved? The aim must be singular, positive, and the utmost than can be achieved under the circumstances. The police, who have a duty to preserve the status quo, may decide upon an aim that uses words like reassure, preserve, restore, or keep, as in 'keep the peace'. A military operation (to which a terrorist operation is akin) must have an active verb, for the aim must be to change and not to maintain.

Military operations follow a standardised planning system, for which the widely used and unlovely but memorable acronym is SMEAC.

SMEAC stands for:

Situation
Mission
Execution
Administration
Communications

The aim is separated from the means chosen to carry it.

The Appreciation

An unusual or especially demanding operation, or one which is of strategic significance, should be the subject of an appreciation, which allows for a more profound analysis of the problem.

As with SMEAC, the appreciation begins with a biref summary of the situation, followed by the statement of the aim. Again as with SMEAC, the aim must be positive, single, and the utmost that can be achieved under the circumstances.

Factors

A factor is anything that affects the aim. Time, ground and weather are constant factors which are relevant to almost any operation. Factors which would certainly be relevant in considering the assassination of an archduke in the centre of a busy city would include the size and likely reaction of the crowd, to the event; the disposition, strength and likely reaction of the security forces deployed to prevent just such an event; and so on.

Impression management as a factor

In the case of a terrorist operation, the operatives may be reckless as to their own fate, or even wish to kill themselves after the event. Therefore, their own survival is not of paramount importance, and an escape plan may not be necessary.[6]

However, a terrorist operation is usually planned with the political context in mind; and so politics, or what we might call impression management, is a factor.

Does the terrorist group wish to create an impression of absolute ruthlessness? In that case civilian casualties will not be a problem, and the terrorists can bomb or shoot their way out of capture after the event, or take hostages, or in other ways behave entirely as they wish.

Or do they wish to convey a reluctant message of absolute necessity in the use of force? In that case only the chosen victim will be harmed, and other casualties are to be absolutely avoided, to the extent that the operation must be abandoned if the target is not a clear one.

This was a dilemma with which the Russian revolutionaries constantly wrestled, and must also have been a consideration in Sarejevo.

Courses Open

To conclude our summary of the appreciation: the factors are combined so as to suggest several courses of action, from which the one is chosen that best matches the aim. This becomes the *course chosen*, and the actual plan follows.

The Sarajevo *attentat* was not planned as the result of any formal appreciation, and the use of bombs in a crowded setting was more-or-less bound to result in unintended casualties. Moreover, the fact that some of the bombers carried suicide pills (even though they did not work) was not intended to contribute to the success of the operation *per se*, but to help to conceal its cross-border origins. As we already know, this was an ill-planned operation.

It is easy to be wise after the event. Unlike several other attempted killings in the same city and province. this assassination was a success. Nevertheless, we might comment that the success gained was despite its plan, rather than because of it. The aim of the operation which is the subject of this chapter, we would suggest, was not to kill the Archduke Franz Ferdinand on 28 June in Sarajevo. The aim might have been stated as follows: *to kill the Archduke during his visit to Saraejvo.*

It is a subtle difference, but an important one. After all, there were means by which this aim might have been achieved, other than by a military-style ambush on a crowded street—and even this tactic might have been improved upon. When the leading Nazi Reinhard Heydrich was assassinated on the outskirts of Prague in 1942, his assassins, who had been specially trained, chose a hairpin bend on a road with no spectators. Even so, the attack nearly failed when the sten gun jammmed—an all-too-frequent occurrence—and a bomb had to be thrown instead.[7]

The Sarajevo assassins did not have the advantage of their Russian counter-parts, who were able to study the movements of their chosen target until they knoew exactly where and when to strike. Nor did they have nitro-glycerine at their disposal. Nevertheless, there were other possibilities to the plan chosen. Franz Ferdinand might have been killed in Ilidze, at the Konak, or in a number of locations in Sarajevo where he would not have been travelling in a convoy at speed and the danger of civilian casualties would have been greatly reduced.

The lone assassin

Terrorists have the advantage over soldiers, that sometimes a single assassin who is both obstinate in his determination and flexible in his approach can achieve what would not be contemplated by a group. In 1910, when the Emperor Franz Joseph visited Bosnia, he was 'stalked' by the would-be assassin Bogdan Zerajic. Zerajic chose not to kill the old man, although he had a perfect opportunity to do so in Mostar. (Two days later, he opened fire on a younger and more suitable target: the Bosnian military governor, General Marijan Varesanin. He fired six shots. The last shot, the only successful one, was the one that killed the assassin himself.)

Four years later, on 27 June 1914, Gavrilo Princip encountered Franz Ferdinand quite by chance, when the heir apparent was making a shopping trip in the city. Had he kept his weapon with him, Princip could have shot his target there and then. But there is a ritual to assassination, as to everything else, and the simple shooting of a middle-aged man examining carpets with his wife might have seemed too close to what it was: a crime.

<u>NOTES</u>

[1] When it comes to his trial, Ilic claims that he had changed his mind about the assassination by 28 June, and was not in favour of it. Not surprisingly, the court fails to accept this account of what happened, from the conspiracy's main organiser,; and he is sentenced to death.

[2] There are, as is only to be expected, different and sometimes coflicting accounts of what actually happened on 28 June 1914, ranging from minor differences to entirely different versions. We have chosen the middle path, and offered an account which ties in with major sources. According to another account, it was the Archduke himself who deflected the bomb into the street. Or he may have believed it had fallen into the car behind him, but did nothing about it, for fear it would alarm his wife. If so, he might have thought it was a missile but not a bomb; but we do not know what the Archduke really thought, for he was to die soon afterwards. We may also note that a bomb with a shorter time fuse, or which exploded on impact, would almost certainly have killed Franz Ferdinand there and then.

[3] Although we ascribe this to a conscious decision made by the young assassin, it is more likely to have been an instinctive reaction without any conscious thought at all. The law requires that we assume responsibility for our actions: but our actions themselves are quite another matter. John Gray's 'Straw Dogs' (Gray, 2002) offers a highly readable provocation on this subject.

[4] 45 minutes later, Princip statess to the investigating judge:

"When the second car arrived, I recognised the Heir Apparent. But as I saw that a lady was sititng next to him I reflected for a moment whether I should shoot or not. At the same moment I was filled with a peculiar feeling and I aimed at the Heir Apparent from the pavement—which was made easier because the car was proceeding slower at that moment. Where I aimed I do not know, but I aimed at the Heir Apparent. I

166

believe that I fired twice, perhaps more, because I was so excited. Whether I hit the victims or not I cannot tell, because instantly people started to hit me."

5 Sopherl! Sopherl! Sterbe nicht! Bleibe am Leben fur unsere Kinder!

6 Here we see the difference between an IRA operation and other more extreme contemporary or past examples. The IRA volunteer does not wish to kill himself, although he may accept that as a possible but unwelcome outcome of his action. The kamikaze pilot, on the other hand, foresees and accepts his own death as an inescapable part of the plan. Kamikaze pilots were not restricted to the imperial armed forces of Japan. Alan Clarke, in his role as a military historian, records the final action of a Fleet Air Arm pilot in firing his air-born torpedo at a German warship from point-blank range: a mission from which Lieutenant Commander Eugene Esmonde, VC (1909-1942) was not to return.

We may note, finally, that a suicide bombing, like a lesson in driving, may be under dual control. The bomber approaches the chosen target, the explosives strapped to his (or her) waist, the self-destruct button in his hand. The choice, it would seem, is entirely his. But is it? Experience has shown that even highly motivated suicide bombers sometimes lose their nerve: and the well-planned operation has an alternative means of detonation, whereby the bomb can be set off by remote control. The choice will prove illusionary. The effect is the same.

7 It is one of the ironies of history with which this study is replete that the Czech Orthodox church in Prague in which Heydrich's assassins sought refuge was in the see of Bishop Gorazd (1879-1942). This clergyman had once served Franz Ferdinand as a Roman Catholic priest before later converting to orthodoxy. Gorazd took responsibility for what happened in his church, and was executed by the Nazis. This information was supplied to the author by Franz Ferdinand's great grandson, Max Hohenberg.

CHAPTER EIGHT

Investigation and Trial

The Investigation

The investigation and trial of Gavrilo Princip, his principal associates, and a large number of other people who were caught up in the event and its consequences, was a very Austro-Hungarian affair.

Some of the accused were possibly tortured by the police, but not with the knowledge and approval of the judges; and if they were tortured, it was soon stopped.

They were held in solitary confinement; but still found a means to communicate with each other.

They were appointed defence lawyers; but those lawyers did not always work in their best interests, for they wished to express their abhorrence of the crime.

By and large, it was a procedurally fair investigation and trial, but was carried out in an atmosphere of mutual incomprehension between those in the dock and those who accused or defended them. The Sarajevo trial was conducted in the spirit of the times, and the Sarajevo assassins called themselves neither terrorists nor freedom fighters.[1] The event was, in the very useful German phrase, an *attentat*. The investigation reflected at least to some extent a confrontation of youth and age, or orthodoxy and ideology; and the attitude of the authorities towards the youths under investigation was a bemused one.

As the officials of a very long-established empire, they simply could not understand what had motivated the young men to act as they did, and their questions in part reveal this. Trifko Grabez, for example, was asked at the trial why the teachings of his father, an orthodox priest, did not encourage him to see that murder was wrong, and that he should have played no part in any conspiracy. Grabez, however, was having none of it, and did not admit that the teachings of orthodox Christianity should have dissuaded him from such a crime. Indeed, he was quite emphatic on the point, in a dialogue with Judge Alois von Curinaldi:

"'Are you an atheist or a deist?"

"I am a believer!"

"How do you reconcile your religion with the murder of a man made by God? From the religious point of view this is a sin."

"My religion does not go so far."

"Your father is a priest. What sort of education did he give you? Did he try to evoke religious feelings in you?"

"He gave me an education in the spirit of the Gospel."

"Did you follow the advice of your father?"

"As a child I listened to him, but when one comes into contact with other boys, then other influences prevail."

Establishing the facts

Franz Ferdinand and his wife had been bombed and shortly later shot at point-blank range in the centre of Sarajevo. The pistol used in the second episode had been seized at the scene, together with a bomb carried by the second assassin which he had not used. The events had been witnessed by a large number of people, including both police and army officers and outraged local citizens who would be willing to bring testimony.[2]

Both Cabrinovic, the would-be assassin who had earlier thrown his bomb, and Princip, the actual shootist, had been seized red-handed and relatively intact at the scene of the crime, for although members of the crowd had attacked them they had been rescued by the security forces.

Moreover, the fact that both young men had taken poison could have been adduced as a further indication of guilty intent, if it were needed.

They had been placed in immediate custody and had been interrogated from then on by the investigating judge, Leo Pfeffer of Sarajevo, an experienced state official who could be presumed to know his job. He certainly knew enough to let them speak without interruption in the euphoria of success and to listen to what they said.

On being first questioned both had immediately admitted what they did. A mere 45 minutes after he had opened fire, Princip stated to the investigating judge: "When the second car arrived, I recognised the Heir Apparent. But as I saw that a lady was sitting next to him I reflected for a moment whether I should shoot or not.[3] At the same moment I was filled with a peculiar feeling and I aimed at the Heir Apparent from the pavement—which was made easier because the car was proceeding slower at that moment. Where I aimed I do not know, but I aimed at the Heir Apparent. I believe that I fired twice, perhaps more, because I was so excited. Whether I hit the victims or not, I cannot tell, because instantly people started to hit me."

This was a spontaneous confession which he would have found it very difficult to retract. Cabrinovic went so far as to boast of his deed and to call himself a Serbian hero. The two young assassins were unlikely to later deny their involvement in the *attentat*, and had they done so, their participation would have been easy to establish. Their trial for murder and probably treason should therefore constitute, if not a mere formality, a relatively straightforward affair.

In fact, however, the Austrian authorities faced a wider series of questions, which might be summarised as follows.

- Were the two assassins in custody operating separately or together?
- Who else was involved in the assassination?
- Where did they obtain the weapons?
- What lay behind the event? What were the motives of the assassins? Was it a political conspiracy, and if so, what did it hope to achieve?
- Was there an outside involvement, and if so, did it lead to Serbia?
- If it did, what should be done?

The combination of legal and political questions to be answered made the investigation of the *attentat* a challenging one. Moreover, by the time that the trial had begun, Austria-Hungary was at war.

As soon as he had fired his two shots, Gavrilo Princip attempted to turn his pistol on himself, as he had planned: for a dead assassin offered fewer leads to the police. There was a frenzied struggle, which under any other circumstances might have seemed almost comic in its intensity: one young man, waving a pistol, was being attacked by the crowd whilst a young Moslem detective sought vainly to arrest him. Smail Spahovic had been ordered to watch the cars rather than the crowd. He had heard the shots fired, and had only realised what was happening when it was too late to prevent it.

Two of the outraged officers who had been accompanying Franz Ferdinand had meanwhile pitched into the fray and were vigorously attacking the young assassin with the flats of their sabres. They were not immune from attack themselves: in the melee, Baron Morsey was struck several times on the back of his helmet with an iron bar.[4] By now Princip had dropped his bomb and lost control of his pistol, but still managed to swallow his cyanide. Just as with Cabrinovic, it caused acute discomfort but failed to kill him. And he was taken into custody, beaten, bloody and exhausted.

We know this for we have the report of the examining magistrate who first interrogated him, and who was to conduct the state investigation into this most sensational and embarrassing of murders from now on. That report is extracted from the memoirs of the judge in question and was clearly written with an eye for posterity. Princip had become a celebrity.

'The young assassin, exhausted by his beating, was unable to utter a word. He was undersized, emaciated, sharp-featured, sallow. It was difficult to imagine that so frail-looking an individual should have committed so serious a deed. Even his clear blue eyes, burning and piercing but serene, had nothing cruel or criminal in their expression. They spoke of innate intelligence, of steady and harmonious energy. When I told him I was the investigating judge and asked if he had the strength to speak he answered my questions with a perfect clearness in a voice that grew steadily stronger and more assured.'

(Judge Pfeffer, describing Gavrilo Princip; Dedijer, page 325.)

Judge Pfeffer may not have been the most brilliant of investigators, but he was painstaking and thorough. Moreover, he was faced with two young men who were not concerned to deny their guilt, but simply to avoid revealing further information. Within a day or so, he was able to establish that they knew each other, but there the matter might have rested: for the Austrian authorities had at first no idea of the size of the conspiracy.

However, standard police procedure was followed, and standard police procedure led to the arrest of Danilo Ilic as a known associate of Gavrilo Princip and therefore a possible suspect. Ilic was brought into the police station, a very badly scared young man. He should have kept his mouth shut. He did not do so. According to Remak's account, as soon as he met the judge he asked for a deal. He would confess everything, he said, if Pfeffer would undertake to save him from the death penalty—a promise which if it were made, was not to be fulfilled.

Pfeffer showed an interest, and it was enough. Ilic cracked completely. There were seven members in the conspiracy, he said, and he named them. Action followed immediately. Trifko Grabez was found near his home in Pale, on his way to Serbia, and immediately arrested. His bomb and pistol were then discovered, where he had hidden them in Sarajevo. The conspiracy was unravelling. Where would it lead?

Cubrilovic and Popovic, who had played no active part in the assassination, and had disappeared as soon as possible afterwards, were as amateurish in covering their tracks as they had been in their part on the Appel Quay—although it was Ilic's confession that put the police in their direction, rather than their own actions. They were soon arrested, and the only member of the assassination team to avoid arrest was Muhamed Mehmedbasic, who had conveniently fled to the neighbouring state of Montenegro. There, he should have been arrested and handed over to the Austrian authorities. But the Montenegrins were Serbs, and sympathetic to the assassination in Sarajevo. Mehmedbasic was able to escape from police custody, and was never re-captured and extradited. Eventually, he crossed to Serbia and enlisted in the partisans under Major Tankosic.[5]

As if he had already not done enough harm, Danilo Ilic revealed further details of the conspiracy to Judge Pfeffer, with the result that the people who had assisted Princip and Grabez to travel from the Serbian border to the Bosnian town of Tuzla were rounded up, arrested, and charged with a variety of offences, some of which carried the death penalty. They included

Misko Jovanovic, Veljko Cubrilovic, and a number of others whose eventual sentences we shall review.

By this time Princip and Grabez, who were held in separate custody but were able to communicate by tapping on the walls, had begun to change their story. They admitted to the names of those who had helped them on the 'underground railway', who were already being arrested: but claimed that any help offered had been given either under duress, or in ignorance of the real intentions of the assassins—which was to provoke much argument at the trial.

The role of Belgrade

By and large, the assassins were able to conceal the role of Serbian military intelligence in the *attentat*, and certainly any contribution to it from Colonel Apis and the Black Hand. In this they were helped by the Austrian authorities, who should have known all about the Black Hand— there were files about it in the headquarters of the Austrian secret service, in Vienna—but made no reference to its existence. Instead, the Austrians were obsessed by the role of Narodna Odbrana, so that Colonel Apis's deception plan was to that extent successful.

The prisoners gave away little pieces of information as the investigation proceeded, and it was not long before Milan Ciganovic was mentioned. This was not of strategic importance, since an obscure employee of Serbian State Railways was unlikely to become the subject for a major diplomatic row that could lead to war. However, worse was soon to come. Danilo Ilic, the compulsive confessor, went on to give away the name of Major Tankosic, whom he obligingly identified as having played a significant role in helping the assassins in Belgrade. That should have given the Austrians what they needed, for Tankosic was in the employment of the Serbian State as an army officer. There was a conspiracy; and it did lead to Serbia. We shall examine the political repercussions of the investigation of the Sarajevo *attentat*, and how it led to a war which almost no-one wanted, in Chapter Nine.

Could murder be justified? Admissions at the trial

The trial began on Monday, 12 October 1914 and lasted until Friday, 23 October. It took place in the barracks in Sarajevo which the Archduke had inspected before his final railway journey. A total of 25 men were charged with various offences, inlcuding murder and treason. Although Princip and Cabrinovic were the star performers, as it were, they did not face the death penalty. Of the seven young men who had been on the Quay, only Mohamed Mehmedbasic and Danilo Ilic were over twenty and therefore qualified for the death sentence.

The accused were seated in rows under armed guard, and the official photograph reveals that the leading offenders assumed much the same attitude. They sat there with arms crossed, looking mildly interested but at the same time mildly defiant, as if it were not they who were on trial, but the judges themselves. They were glad to be together, for they had been held in solitary confinement since arrest. Perhaps they welcomed the opportunity to put their side of the story, and shock officialdom with their radicalism: some were atheists as well as assassins. They were extremely young; they were defiant; and they were vulnerable.

The men who had assisted in the conspiracy, according to the authorities, tended to take a different stance. Their best hope was to plead ignorance as to what had really been going on, or to claim that they had been coerced; and to be as vague as possible. Not for them, the heroic stand in the court-room. Unlike the young assassins, they had wives, children and property to protect; and it is impossible to read their testimony without sympathy.

There were others who might have been placed on trial, and were not: for the Austrian judicial investigation failed to uncover all the facts. Mihailjo Pusara, for example, was a possible conspirator who according to Dedijer and others assisted in the *attentat* by distracting a policeman at the vital moment by kicking him on the knee, and after the event tried to prevent the police from arresting Princip. This behaviour may have been the spontaneous reaction of a by-stander. Or it may have indicated an informed and premeditated commitment, for Pusara was a member of Young Bosnia and may have been an ancillary conspirator. According to Dedijer, Princip was determined that Pusara should not be implicated in the plot, and he went out of his way to avert the authorities's suspicions, as his testimony to Judge Pfeffer indicates—a testimony which was successful in its deceptive intent.

"After Cabrinovic was caught, I went to the corner of the Appel Quay and Franz Josef Street, just at Schiller's shop, when Mihajlo Pusara came to me, saying: "Look what has happened!" I replied: "I have seen it. What nonsense to commit such a thing at this time!" He then said that this had not been a good thing to do, and he invited me to go to the Sloga society, because there was a celebration. I was very much afraid of Mihajlo Pusara, because he was often in our company. I thought he was a spy, because he used to dine at his relative Simon Pusara's, who is an innkeeper and a detective, and therefore I thought that when Pusara took me by the arm he wanted to take me to somewhere and search me. Therefore, I did not let myself be taken by the arm and when a moment later "Long Live" was heard, I succeeded in getting through the crowd to the corner of Schiller's shop."

In accordance with Bosnian law there was no jury: a panel of judges were to decide on the guilt or innocence of the accused, and the appropriate penalties for those found guilty.

In addition to the three judges, a number of defence lawyers were also present.

The status of the trial was somewhat odd. It was not held in secret, but neither was it open to the public at large. The press was minimally represented, and there were no special correspondants in court. Finally, although a record of the proceedings was kept, it was not published until long afterwards, and there are several variations (and translations) of what should have been one transcript. Nevertheless, what occurred seems reasonably clear.

The three leading conspirators, Cabrinovic, Princip and Grabez, did not deny that they had intended to kill Franz Ferdinand, although only one of them had been successful in doing so. However, they did not therefore believe themselves to be guilty, and indeed Princip disputed this status, claiming that he did not feel guilty, as he had acted to rid the world of an evil person—although he admitted that he had not intended to kill the duchess.

We may note that here as elsewhere, Danilo Ilic was the odd man out. He admitted that he had been present on the quay, that he knew the conspirators, that he had armed them with their weapons, and that he had assigned them to their places. But he also claimed that he was by then opposed to the assassination, and had done his best to try and stop it. The reaction of the court to this claim for mitigation, if claim it were, may best be judged by the death sentence passed against Danilo Ilic, the reluctant assassin.

The admissions of the accused rested on a distinction between legal and moral guilt.

Legal guilt

In general terms, a person is guilty of a crime if it can be shown that he chose to carry out an act that is classified as a crime and that he was aware of that fact. It is assumed that the normal person has free will, and must accept responsibility for what he has chosen to do. A more penetrating analysis is to separate what happened into two parts: *actus reus* and *mens rea*, or the guilty act and the guilty mind.

Suppose a person (like Franz Ferdinand) is out shooting game-birds, and he shoots at a pheasant in flight and hits his fellow shooter instead (and that person dies as a result). The shooter may be guilty of carelessness, or even recklessness; and he may be charged with manslaughter. But he cannot be convicted of murder, for there was no guilty intent. He did not intend to shoot at his companion; and he certainly did not intend to kill him or cause him serious harm. In terms of Roman law, *actus reus* has been established, but not *mens rea*.

The aim of a criminal trial under common law is to establish whether or not both *actus reus* and *mens rea* can be proved to have existed, beyond reasonable doubt, in regard to a specified offence. It is the jury that decides on the facts and not the judge, who is there to ensure a fair trial and to make sure that the jury is properly briefed as to its duties.

Passing over, for the moment, the fact that this trial did not take place under common law traditions but within the legal framework of the Austro-Hungarian empire, where there was not the same emphasis on a jury and the legal tradition was nore investigative than adversarial, let us apply some general principles to the administration of justice in this case.

In so doing, we shall review both the defences of the seven young men who were identified as having been present on the Appel Quay on 28 June, and also the defences open to the large number of 'associates' who were also on trial as a result of extensive police enquiries. The same principles might be applied to the defence (or prosecution) of anyone who was on trial for any offence connected with the murder.

Under the law, a person who is an accessory to a murder is as guilty as the man or woman who actually pulls the trigger. Ignorance of the law is not an excuse. An ignorance of the facts which is shown to be reasonable, however, may be accepted. (If I am passed a murder weapon and know it to be a murder weapon, I should immediately report it to the police. However, I may not know what has been given to me, nor have any reason to suspect what it is.)

Some associates were charged with in some way having contributed to the success of the murder <u>beforehand</u>, in assisting the three main conspirators to travel from Belgrade to Sarajevo with their pistols and bombs. Other persons were charged with offences <u>after</u> the murders, for example by taking charge of the weapons as the young conspirators left both the scene of the crime and the city of Sarajevo. In both cases, the penalties they faced were severe, and included the death penalty. The defences available to them were limited, but the court showed some discretion in its judgements, both as to guilt and penalty.[6]

The defence

According to Professor H L A Hart of Oxford University (Hart, 1968), 'in the criminal law of every modern state responsibility for serious crimes is excluded or 'diminished' by some of the conditions we have referred to as 'excusing conditions.' ... These matters come up under the heads known to lawyers as Mistake, Accident, Provocation, Duress and Insanity, and are most clearly and dramatically exemplified when the charge is one of murder or manslaughter.

'Though this general doctrine underlies the criminal law, no legal system in practice admits without qualification the principle that *all* criminal responsibility is excluded by *any* of the excusing conditions.' (Hart, 1968, page 31.)

Professor Hart's analysis, although paying especial attention to Anglo-American law, may be applied more generally; and it is clear from both the process and results of the Sarajevo trial that it may be considered an example of a modern legal system, in which some attention was paid to the mental state of the accused and their degree of responsibility for the crime.

The legal possibilities for the defence included the following options and possibly others:

- That the accused had been mistakenly arrested and had nothing to do with the crime, which must have been carried out by others (there was no *actus reus* by those who were accused);
- That they had carried out the act, but had been coerced into doing so (they therefore lacked *mens rea*);
- That they were able to claim diminished responsibility (and therefore a reduced *mens rea*);[7]
- That the trial was in some significant way improperly conducted, for example because inadmissible evidence was accepted, and that therefore any conviction arising from it was unsafe;[8] or
- That the court had no jurisdiction to try the offence.

The last point was seized upon by the actively-minded defence lawyer Rudolf Zistler, who argued that Bosnia had not been fully incorporated into the dual monarchy and that therefore the assassins could not be charged with treason (although this did not exclude, presumably, the possibility of the charge of common murder.) However, the President of the Court, Judge Alois von Curinaldi, summarily rejected this argument and ordered the lawyer in question to pursue it no further.

In regard to the other possible legal defences, some of them appeared more applicable to the associates who were on trial for a secondary role in the conspiracy. They could claim, at least in some cases, that they had been coerced or tricked into doing what they had done, or that they had simply acted in ignorance—although none of these claims, even if true, was likely to be a cast-iron defence against a charge of being an accessory to murder.

However, the seven leading offenders faced a greater challenge. They had not been arrested in error. They had carried out the act, or had intended to do so, and had been not been coerced in their intentions. They were not mentally disabled or in some other way incapacitated. They freely admitted that they had intended to kill, or had killed, the Archduke and his wife (which was regretted as a casualty of war); but did not regard this as a criminal act.

Nedjelko Cabrinovic, the most emotional and outspoken of the accused, said that they (the court) could call them what they liked, but they were not criminals. He was especially sorry to learn that the archducal couple had young children, of which he had not been aware, and which might have stayed his hand. His argument was stronger for its rhetoric than its reason, although his sincerity impressed the court. His words at the end of the trial were as follows:

'I would like to add something else. Although Princip is playing the hero, and although we all wanted to appear as heroes, we still have profound regrets. In the first place, we did not know that the late Franz Ferdinand was a father. We were greatly touched by the words he addressed to his wife: "Sophie, stay alive for our children." We are anything you want, except criminals. In my name and the name of my comrades, I ask the children of the late successor to the throne to forgive us. As for you, punish us according to your understanding. We are not criminals. We are honest people, animated by noble sentiments; we are idealists; we wanted to do good; we have loved our people; and we shall die for our ideals.'

To argue that a person has carried out an assassination or is legally guilty of that crime as an accessory to it, but that he is not in fact a criminal, allows for only two valid foundations.

History will absolve me

Firstly, it might be argued that the legal system on which the prosecution is based is itself unlawful, and that the supposed criminal has a right to be tried by a greater judge than the president of the court. This defence was eloquently summarised by the young Fidel Castro (born 1926), on trial for attempting an uprising against the Cuban dicator Fulgencio Batista in 1953, under the phrase 'la historia me absuelta.'

We may see this as a political argument rather than a legal defence. The person putting it forward must hope to live long enough for history to have the opportunity to absolve him whilst he is still able to take advantage of that opportunity. (Unless he is executed first, and is forced to accept the melancholy solace of martyrdom. In Castro's case, he was released under amnesty and later overthrew Batista as a result of a guerrilla campaign.)

Secondly, there is the argument that assassination may be justified on moral grounds, if there is no other means to rid society of a tyrant. In this case, the Austrian heir apparent was not a tyrant, whatever else he may have been; for at the time of his assassination his only official appointment was of inspector general of the imperial army, and he had had no opportunity to tyrannise.

Princip and company might and did argue that the Austrian regime in Bosnia was oppressive, and that the population of the rural areas were suffering; but they did not tend to argue that the administration was tyrannical. If they had, those Bosnians with longer memories could have put the counter-argument that the Bosnians were better off under the Austrians than under their predecessors, the Turks, who had been capable of systematic oppression and brutality, both as an occupying power and through their local agents. If the Bosnians were better off than under the Turks, the prosecution might have argued, how could the Austro-Hungarian empire be described as a tyranny?

It might also be argued that the plight of the rural Bosnians in 1914 did not relate to specific Austrian policies, but to the overall economic climate in the Balkans at the time. Criminal trials, however, do not usually concern themselves with socio-economic conditions, but with the individual responsibility of the accused.

Not surprsingly, Princip's argument that the oppressive Archduke Franz Ferdinand deserved his assassination was not accepted, and he was convicted of the offence.

Remorse and forgiveness

Part of the result of a criminal process is that the person convicted of a crime should be brought to feel remorse for what he has done and an urge to make amends. Where a political trial for murder is concerned, remorse is less likely, for the killer feels justified in what he has done, and may compare his actions to those of a soldier in war.   However, remorse, or something very close to it, was expressed by the two leading assassins. From Cabrinovic, it was to be expected. From Princip, it was a glimpse into an aspect of his personality that was normally hidden.

On the last day of the trial, when the presiding judge asked if there were any final statements to be offered, Cabrinovic expressed his regrets for what had occurred and with tears in his eyes begged the children of Franz Ferdinand and Sophie to forgive him. In Dedijer's account, his words were as follows.

"I would like to add something else. Although Princip is playing the hero, and although we all wanted to appear as heroes, we still have profound regrets. In the first place, we did not know that the late Franz Ferdinand was a father. We were greatly touched by the words he addressed to his wife: "Sophie, stay alive for our children." We are anything you want, except criminals. In my name and the name of my comrades, I ask the children of the late successor to the throne to forgive us. As for you, punish us according to your understanding. We are not criminals. We are honest people, animated by noble sentiments; we are idealists; we wanted to do good; we have loved our people; and we shall die for our ideals."

'After this, as one of the lawyers recorded, Cabrinovic sat on the bench with his head bowed, barely controlling his feelings, while "Princip's giant nature, his enormous vitality, would not let him accept Cabrinovic's words unchallenged.... Princip jumped up and said briefly that Cabrinovic had not been authorised to speak in his name."

'The proceedings were interrupted for five minutes; one of the lawyers came up to Princip and asked him what he thought about Franz Ferdinand's words. Princip answered: "What do you think I am, an animal?"'

When it came to making a formal statement, however, the mask was back in place. Princip followed Cabrinovic and spoke quietly and to the point, in order to protect the Black Hand to the end.

"In trying to insinuate that someone else has instigated the assassination, one strays from the truth. The idea arose in our own minds, and we ourselves executed it. We have loved the people. I have nothing to say in my defence."

The contrast between the two men could not have been greater.

Convictions were as follows:

Treason and murder

Gavrilo Princip	20 years
Nedjelko Cabrinovic	20 years
Trifko Grabez	20 years
Vaso Cubrilovic	16 years
Cvetko Popovic	13 years

Popovic and Cubrilovic were judged to have played a lesser role on the day and received lighter sentences.

Treason and accessories to murder

Danilo Ilic	Death by hanging
Veljko Cubrilovic	Death by hanging
Misko Jovanovic	Death by hanging
Nedjo Kerovic	Death by hanging
Lazar Djukic	Ten years

Treason but not murder

Mitar Kerovic	Death by hanging
Jakov Milovic	Life imprisonment

A further four associates were convicted of being accessories either to treason or murder by virtue of having failed to inform the authorities of the plot.

Nine of the defendants were acquitted on all charges.

Under Austrian law, no-one under twenty could face the death penalty. Most of the conspirators were either clearly above or below that age, and the only dispute that arose was in regard to the age of Gavrilo Princip—an issue that would decide his life or death.

How old was Gavrilo Princip? This issue has already been addressed in Chapter Four, and although the evidence was not wholly conclusive—the mother's evidence was hardly objective, and the parish priest may or may not have kept accurate records—the court gave him the benefit of the doubt when sentence was passed. He was stated to be 19 years and 11 months old at the time of the murder. He could live.

The sentences were reviewed by a higher court and confirmed by the emperor, and the sentences against Nedjo and Mitar Kerovic were changed from death by hanging to imprisonment.

On 3 February 1915 Veljko Cubrilovic, Misko Jovanovic and Danilo Ilic were duly hanged. Their executioner claimed to be a master of his trade, and no difficulty arose.[9] The remaining prisoners, meanwhile, had been desptached to various jails.

The trial was over and sentence had been carried out. Further trials were to take place in war-torn Bosnia, as the Austrian authorities strove in increasing desperation to address insurrection, real or supposed, in the province; and some of the Bosnian Serbs who had found themselves on trial in 1914 where to find themselves again in the dock, two years later.

Conclusion

The investigation of the murders of Franz Ferdinand and his wife, and the subsequent trial of those accused, was a comparatively civilised affair, in which the rule of law was respected—by and large. The accused were given not only the opportunity to claim their innocence, if they wished to do so, but also to expound their political views; and they spent at least part of their time arguing with each other as much as with the court.

Their convictions were justified under law, and the sentences imposed were not overly harsh by the standards of the time, whether in the Austro-Hungarian empire or elsewhere. Indeed, had the three young assassins Princip, Grabez and Cabrinovic been convicted of the same offences under English law they would almost certainly have been hanged forthwith. As all three were over 18, they would have been considered adults with full criminal responsibility; and treason was the most serious crime on the list of possible criminal offences.

We might also consider it nothing less than remarkable that the court gave Princip the benefit of the doubt in regard to his age, considering the seriousness of his crime.

However, if the Austrian legal system did not deprive three of the main conspirators of their lives, then the Austrian prison system was easily capable of achieving that result, by neglect as much as by intent—as we shall see.

NOTES

[1] That debate had not yet begun: at least, not in those terms. Had the crime occurred in the United Kingdom to-day, its perpetrators and their associates might have been charged with a variety of terrorist offences which were not available to Austria-Hungary in 1914, including the offences which came into law in 2006 as a result of Islamist suicide bombings and which deal with the promotion of terrorism..

[2] Those outraged citizens included the majority of Bosnian Serbs, who had every reason to condemn the murder and to testify, if needed, against those who were behind it. Firstly, they did not approve of murder; and secondly, the event rendered

them liable both to the reprisals of the mob, as in fact occurred, and the lingering suspicion of the authorities.

3 Princip had also considered using his bomb, but decided that the location was too crowded and it would have been awkward to extract and strike.

4 This may have been wielded by Mihailjo Pusara, a member of Young Bosnia who was present at the scene.

5 Mehmedbasic survived the sufferings of the Great War, as he survived everything else, and was to die a peaceful and obscure death in the Second World War. However, he was put on trial in Salonika in 1917, although this time for a crime which he did not commit. See Chapter Six.

6 Courts may refer to either mitigating or extenuating circumstances, or both. If I steal medicine to treat my sick child, I am, notwithstanding my intentions, guilty of the crime of theft. However, the court is more likely to be sympathetic to me than if I had stolen the medicine and sold it on the black market: and my penalty may be adjusted accordingly.

7 Diminished responsibility was first introduced in England by statute in 1957. It has resulted in some murder charges being reduced to manslaughter.

8 This might be grounds for an appeal rather than a defence put forward at the trial itself. What a fair trial requires is clearly laid out in the European Convention of Human Rights (1951). Although this convention did not exist in 1914, the principles upon which it is based have long been enshrined in common law.

9 The bodies were buried in an unmarked grave, so that the site should not become an inspiration to future enemies of the state. After 1918, they were disinterred and re-buried in Sarajevo.

CHAPTER NINE

World War One: Causes, course and consequences

The causes of the First World War

The underlying causes of the First World War may be ascribed to imperial rivalry between the great powers; the absence of an effective diplomatic means to resolve potential conflict; and the arms race between the United Kingdom and Germany, especially over battleships. For while competitive naval construction does not necessarily lead to war, and is in fact intended to prevent it, the opposite may occur.

However, the immediate cause of the war was the assassination in Sarajevo, which triggered off the declaration of war by Austria-Hungary on Serbia; the consequent mobilisation of troops by the great powers, as a series of defensive alliances swung into place in semi-automatic response; and the bloodshed that almost inevitably followed as the soldiers confronted each other at the point of contact and the general staffs considered the dangers of <u>not</u> acting and decided that there was no alternative to action if the advantage were not to be lost.

Austria-Hungary used the assassination of the heir apparent and his wife as a pretext to declare war on Serbia, an action that they had long intended. Their aim of conquering Serbia was based on three main suppositions:

i   That Serbia posed a strategic threat to Austrian interests in the Balkans, which must be addressed by force;

ii That Serbia was a minor military power with a backward political directorate and a weak or non-existent industrial base, which could easily be conquered without undue effort; and

iii That this conflict could easily be restricted in its wider consequences, and would not lead to general war (and) the collapse of the Austro-Hungarian Empire.

The last assumption, as we know, was disastrously wrong. The middle assumption was also wrong. The first assumption was arguably true, but should not have been addressed in July 1914, when the other great powers were likely to intervene. Furthermore, Austria dallied too long and failed to respond spontaneously to the outrage. The declaration of war against another country a month after the provocation has taken place is not quite the same as a reaction in the heat of the moment, and attracts less sympathy.

It is arguable that the Austrians did not so much weigh up the risk of adverse consequences to their declaration, as act recklessly. In 1914, Franz Joseph was 84 years old; and whilst old men do not necessarily act recklessly, they may simply be tired, and let events take their course which they might otherwise have prevented by stopping younger men from being foolish. The war party in Vienna won. Ironically, the Archduke himself had not belonged to the war party: and had the heir to the imperial throne left Sarajevo as soon as Cabrinovic had thrown his bomb, and returned scared but unharmed to Vienna, he would have worked to prevent war.

There was a contradiction lying at the heart of the dual monarchy's engineering of a war with Serbia. In order to justify a declaration of war before international opinion (and especially to gain the support of the other Great Powers), the Austrians had to show sufficient cause. The murder of the heir apparent and his wife was a good start, but on its own it was not enough. The men who killed Franz Ferdinand might have been simply mad, as were many such killers, including the Italian Luigi Lucheni who stabbed to death the Empress Elizabeth of Austria in 1898, sixteen years before. Or the assassins might have been acting entirely on their own initiative, without any direction or influence from a foreign power such as Serbia; and thus no foreign power such as Serbia could legitimately be blamed for their actions.

Vienna needed to show that Serbia was behind the assassinations and that a declaration of war was therefore justified. She set out to do so by several means. Firstly, diplomatic pressure was brought to bear, to ensure that Austria's policy was understood. Secondly, the interrogations of the captured prisoners were closely monitored for signs of Serbian involvement in the plot. And thirdly, a senior Austrian official, Friedrich von Wiesner (1871-1951), was sent from Vienna to Sarajevo, specifically to find evidence of a conspiracy linking the Serbian government to the assassination.

Von Wiesner's mission

Von Wiesner should have been able to find evidence, or at least to present a convincing argument, that the Sarajevo conspirators were funded, trained, equipped and transported with the help of a semi-official Serbian secret society, Unification or Death – popularly known as the Black Hand – which had decided to mount the assassination of the heir apparent to another state. This Black Hand, despite its melodramatic name, did not belong in the music-hall; it was a serious and deadly organisation which contained within its ranks some of the most senior people in the Serbian apparatus of government, including its chief of military intelligence, Colonel Apis – the man who was generally believed to be the puppet master who pulled the strings at the ministry of war.

The government in Vienna knew of the existence of the Black Hand at this time, as its files were able to show to the relevant investigators after the war. If Vienna had been able to prove that the Black Hand was guilty of an active part in this conspiracy, it seems hard to believe that the First World War would have followed; for an Austrian assault on Serbia would have been justified.

Von Wiesner, the official sent from Vienna to Sarajevo on 10 July 1914 was intelligent, motivated and hard-working. He spent spent two days in Sarajevo, going through the files and talking to the relevant officials (although he did not interview the prisoners in custody). After completing his research and coming to his conclusion, von Wiesner wrote his report and telegraphed it to Vienna.

Contrary to the war party's wishes, his report said that:

'There is nothing to show the complicity of the Serbian government in the direction of the assassination or in its preparations or in the supplying of weapons. Nor is there anything to lead one to even conjecture such a thing. On the contrary, there is evidence that would appear to show such complicity is out of the question... '

It was a conclusion that the writer was destined to regret for the rest of his life, during which he repeatedly tried to deny, re-interpret or discount what he had said. Moreover, his report was contradictory, for having found against Serbian involvement, he recommended criminal proceedings against Ciganovic and Tankosic, Serbian officials who had both been named by the prisoners under interrogation. Nevertheless, his report was made: and it did not justify war.

Vienna was now in a difficult position. Von Wiesner had succeeded in the almost impossible task of <u>not</u> finding evidence, or at least something close to it, against the Serbs, and of <u>not</u> identifying the Black Hand, a known terrorist organisation, as having been involved in the conspiracy.

Narodna Odbrana and the Black Hand

Instead of fastening upon Unification or Death for all it was worth, both at this stage of their investigation and in the trial of the leading conspirators and their associates that followed, the Austrians became obsessed by asserting that Narodna Odbrana was behind the conspiracy. This was to play into Colonel Apis's bloody hands, for Narodna Odbrana was what would later be called a 'front organisation': the respectable face of Serbian nationalism, formed in a spontaneous outburst of popular opinion against the dual monarchy's formal annexation of Bosnia-Herzegovina in 1908. Narodna Odbrana may or may not have approved of the assassination. It did not instigate it. Colonel Apis, concerned as always to muddy the waters, made sure that at least some of his agents, such as the customs officials who helped the young assassins to cross the border between Serbia and Bosnia by impromptu means, were openly members of Narodna Odbrana as well as secretly members of the Black Hand.[1]

Narodna Odbrana was frequently mentioned in the trial of the conspirators that took place in October 1914, but the Black Hand did not receive a mention. Remak (1966) describes this as the final triumph of Apis's planning. It is certainly a reflection of Gavrilo Princip's determination, and his command over his fellow-prisoners: for it was he who was able to prevent his fellow accused, Nedjelko Cabrinovic, from unwittingly betraying the entire plot, and indicating an official Serbian involvement in the attentat.

It was mid-July in the long, hot European summer of 1914. Time had gone by, and the dual monarchy had still not attacked Serbia. Now, it had failed to assemble the crucial information it needed to justify an attack. It was time to force the Serbian hand, black or otherwise. The dual monarchy presented a list of demands to the Serbian government, which consisted of ten points. The sixth demand was that the Serbs were:

6. To open a judicial inquiry against those implicated in the murder, and to allow delegates of Austria-Hungary to take part in this.

The Serbian reaction, under its canny and cautious Prime Minister Niclola Pasic, was first of all to play for time. When the demands were presented, it was the week-end. His cabinet was not available. The demands had implications. He needed more time to consider them. However, this ploy was bound to fail, for the Austrians had issued an ultimatum, rather than a basis for negotiations at which Pasic, with a lifetime of political experience behind him. would have proved adept. They demanded a reply by a certain point, whether or not he were able to consult his colleagues. In the end the Serbian government capitulated to the great power, for they did not want to go to war, and least of all for an action for which they were not officially responsible. The offical Serbian reaction was not to reject all ten demands all out of hand, but to accept all save the sixth demand, which they declared to be constitutionally impossible.

Their partial rejection of Austria's demands was enough. War was justified, and was declared precisely one month after the assassinations. The war which was at first known as the Third Balkan War, and then the Great War, and then the World War, and finally the First World War (1914-1918), which was to lead to millions of deaths, to destroy four empires, and to change the map of the world for ever, had begun.

Greater involvement

A war between Austria-Hungary and Serbia might have remained simply a local affair, in which Austria mounted a swift and crushing military victory, and the Serbs sued for peace almost before the other powers knew what was going on. Why did the war spread to becoming a major European confrontation? In the first place, the Austrians did not achieve a swift and crushing victory. But in any case, this was a general war waiting to happen.

Military planning

   In essence, we see no reason to disagree with AJP Taylor's aphorism, that the Great War began at least in part as a matter of railway timetables. This was the age of rigid military planning, and the various general staffs, then as now, had made contingency plans for war. Those plans could not be partially activated; they had to be activated in full, for example in regard to mobilisation. Moreover, they relied upon the logic of what came to be called the pre-emptive strike, whereby A must attack B if A thinks that B is likely to attack him, <u>before</u> the event has actually happened; since unless A takes the initiative he will be unable to mount an effective counter-attack, if or when B's anticipated attack does take place. (The problem with this sort of logic is that it actually brings about a result which was in the real interest of neither A nor B. Its culmination was the Mutually Assured Destruction which was intended to deter the cold war from becoming a hot one, and which is best summarised by the word formed from its initials.)

Rival alliances

   Secondly, we must recognise that Europe in 1914 was already divided into rival alliances, so that once any conflict began, it was likely to spread: the sequence of events thus becoming a seemingly inevitable involvement of the great powers in war. The great powers were united in two alliances, consisting of the United Kingdom, France and Russia (the Entente Powers, to which we should add smaller powers such as Serbia and Belgium, to be joined by Italy in 1915) against Austria-Hungary and Germany (the Central Powers, to whom Turkey and Bulgaria also became allied.)   Although it could be argued that these were defensive alliances (like NATO to-day), defensive alliances may also become offensive under the right conditions.

Diplomacy and its drawbacks

   Thirdly, there was no established, permanent institution for preventing war, such as the Security Council of the United Nations (founded in 1945, after another world war) or even the League of Nations, its much less powerful predecessor, founded as a result of the enthusiasm of President

Woodrow Wilson of the United States at the Treaty of Versailles in 1919.

War as Mystery

Finally, we must agree in principle with the conclusion reached by the military historian John Keegan (Keegan, 1998) that the First World War remains a mystery. Its consequences were catastrophic for all concerned. Even if the war aims of its constituent parties could have been clearly identified in 1914, none of them was achieved. It destroyed four empires which had provided an element of stability in a warlike continent. Some observers forecast its dreadful consequences in advance; but that did not prevent it. And it led to another war. Why did it really happen? The outbreak, duration and scale of destruction of the First World War remain a mystery.

The Benefit of Hindsight

None of the belligerent parties, had they known what was to happen, would have gone happily to war in an outburst of patriotic enthusiasm, such as was to be seen in Great Britain in August 1914. They could not have known, we might say. There had not been a major war in Europe since the Napoleonic wars. The new weaponry had not yet been tested. War was still a limited affair: a conflict between professional armies, with no national involvement. And yet, it could be argued they should have known. The American civil war had shown the suffering to be expected on the modern battlefield. The Russo-Japanese war of 1905 had been a warning of the slaughter ahead. So had the first and second Balkan wars. Astute military commentators, whether or not they were part of the military establishment, had already anticipated the bloody stalemate of trench warfare. This war was never going to be over by Christmas. How, then, did they all become involved?

Greater Involvement

Austria-Hungary declared war on Serbia on 28 July 1914, one month after the assassination of Franz Ferdinand for which Serbia was held responsible. In reality, Austria had long desired to crush Serbia, and saw this as its last chance to do so, to strengthen its position in the Balkans, and to remain a Great Power. Moreover, the Austrian Emperor had the so-called German blank cheque in his pocket; for Kaiser Wilhelm had promised his unconditional support for the dual monarchy's reaction to the murder of the Archduke (and this, despite the fact that his own ambassador in Belgrade did not believe that the Serbian government had planned the assassination, which was not in their interest.)

Russia, which did not wish to see the dual monarchy become more powerful in the Balkans, came to Serbia's defence and declared war on Austria-Hungary.

In order to implement its plans to make war on Austria-Hungary, it had also to mobilise its troops for war with Germany; and, in effect, to declare war on Germany.

Germany followed suit and declared war on Russia. In order to implement its plans to declare war on Russia, Germany had to order general mobilisation: which meant making ready for war with France. Because of the Schlieffen Plan, in order to attack France, Germany had to attack Belgium.

The United Kingdom was committed to the defence of Belgium by mutual defensive alliance. Once Belgium's neutrality was violated, The UK had to come to its defence. In any case, the UK was already generally committed to war, in its obligations to France and Russia under the extended entente cordiale.

Turkey entered the war to protect her own interests by supporting the central powers.

Italy was still neutral in August 1914. She might have been expected to fulfill her obligations under the Triple Alliance of 1882, and to fight with the Central Powers: but in fact she had designs on Austrian territory, and joined the Entente in 1915. The war between Italy and the dual monarchy became a major commitment for both sides, and the decisive victory for the Italians of Victoria Vennetto in 1918 was to prove the last straw that broke the back of imperial Austria.

The United States remained resolutely neutral until 1917, when it entered the war on the side of the Entente Powers. Its apparently limitless resources were to prove crucial to the outcome of the war, in convincing the German High Command that it could not continue the struggle indefinitely on the Western Front.

Other countries became involved for a mixture of reasons. Troops from the British Empire, for example, supported the motherland more or less as a matter of course, although there was some opposition; and they included huge numbers of Indians as well as white settlers from the old commonwealth of Canada, Australia, New Zealand and South Africa, who might be expected to respond to the need to support kith and kin.

Ireland proved a special case. It was still part of the United Kingdom, to which home rule had been promised. Ireland produced a huge number of volunteer soldiers from both parts of what was to become a divided country, who fought loyally throughout the conflict. Sinn Fein, however, was opposed to the war, and conscription was an extremely controversial issue and was never applied in Ireland.[2] The Easter Rising of 1916 (England's difficulty was, as always, Ireland's opportunity) was almost entirely restricted to action by a small number of die-hard republicans in Dublin itself and did not become the national insurrection for which they had hoped. Indeed, it was at first thoroughly unpopular, and the Dublin crowds jeered the rebels who claimed to be dying on their behalf.

The uprising was over within a week, and had no effect on the First World War beyond proving a minor distraction to the War Office. But it did achieve its architects' ambitions, in creating an atmosphere in which further conflict was perceived to be justified; and it was to lead to the Irish War of Independence (1919 to 1921) and the creation of the Irish Free State in 1922. This was the culminating if incomplete triumph of Sinn Fein, whose leader Arthur Griffith had once been inspired by the Austro-Hungarian 'compromise' of 1867.

The First World War was thus essentially a European civil war with global consequences. Its major effect was to lead to the collapse of the four great imperial powers, Russia, Germany, Austria-Hungary and the Ottoman Empire, and the re-drawing of the map of Europe and the middle East. It did not lead to the end of empire *per se*, for the British and French overseas colonial empires survived the war: as did those of the Dutch, Spanish and Portuguese. (Germany lost its new colonies in Africa, but that was hardly surprising) Before we examine its consequences, however, we need to look at the course of the war.

The Course of the First World War:
The Western Front

The Western Front (which did not directly involve the forces of the dual monarchy) rapidly became a stalemate, as the (German) Schlieffen Plan to conquer France proved ineffective and the armies dug themselves into Northern France, to dispute small territorial gains and losses with massive loss of both life and materiel for four years. Cavalry finally proved themselves obsolete, as military experts should have recognised long before: neither cavalry nor indeed infantry could succeed in fixed attack against the deadly combination of machine-gun fire from defended positions, protected by barbed wire, and periodically bombarded by indirect artillery fire, using timed fuzes for greater effect. (These techniques had begun to prove effective in the American Civil War, 1861 to 1865, and had also shown themselves in the Russo-Japanese War of 1904 to 1905 and the First and Second Balkan Wars of 1912 and 1913.)

The situation called for the armoured fighting vehicle, or tank, propelled and steered by its own tracks, and capable of crossing a muddy, obstacle-dominated area under machine-gun fire; but tanks were not to be used in any numbers on the battlefield until 1917, and they were not to finally prove effective until 1918, when they became the spearhead of a combined arms advance following in time an effective three-dimensional artillery barrage (or indeed following at a distance, a so-called creeping barrage, in which 'friendly fire' falls ahead of the advancing troops.)[3]

The Eastern Front

The Eastern Front was more fluid, but nevertheless stalemate was reached on some occasions and in some places, as the Central Powers and Russia confronted each other in a long line stretching right across Europe, from Riga in Latvia, in a long, gentle curve south east to the Black Sea.

Conflict elsewhere?

The combined operations attack on the Dardanelles in 1915 proved an expensive failure. Churchill and Fisher's attempt to attack the Central Powers through their 'soft underbelly' proved unsuccessful. Other related conflicts took place, including war in the middle East and in East Africa, and in the war at sea. However, it is usually argued that the First World

War began, and was won, on the Western Front. Was it? Glenny claims (Glenny, 2002, page 346), that the Macedonian Front was significant to the overall outcome of the war. The German military leader, General Ludendorff, 'bitterly regretted his neglect of the Macedonian Front' (Glenny, page 354) which opened in September 1918, after the German Spring Offensive on the Western Front had failed and the Entente had replied with its own 100 day advance, in which they finally made a decisive break-through on the muddy fields of Flanders. Nor can we cannot ignore General Hindenburg's statement of 3 October 1918, as follows:

'As a result of the collapse of the Macedonian Front and the weakening of our western reserves which this has brought about, and now that it is impossible to make good the very considerable losses which have been incurred in the battles of the last few days, there is, so far as can be foreseen, no longer a prospect of forcing peace upon the enemy.' (Glenny, page 354). Glenny then added that 'two days later, the Germans appealed to President Woodrow Wilson to arrange an armistice. The war was effectively over.'

The dual monarchy at war

As far as Austria-Hungary was concerned, the war began well but soon turned sour. Its main target was Serbia, and the war with Russia was an expensive distraction. Austrian soldiers attacked and invaded Serbia in August 1914, expecting an easy victory. However, the Serbs proved a patriotic and highly motivated enemy; and by September 1914 had turned the tables on their aggessors and crossed into Austrian territory, at one point racing towards Sarajevo. The Austrians counter-attacked in strength and on 2 December 1914 occupied Belgrade, only to be driven out of Serbia once again by a renewed Serbian counter-offensive.

Serbia had gained a breathing-space, but it was not to last: in 1915 a combined German-Austrian offensive crushed the Serbian armed forces, and the battered remnants withdrew in disorder firstly to Corfu, and then on to the Greek city of Salonika where the Serbs formed a government in exile. Salonika was still officially under Greek control, and the Greeks were officially committed to supporting the Entente. In reality, Salonika was an occupied area, where the United Kingdom and France maintained a joint administration to pursue their wartime strategic aims. (The Serbian government in exile remained in Salonika until the end of the war, staging its trial and execution of Colonel Apis and two colleagues during this period.)

Meanwhile, further north, the Central Powers were at war with Russia in East Prussia and Galicia, which the Tsar's forces had invaded. The Central Powers defended East Prussia effectively and chased out the invaders. They managed to expel the Russians from Poland as well, gaining Warsaw in August 1915 and the whole of Poland by the end of the year, as well as capturing Bucharest (Romania had joined the Entente) in December 1915.

The Brusilov Offensive

The Russians were not finished yet, and replied with the Brusilov Offensive in June 1916 – a massive attack on a massive front. Well-led Russian troops inflicted huge losses on the ill-prepared forces of the dual monarchy, as well as killing or capturing a large number of German troops. However, the Russian initiative and military success was not followed up. Nor could it stop what was happening at home, where the Tsarist autocracy could not cope with a sustained war, and demonstrations, strikes and mutinies were bringing Russia to the point of revolution. In March 1917, the first Russian Revolution took place, and the Tsar abdicated, to be replaced by a provisional government which in theory was committed to continuing the war, but in practice was finding it practically impossible to do so.

Bread and Land

The Bolsheviks came to power in Moscow and Petrograd as a result of a second revolution in October 1917, orchestrated by Vladimir Ilych Lenin, and having taken full advantage of the chaos prevailing under the provisional government. Their appeal to the people was simple: Bread and Land! (an echo of Narodna Volya) and they promised the peasants and factory workers what they most wanted to hear. The Bolsheviks were unwilling to continue a war that they had not begun and which was in the interest of the imperialist powers (Lenin saw imperialism as the last stage of capitalism) and not in the interests of the proletariat.

The new Russia declared an armistice with the Central Powers in December 1917. This was followed by the Treaty of Brest-Litowsk on 3

March 1918, at which the communist firebrand Leon Trotsky (who had once been a foreign correspondent in the Balkans) negotiated a settlement that would enable the Bolsheviks to concentrate on their internal problems and not in defending themselves against Germany.

The Treaty of Brest-Litovsk

The treaty of Brest-Litovsk marked a massive victory for Germany (rather than the Central Powers) on the Eastern Front. Under its terms, the war was over, and Germany gained a huge amount of territory from Russia, including a large part of Poland and the Ukraine. However, the victory was not to prove as beneficial as it promised. Firstly, the Germans had to garrison and administer the new territories, which removed soldiers and other resources from the Western Front. Secondly, their new possessions brought them few assets, since agricultural and industrial production had been devastated by war. And thirdly, its gains were reversed at the Treaty of Versailles – although no one was yet to know that in March 1918, when the Germans were still hoping to make a decisive break-through on the Western Front, and to sue for peace on favourable terms, before American intervention proved decisive.

Despite its colossal victory on the Eastern Front, consolidated by the Treaty of Brest-Litovsk in March 1918, Germany soon faced military defeat on the Western Front, and the generals negotiated for an armistice, to be followed by a peace settlement. Impending military catastrophe, acute shortages of basic necessities, radical propaganda, and the example of what was happening in Russia led to revolution in Germany itself, and for a short while it seemed as if a revolutionary government on the Russian pattern might come into power. Kaiser Wilhelm 11 abdicated, and moved into exile in Holland. Order was restored, and the extreme revolutionaries were defeated. The Weimar republic was born. An entirely obscure Austro-Hungarian lance-corporal, who had volunteered to serve in the German army for the war and had been gassed and temporarily blinded for his pains, began to take an interest in politics...

Austria's War with Italy

The dual monarchy gained nothing from the Treaty, although it did at least mark the end of hostilities with Russia. However, by March 1918 Austria-Hungary (still linked to Germany, and with the assistance of the

Fatherland) was locked in a life or death struggle with Italy. The Central Powers defeated Italy at the Battle of Caporetto in October 1917, and for a time it seemed as if the dual monarchy would survive this latest crisis, as it had survived so many others. But the Italians regrouped, and called up almost the entire adult male population to fight. In October 1918, the Battle of Vittorio Veneto was a decisive victory for the Italians and marked the end of the Austro-Hungarian Army as an effective fighting force against Italy. This culminating defeat led to the disintegration of Austro-Hungarian Empire. During the last week of October 1918 declarations of independence were made in Budapest, Prague and Zagreb. A month later, the Emperor Karl resigned his post. Kakania was dead.

NOTES

[1] This was the equivalent of being a member both of Sinn Fein and the IRA in Northern Ireland at the height of the recent troubles in what was officially part of the United Kingdom. The IRA was a proscribed organisation, and to belong to it was a criminal offence which warranted a sentence of imprisonment. Sinn Fein was not proscribed, and could act as a cover or front organisation for the IRA, articulating its aims, gathering political support overseas, and raising money for the cause.

[2] Meanwhile, its Dublin recruiting office set a record for recruiting volunteers: for the British Army. Information supplied by Maj. Gen. Jonathan Bailey, CB, MBE.

[3] It was not until 1918 that British, French and American infantry finally achieved the eerie experience of being able to walk unshot across an undefended battlefield.

CHAPTER TEN

The end of Gavrilo Princip, and his legacy

About two hours' drive from Prague, the capital of the Czech Republic (formerly the capital of Czechoslovakia, and before that a regional capital of the Austro-Hungarian Empire) is the small town of Terezin. Among Terezin's monuments is its former prison, still called by its German name of Theresienstadt. Like Auschwitz, it is on the tourist circuit.

Theresienstadt was planned as a fortress by the Emperor Joseph 11 in 1780, and completed ten years later. It was never needed for its original intention, and was later used as a prison. During the Second World War, under the Nazi occupation, Theresienstadt was used as a holding centre for both political dissidents and Jews. Although it was not a designated extermination camp, and was inspected by the Red Cross in 1944, many inmates met their deaths there at the hands of the SS.

Its most famous former inmate is the subject of this book.

Gavrilo Princip, Nedjelko Cabrinovic and Trifko Grabez, the three chief conspirators of the Sarajevo *attentat*, were sent to serve their sentences in Theresienstadt in Bohemia under conditions of maximum security, while the remaining convicted conspirators were incarcerated in Zenica in Bosnia. (They were all later dispersed to other prisons, as the situation in Bosnia deteriorated from the point of view of Austria.)

The three young Bosnians left Sarajevo on 2 December 1914, chained to their seats in a special railway coach and under armed guard. They stopped overnight in Vienna, where a mob tried to attack them, and arrived in Theresienstadt on 4 December.

Theresienstadt, as Dedijer (Dedijer, page 352) describes it, was 'an old fortress converted into a military prison, a few miles from the town of the same name. The fortress was of stone and brick, and in front was a deep moat full of water from the surrounding marshes, which received the fortress sewage. The outside wall was over four feet thick; the inner ones were of normal thickness. All the cells were built within walls. The casemates were large rooms in each of which were from twelve to fifteen men [far more under the Nazis] and the solitary cells were between the casemates.'

Bleak, forbidding Theresienstadt was to accommodate Austria-Hungary's most famous offender, together with his two closest companions, amongst a large number of political prisoners from throughout the empire.

The ends of Cabrinovic and Grabez

The tall, athletic and sociable Nedjelko Cabrinovic, the constant irritation to his father and apple of his sister's eye, soon fell ill, unable to cope both with the physical conditions and the mental consequences of solitary confinement—a condition for which he was spectacularly unsuited.

In 1915, Cabrinovic was removed to hospital in the near-by town, but the respite was purely temporary. The young Bosnian Serb was diagnosed with tuberculosis, then returned to prison as incurable. He lasted very little longer, and died on 23 January 1916—to be followed little more than a month later by Trifko Grabez, who died of exhaustion and malnutrition, exacerbated by tuberculosis.

After his death, Cabrinovic's skull was requested by the department of police in Sarajevo, but this request was not complied with, probably because of the bureaucratic difficulties it raised, rather than any humanitarian disquiet.

- Which department of state had sent the prisoner to Theresienstad, and could therefore properly deal with this request?

- Who would be responsible for the decapitation?

- Who would pay for its cost?

The questions multiplied, and the chief of police in Sarajevo, Viktor Ivasjuk, had to content himself with the skull of the failed assassin Bogdan

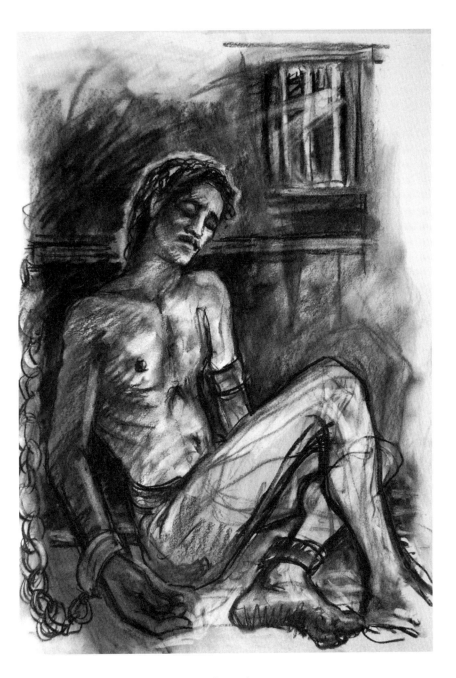

The end of Gavrilo Princip

Zerajic, which he had obtained by non-bureaucratic means, and which he used as a ploy during interrogations.

Princip's condition

Princip was held in solitary confinement throughout his imprisonment. His jailers kept to the terms of his sentence and he was kept in chains weighing ten kilograms unless being treated in the prison hospital. On 28 June every year, the cell was darkened and he was left to meditate on his misdeeds and repent of them: and no doubt he did so, but not in the manner in which the authorities intended. He did not regret his intention in planning the assassination, as far as we know: but he did regret its consequences.

Whether or not Princip took the seeds of tuberculosis into prison with him, conditions there soon enabled the disease to develop.[1] On 27 February 1916 an Austrian official was reported as saying of the empire's most notorious prisoner, to a Sarajevo journalist:

'Princip is very ill and suffering from consumption… He is a finished man; his chest is sunken, his eyes are deep in their sockets, he has wasted away completely and is now in the prison hospital. The news that Serbia has been conquered and that King Petar has fled profoundly distressed him. When he learned that Cabrinovic was dead he was quite overwhelmed.'

Princip had no official access to any form of information and was not entitled, it would appear, to visitors or letters from home. Nor is there any suggestion that any friend or relative attempted to visit him, partly, no doubt, because he was so far from Bosnia. Under such conditions, amounting almost to sensory deprivation, the prison authorities could drip-feed the young political prisoner whatever information they chose.

But the authorities did not succed in keeping the young Bosnian assassin in total isolation, and there were occasions when he was able to make contact with other prisoners, or with officials from another of the minority races of the empire who might be sympathetic to him; especially as he was transferred between his cell and the prison hospital from time to time. (The prison hospital was not part of Theresienstadt prison itself, but was a ward designated for prisoners in the general hospital of the near-by town.)

A fellow prisoner who obtained access via a Czech guard, commented:
'Gavro was ill, losing strength more and more, but spiritually he

remained alert. He was very pleased he had been put in the same cell where Hadzi Lojo [leader of the insurgents against the Hapsburgs in Bosnia in 1878] served his term, because "it is a special privilege that he, the last Austrian prisoner from Bosnia, is put in the cell of the first prisoner.".... He was convinced that he would not live long enough to see the end of the war, but he was sure that the end of Austria was certain.'

Conversations with a psychiatrist

In hospital, Princip told the Viennese psychiatrist, Dr Pappenheim, who interviewed him on four occasions in 1916, that he most regretted the absence of books, for without books to read he did not feel himself fully human. There is no evidence that his spirit was broken. However, he knew that his life was coming to an end, and it is doubtful if he regretted it: for how could he face a world in which his act had led to so much suffering?

The meetings between the sophisticated Viennese psychiatrist and the Bosnian assassin were recorded only in note form (Armstrong, 1927), for Dr Pappenheim never fulfilled his intention of turning his interview notes into a complete record. They form an incomplete and in some ways a frustrating account, but do tell us something about Princip's family; his enduring convictions; his resignation to his fate; his love of books, and inability to commuicate without them; and his inner world. True to himself, he does not reveal anything of security interest about the assassination, although he does describe it in brief; and he emphasizes Ilic's uncertainties.

The four meetings took place between February and June 1916, and the dates were 19 February, 12 May, 18 May and 5 June. At this point we must assume that Dr Pappenheim returned to Vienna, or at least ceased his prison work at Theresienstadt whilst completing his military service in the imperial army. Here is part of what Dr Pappenheim recorded in note form from his penultimate interview with the assassin, Gavrilo Princip.

'Wound worse, discharging very freely. Looking miserable. Suicide by any sure means is impossible. "Wait to the end." Resigned, but not really very sad.

'...Sometimes in a philosophical mood, sometimes poetical, sometimes quite prosaic. Thinks about the human soul. What is the essential in human life, instinct or will, or spirit—what moves man?

'Many who have spoken with him think he is a child, think that he was inspired by others, only because he cannot express himself sufficiently, is not in general gifted as a talker. Always a reader and always alone, not often engaging in debates....

'...Read much in Sarajevo. In Sarajevo used to dream every night he was a political murderer, struggling with gendarmes and policemen. Read much about the Russian revolution, about the fightings. ... Had a nice library, because always was buying books. *Books for me signify life.* (Author's emphasis). Therefore [life] now so hard without books.

'Thought that as a result of repeated attempts at assassination there could be built up an organization such as Ilic desired, and that then there would be general revolution among the people. Now comprehends that a revolution, especially in the military state of Austria, is of no use. What he now thinks the right thing he would not say. Has no desire to speak on the matter. It makes him unquiet to speak about it. *When he thinks by himself, then everything is clear, but when he speaks with anybody, then he becomes uncertain.*

'*If he had something to read for only 2-3 days, he could then think more clearly and express himself better.* (Author's emphasis.) Does not speak to anybody for a month. Then when I come he wants to speak about ideas, about dominating thoughts. He considered that if he prepared the atmosphere the idea of revolution and liberation would spread first among men of intelligence and then later in the masses. Thought that thereby attention of the intelligentsia would be directed upon it. As for instance Mazzini did in Italy at the time of the Italian liberation.'

In summary, Princip did not like to think about the consequences of what he had done, and tried to block it from his mind. At the same time, he constantly returned to the need for revolution, and how it could best be achieved. He suffered acutely from the absence of the written word, and found it extremely difficult to articulate his thoughts. Although his life in solitary confinement was not one of continuous misery, he had nothing to live for and was resigned to his impending death.

Dr Pappenheim continued in his profession as a psychiatrist after the Great War, and continued his membership of the Vienna Psycho-Analytic Institute which had been founded by Sigmund Freud, the father of psycho-analysis.[2] Dr Pappenheim emigrated to Israel in 1933, where he became a member of the Israel Psycho-Analytic Society and a well-known person in

Tel-Aviv. His daughter Elsa, who died in January 2009, emigrated to the United States and became a psychiatrist in her turn, belonging to the New York Psycho-Analytic Institution. This author has found no trace of any subsequent interview with Dr Pappenheim on his work at Theresienstadt in 1916.

The end of Gavrilo Princip

In late 1917, all the remaining Bosnian political prisoners in Theresienstadt, save Gavrilo Princip, were sent back to the Zenica prison in Bosnia. Princip was presumably too ill and still too dangerous to be moved, and remained in the prison hospital. His end, as he knew better than anyone, was near. A prison doctor late wrote his recollections of this period, as follows:

'Already... Princip was a candidate for death, a living corpse with his meagre body wasted to the bone with several tuberculosis ulcers as large as a hand.... In my presence he never uttered any repentance for his deed... On the lines of his face was an almost solemn earnestness, the eyes sunken in their sockets had lost their brightness and the fire of youth. Except when he was speaking about the liberation of his people, then they would brighten up for a while... In good German he talked to me about his family and his youth, but he never mentioned the man from the Black Hand who, in the opinion of the Austro-Hungarian secret police, had provoked him to doing what he did... The disease had destroyed the elbow joint of his left arm to such an extent that the lower part had to be connected with the upper part by a silver wire...'

The arm was amputated, although only after the full bureaucratic procedures had been complied with. Austria-Hungary kept its forms to the end. But the amputation came too late to do any good. Princip's death certificate states that he died at 1830 on 28 April 1918, in Room 33 of the closed part of Hospital Number 13 at Theresienstadt.[3]

Burial and resurrection

After Gavrilo Princip died, his body was buried at dead of night in an unmarked pit dug for the purpose, as the authorities did not intend that his grave become a source of inspiration to other dissidents. Their fears were not unfounded: Princip himself had been in the habit of laying flowers at

Bogdan Zerajic's grave, and had marked each such occasion by swearing to avenge his death—part of his motivation for the attack on Franz Ferdinand. His last visit had been on the night before the assassination, at the cemetery in Sarajevo where he renewed his vow that Zerajic would be avenged, and that his death had not been in vain. (As Gavrilo Princip's psyche had been steeped in Serbian tradition, we may be sure that he had the legend of the battle of Kosovo in mind when he swore to attack the Archduke, as an enemy not only of Bosnia but of Serbia.)

Princip was buried secretly, but a Czech soldier noted the location of his grave and marked it on a hand-drawn map. After the war Princip's remains, together with those of the other conspirators who had perished during the war, were transported to Sarajevo and buried in a common grave.

The three main conspirators were later buried together in St Mark's cemetery and a headstone was added with an heroic inscription. However, Princip's grave did not become a symbolic location for young Bosnians, as had Bogdan Zerajic's before him. After all, Bosnia had gained a new status, as part of the new, post-war Yugoslavia: and besides, no-one was quite sure how to decide the reputation of the young Bosnian Serb who had shot the Archduke and his wife. Was he to be venerated as a hero? Or condemned, as an assassin working for what was at the time a foreign power? Or quietly forgotten, as something of an embarrassment?

Had he survived the war, Princip would have been due for release in 1934. However, he would probably have been released in 1918, like the two Sarajevo students Cvetko Popovic and Vaso Cubrilovic, who had been reccruited to the conspiracy at the last minute by Danilo Ilic, and who survived the war.[4] (They had received lesser sentences in 1914, were not already infected with tuberculosis, and had not been sent to Theresienstadt.) The world into which the young assassin had fired his two shots on 28 June 1914 had disappeared.

The Decline and Fall of the Hapsburg Empire

Franz Ferdinand died in the Governor's Palace or Konak in Sarajevo shortly after he was shot. His wife Sophie was already dead. The bodies were taken back to Vienna by the same route as Franz Ferdinand had used to travel to Sarajevo, with mourners at every stage of the journey.[5] The funeral service for the murdered couple took place at the Hofburg in

Vienna. It lasted a mere 15 mintues, and was not attended by foreign dignitaries—although, as we would have expected, the Archduke's mother-in-law was present. The emperor himself expressed no very great grief at the death of the heir apparent. Indeed, he does not seem to have expressed any sentiments at all.[6]

Franz Ferdinand and his wife were transported to his favourite castle at Artstteten, and laid side by side to rest in the crypt he had himself designed. He is reported to have urged its completion, and he wrote to his chamberlain when the work was finished: "You have managed, that well, as I like it. It is airy and light. Only the entrance is not well designed. It makes too sharp a turn. Awkward bearers will knock off a corner with the coffin. Then I shall turn in my grave." (Dedijer, page 97.) As Remak (Remak, page 181) reports the occasion, at least part of the Archduke's prediction proved accurate: the soldiers carrying his coffin to its final resting-place did indeed knock against the wall.[7]

The plan of succession was changed, and the Archduke Karl, son of Franz Ferdinand's younger brother Otto, became the heir apparent. He was given no more training in the art of emperorship than his cousin Franz Ferdinand, and the emperor, ageing but never senile, continued to immerse himself in his duties—although it was noticeable that he was no longer able to work quite so long or so hard as in his prime.

The Emperor Franz Joseph died on 21 November 1916—a death which had little or no impact on the war in progress. Franz Joseph had been born in 1830, and had ruled for 68 years—five years longer than Queen Victoria. During that time, his empire had seen many changes, none of which had been to his advantage: but he had been able to live up to the Hapsburg creed, and to remain in power.

The Emperor Karl 1 was judged, at least by some, to prove a weak and incompetent director of an empire at war. Even had he possessed greater leadership qualities, however, it is likely that events would have defeated him. By 1918, the Austro-Hungarian Empire was facing its final crisis, as the forces that had held it together were finally overcome by the forces that had been driving it apart.

War was the catalyst. Austro-Hungarian empire was not destroyed by conquest, and many of the Emperor's soldiers, sailors and airmen fought loyally to the end. They included intellectuals such as the philosopher Ludwig Wittgenstein, who had returned home from Cambridge as war broke out, and served on the Eastern Front until imprisoned—completing his *Tractatus Logico-Philosophicus* whilst in captivity. His patriotism contrasted strongly with the attitude of his philosophical mentor and colleague, Bertrand Russell, who was a pacifist in the First World War—although he saw the need to defeat Hitler in the Second.

Ludwig Wittgenstein, a millionaire until he gave away his inheritance, and a cosmopolitan who was nevertheless patriotic, was an isolated if not unique example. A more general assessment of morale in the imperial armed forces was made by the distinguished military historian John Keegan, in his comprehensive analysis of the First World War. According to Keegan (Keegan, 1998, page 169):

'Of the nine language groups in the army, of which 44 per cent was Slav (Czech, Slovak, Croatian, Serb, Slovene, Ruthenian, Polish and Bosnian Moslem), 28 per cent German, 18 per cent Hungarian, 8 per cent Romanian and 2 per cent Italian, the Germans were always dependable, if some never wholly enthusiastic; the Hungarians, non-Slavs, and privileged co-equals remained reliable until defeat stared them in the face at the end; the Catholic Croats had a long record of loyalty to the empire, which many of them maintained; the Poles, hating the Russians, distrusting the Germans and enjoying large electoral and social privileges under the Hapsburgs, were *kaisertreu*; the Bosnian Moslems, sequestered in special, semi-sepoy regiments, were dependable; the Italians and the rest of the Slavs, particularly the Czechs and the Serbs, rapidly lost the enthusiasm of mobilisation. Once war ceased to be a brief adventure, the army became for them "a prison of the nations", with the ubiquitous German superiors acting as gaolers.'

Once the imperial army was actually required to fight, and not simply to constitute an instrument of imperial solidarity, its deficiences became crucial; and military defeat was linked to social unrest and political agitation, based on a very understandable upsurge of nationalism. What, the Czechs, Poles, Bosnians, Croats, Hungarians, and all the rest were entitled to reflect, was the empire doing for them? And the answer was, very little. Were they now permitted, as a Czech delegation is supposed to have respectfully asked the emperor in 1918, to make a revolution?

Was the end of empire inevitable?

Was the Austro-Hungarian Empire already doomed in 1914, and was the assassination of Franz Ferdinand merely the coup-de-grace? Given a sufficient time-span, the decline and end of any empire is inevitable. But the Austrian empire had survived crises in the previous 100 years, for example in 1848, 1866, and 1867; and it might have survived longer where it not for the catalyst of war.

Alan Sked (Sked, 2001) argues against the hypothesis of inexorable decline. In his view the empire in 1914 was not doomed, but in reasonably good shape. In Chapter Seven of his reflections on the decline and fall of the Hapsburg Empire, Sked writes that its foundations were not smashed by the war. In war as in peace, the empire continued. The rule of law was maintained. Social and economic administration endured. The highly developed Hapsburgian version of a welfare state continued to function, and a vast civilian army of bureaucrats, administrators and needy dependents continued to derive both purpose and substance from the continued reign of the Hapsburgs.

Political repression was restrained, and was not in any case a primary consideration. Contrary to the libertarian dream, most people in most countries rate security and economic prosperity more highly than abstract political ideals, and are quite prepared to live with a degree of repression, including formal censorship, and certainly a restriction of their right to the freedom of expression, provided that they are able to live and work in peace and to have some belief in a future for their family. (For a contemporary example, let the reader consider the success of current government policies in China, where political expression is severely restricted but where there has been a necessary development of economic freedom, without which the current Chinese economic miracle could not have occurred.)

But the empire fell. Why? We may attribute its final collapse to the destruction of war; to the growth of nationalism in the late nineteenth century, which meant that the constituent elements of the empire began to see themselves not only as ethnic groups, but as political entities in their own right; to the policies of the American President, Woodrow Wilson, as put into practice at Versailles; and finally, to the spirit of the times. Empires end, not so much though external pressures, as when the imperialists themselves cease to believe in their mission.

The Departure of the Hapsburgs?

Influenced by the views of his wife Zita and his own desire to end the suffering and bloodshed of the war, the Emperor Karl engaged in secret diplomacy which went against him. His intrigues included suggesting that Alsace and Lorraine remain part of Germany after the war. This supposedy confidential suggestion did not impress the French, when they soon heard of it, for they were determined to regain the lost territories of Alsace and Lorraine that had been seized from them in the Franco-Prussian war of 1870, and were part of the reason for their involvement in the current conflict. Nor did it impress the Germans, who were angry that the Austrians were negotiating behind their back. The emperor Karl may have been acting like a Hapsburg in making this offer, but he was not Hapsburg enough: his character lacked that element of ruthless cunning that had been the most effective characteristic of his more successful forbears.

The dual monarchy collapsed in November 1918. Karl resigned his position but not his rights on the same day that the general armistice was declared, and went into exile. He died in poverty in Madeira in 1922 at the age of 34, leaving his wife and eight children, some of whom are still alive. His wife Zita died in 1989 at the age of 97, having outlived her husband by 67 years.[8]

The former emperor Karl, who renounced his powers but never abdicated, has since been beatified by the Roman Catholic church for his devotion to the faith. His oldest son, Otto von Habsburg, was brought up in exile—thus avoiding the Nazis' treatment of Franz Ferdinand's two sons Max and Ernst, who were seized by the Gestapo and imprisoned in Dachau concentration camp for the duration of the Second World War.[9] Otto von Habsburg renounced his claims to imperial succession in 1961, returned from exile, and served as a member of the European Parliament for a German constituency for twenty years, from 1979 to 1999. He is a conservative.

His children and those of his siblings remain noteworthy in European society, including both culture and politics, and the name Hapsburg, Habsburg, von Hapsburg or any other recognized variation remains one with which to weave spells.

'The claim to set up new states according to the limits of nationality is the most dangerous of all Utopian schemes. To put forward such a pretension is to break with history; and to carry it into execution in any part of Europe is to shake to its foundations the organized order of states, and to threaten the Continent with subversion and chaos.'

Austrian Foreign Office, 1853

Gavrilo Princip and his colleagues had not propounded a clear and comprehensive plan for the future of the former Austro-Hungarian possessions that had been located in the Balkans, because they had not articulated one. They wished Bosnia to be independent of Austria, and perhaps part of something called Yugoslavia. But of what Yugoslavia would actually consist, and what would be the details of its constitutional settlement, had never been made clear. Was Bosnia to be part of a greater Serbia, as Colonel Apis would certainly have intended? Or part of a greater Croatia—as Apis would certainly have opposed as far worse that the *status quo*, and to which Young Bosnia, despite its ideals, would in practice have been equally opposed? Or was it to become part of a mysterious new entity, the kingdom (or republic) of the South Slavs, or Yugoslavia? Who knew?

In the end, events dictated a solution which had not been anticipated, although it was consistent, in broad terms, with those who had wished for a greater Serbia. The new state included other nationalities, but the Serbs were a favoured group; for their king was to rule the whole country and their officers were to dominate the army.

The Treaty of Versailles resulted in the creation of the Kingdom of the Serbs, Croats, and Slovenes. Significantly, the official date of its creation was 28 June 1919. It became the Kingdom of Yugoslavia in 1929. Its constituent areas included the former Bosnia. However, the administrative areas of the new state were redefined, and for a generation Bosnia became a territory of purely historical significance, like a former kingdom within the heptarchy that had once preceded England, such as Northumbria or Mercia.

Political developments between the wars

Like other European governments, the government of Yugoslavia became increasingly authoritarian and anti-democatic, although it did not embrace fascism. Instead, it became almost by default something very close to a royal dictatorship. During the 1920s, Yugoslavian politics became increasingly polarised between left and right, and the traditional rivalries of the Serbs (who favoured centralisation) and Croats (who favoured regionalism or federalism) were never resolved.

What sort of state was Yugoslavia was intended to become? This was never fully resolved. In the first instance, was it be centralist (and therefore under overt Serbian control) or federalist? And if it were to be federalist, what sort of federalism was implied?

Federal or confederal?

There were two understandings of federalism. Under federalism proper, the state was the original source of power and ceded or conceded power to its constituent republics or sub-units on agreed issues. Thus, the state might be responsible for the currency, national defence and foreign policy, whereas the sub-units were authorised to decide local issues of policing, education and health. Under a confederal system, on the other hand, confederal republics or sub-states held original power and ceded or conceded power to the state on agreed topics. What this subtle distinction meant in practice was that when it came to an issue of disputed power or authority, a federal state would incline one way and a confederal state, another.

Such arcane issues were not resolved, or even addressed, as the 1930s wore on and Europe became increasingly polarised, with fascism exercising a fascination not only for the dispossessed, but also for a section of the intelligentsia, then as always ready to be seduced by new ideas. However, the federal question was to arise again in Yugoslavia in the 1980s, and finally to destroy it altogether.

The Rise of Hitler

The Second World War was a continuation of the first, from which it was separated by a mere 21 years. Its primary cause was the accession to power in Germany of Adolf Hitler (1889 to 1945), who created a national socialist Germany which was intent upon conquest and world power, and which was determined to reverse the humiliations of the Treaty of Versailles.

Hitler believed in war and was determined to promote it. Hitler himself, perhaps ironically, had been born an Austrian: but he showed no allegiance of any kind to the multi-racial and multi-cultural empire of his birth, and instead proved himself a fanatical 'Germanist,' who believed that the weak and ineffective Austrians should be absorbed into a greater Reich.

Adlof Hitler was the fourth child of the third marriage of an Austrian customs official, Alois Hitler, who was already fifty years old when his son Adolf was born. Age did not mellow Alois, who was consistently violent to both wife and son. Hitler proved an indifferent student at school in Linz (where he overlapped with Ludwig Wittgenstein) and left without a diploma. He drifted towards Vienna, where he lived the life of a penniless bohemian, without qualifications, skills (apart from the production of a few water-colours) or prospects; and it was in Vienna that he began to develop and express the virulent anti-Semitism[10] which was to be his fundamental characteristic. He left Vienna for Munich in 1913, and never returned to live in Austria, although he was not to become a German citizen until 1933.

Again ironically, for someone who was to glorify war as a necessity for the triumph of the race, Hitler does not appear to have been willing to do his military service for the Austro-Hungarian Empire. As a result, he was arrested by the relevant military authorities, and failed the medical. However, the outbreak of war changed all that; and Hitler volunteered and was accepted by a Bavarian regiment, serving with honour throughout the First World War.

War was the making of this failed artist. For the first time, perhaps, he earned something like the respect of his fellow men, or was at least able to rise in his own self-esteem. He was able to discover a nationality, a cause and a set of aptitudes which had hitherto eluded him; for the former lance-corporal was recruited into military intelligence in 1919, and ordered to infiltrate the new German National Socialist Workers' Party.

The young secret agent found, like other secret agents had done before him, that the ideals of the organisation he had been commissioned to penetrate were of greater appeal than anything he had hitherto worked out for himself. His mind was virgin territory, and national socialism took easy root there. Hitler found that he had a passion for politics and an ability to move others through the power of oratory, which was to propel him from profound obscurity to absolute power as Chancellor of Germany within the space of 14 years.

In 1938, he united Germany and Austria by the simple expedient of occupying Austria. His ambition thenceforward was to create a larger and larger Germany, united under one leader. That empire was not to be a fixed (if gradually expanding) territorial area, like the old Austro-Hungarian empire. Hitler thought it would be beneficial to the race, or 'folk', to be in a state of permanent war with the slavs to the east, where German warrior-settlers would dominate a slav or slave population, like the Teutonic Knights of old in the Baltic.

The Second World War and The invasion of Yugoslavia

Despite his quasi-mystical plans for world domination by a thousand year Reich, Hitler was perfectly capable of rational calculation, at least until his war started to go against him in Russia in 1942; and until that point his expansionist policies were dramatically successful. The Third Reich absorbed Austria and Czechoslovakia without warfare, and conquered Poland, Norway, Holland, Belgium and France with an almost contemptuous ease. Operation Sealion, the attempt to conquer the United Kingdom, was abandoned when the preliminary air offensive was unsuccessful. Hitler accepted this with comparative equanimity: his fellow Anglo-Saxons were not really his enemies, and perhaps a joint empire overseas would still be possible.

The invasion of Yugoslavia by German, Italian and Hungarian troops in 1941 was a pragmatic collaboration, brought about by other issues, primarily the failure of Italian actions elsewhere in the Balkans. Hitler and Mussolini were supposedly allies, but it was an alliance more of convenience than ideological conviction, although fascism and nazism were based upon the same fundamental belief in racial superiority—a superiority which the Second Rome had found it harder to display, in action, than the armed forces of the Third Reich.

Having conquered Ethiopia with great difficulty, Italy had become bogged down in its campaign to conquer Albania, and invaded Yugoslavia to assist its progress—only to encounter fierce resistance. Hitler came reluctantly to the aid of his ally. He thereby postponed his attack on his supposed ally, the Soviet Union[11] at a a vital moment, and arguably deciding the outcome of the whole war.[12] Yugoslavia was in effect partitioned between Italy and Germany until 1943, when fascist Italy collapsed and the Italian military presence in Yugoslavia ceased to be significant.

Croatia and the Ustase

The Nazis were also able to create a local puppet fascist state, based on a greatly enlarged Croatia, which was nominally independent. The Ustase, the native Croat Fascists who dominated the new creation, had been a very small group up to 1941. However, by using the perverted ideals of national socialism as a sort of ideological cloak for their own, home-grown, racial hatreds, they were soon able to make up for a comparatively late start.

The new Croatia became a hell on earth for those of its inhabitants who displeased the regime. Serbs and Moslems were killed in large numbers, in what would later come to be called ethnic cleansing, with the aim of creating a 'racially pure' Croatia; and the Jews were wiped out en masse, either locally or by deportation to the formal extermination camps of the Third Reich, largely stationed in eastern Germany and Poland. The Second World War was a very bad time to be living in Croatia; and it was not much better in the rest of Yugoslavia.

From the allied point of view, it was a good thing that Hitler had invaded Yugoslavia, since it delayed Operation Barbarossa, his invasion of the Soviet Union, and was to tie down a large number of his troops in the Balkans. According to Malcolm's commentary (Malcolm, 2002) few of those troops were first-class, front-line fighting units such as the Waffen SS; but it was still a drain on Nazi manpower; and any local resistance movement was to be encouraged. However, the problem with the resistance movement was that it was split into two camps who tended to spend more time in fighting each other than in fighting the supposed common enemy, since their aims were fundamentally different.

Chetniks and Partisans

The local resistance movement to both Germans and Italians was split into two main groups: the Chetniks, led by the Royalist army officer Draga Mihailovic, and the Partisans, a communist resistance movement led by the hitherto obscure Josip Broz, a former corporal in the Austro-Hungarian army and communist agitator who was best known as Tito. Tito (1892-1980) was a died-in-the-wool communist who had been indoctrinated in Moscow, and was regarded as Stalin's man in the Balkans.

The Chetniks sought to expel the Nazi invaders and re-establish the monarchy. However, they avoided attacks which led to savage civilian reprisals by the Nazis. The Chetniks, like their leader Mihailovic, were mainly Serbs. The Partisans, on the other hand, were united on ideological rather than ethnic grounds, and indeed Tito made much of the fact that he had a Croat father and a Slovene mother and was therefore an authentic Yugoslav. They were determined to create a communist Yugoslavia, or indeed a wider area under communist rule, and quite rightly perceived the Chetniks as a strategic threat to this ambition. Both sides, therefore, attacked each other, and both entered into negotiations with the Germans who were their supposed enemies.

Whom to support?

Whom were the allies to support? Churchill asked the key question: Which of the two groups is killing more Germans? It would seem to have been the Partisans, for they were more ruthless than the Chetniks as to the consequences of their actions. (Nazi reprisals against the local population, carried out as a result of Partisan attacks, tended to increase support for the Partisans.) In 1943 Churchill swiched his support from the Chetniks to the Partisans, usiing first-hand knowledge from the SOE officer William Deakin (1913-2005) to make his choice.

It is likely that the information that Churchill and the allies were receiving was not unbiased, since amongst the officials working for MI6, the secret intelligence service which had been entrusted with the long-term cultivation of secret agents in the Balkans, were communists or communist sympathisers, including the self-confessed communist James Klugman. They had been recruited into MI6 by Anthony Blunt and the so-called Cambridge spies, in order to destroy the establishment from within. They would have no reason to present Mihailovic in a good light, and every reason to embellish Tito's achievements. (Their influence persisted. After the war the traitor Kim Philby was able to betray British agents in Albania and elsewhere for some time, without being detected.)

However, Churchill also had access to information from the Special Operations Executive, an alternative organisation to MI6 which he had himself created in order to 'set Europe ablaze;' and SOE had not been infiltrated by traitors. In addition to Deakin, liaison officers such as Sir

Fitzroy MacLean, MP, and Churchill's son, Major Randolph Churchill, were able to continue to report that the partisans were killing more Germans than the Chetniks, and there was no reason to doubt their integrity—especially as neither was temperamentally inclined towards communism.

In summary, the Partisans were capable of savage fighting against a savage enemy, and therefore merited support; and whilst their campaign did not decide the outcome of the conflict in the Balkans, it played a part. Whether or not the Chetniks were patriotic, neutral, or collaborationist is not something we are called upon to decide; and there is quite enough controversy in Balkan history without our adding to it.

Yugoslavia under President Tito

Yugoslavia had been ceded by Churchill to Stalin at the Yalta conference of allied leaders in 1943, as an area of legitimate Russian influence—which meant in effect that Tito would have a free hand to establish a Moscow-orientated socialist state. In 1945, he proceeded to do so. The communists seized power by their usual tactics of oppression, intrigue and thuggery, aided in this case by Tito's genuine popularity as a liberator. The opposition, real or potential, was routed out and the monarchy was never restored. General Mihailovic was hanged as a war criminal in 1946 and the Ustase were crushed or driven into exile. This left Tito and his closest advisers free to build the state they chose.

Tito was an ardent communist, and not a Serb, Croatian or Slovene nationalist. He was determined upon a federal Yugoslavia, in which the rival interests of the various groups and factions were evenly balanced under his wise and necessary leadership. At the same time, the ideology of communism was a genuine inspiration for at least some of the partisan guerrilla commanders turned politicians who supported Tito.

They included Milovan Djilas (1911-1995), the guerrilla leader, politician and writer who provides us with a chilling picture of what it was like to be at the centre of communist power in this period. *Conversations with Stalin* was first published in 1962, after Djilas had been tried, convicted and imprisoned as a political prisoner by the communists, just as he had previously been imprisoned under the Royalist regime. His crime was to question the continuing dedication of its officials to the ideals of the revolution and to point to the corruption of the new holders of power.

Milovan Djilas: The corruption of the 'new class'

Milovan Djilas, a Montenegrin by origin and an ascetic by inclination, wanted a greater freedom of speech in Yugoslavia, in order to achieve proper reforms and genuine progress—just what President Gorbachev was later to desire for Russia.

Djilas's ideas were of course, anathema to any traditionally-minded communist official and could easily be written off under Marxist-Leninist dogma. The offender could then be punished as a criminal or re-educated as a deviationist: a distinction without a difference, as far as the deprivation of his freedom was concerned.

Djilas, like Princip before him, was a revolutionary idealist, although a much more articulate one; and such people are always a thorn in the side of the ruthless and often paranoid autocrats such as Lenin or Stalin who concentrate on the main issue, to seize and hold power. Like the more recent dictator Fidel Castro, they will never actually submit themselves to the scrutiny of popular endorsement for their regime: for somehow the revolution has never *quite* been achieved, and there will always remain enemies within the gate.

In 1945, Djilas's fall from grace was still seven years away. Tito was the man of the hour, who could almost be said to have attempted to out-Stalin the Georgian dictator himself, at this crucial moment in history. When Stalin and Tito (or Djugashvili and Broz, to give their real names) did fall out, in 1948, it was not over ideological differences in their interpretations of Marxism-Leninism. Tito resented Stalin's attitude of superiority towards Yugoslavia and his fundamental conviction that the South Slav People's Republic existed purely to serve the economic and political interests of the Soviet Union.

The Red Army had not liberated Yugoslavia, and Tito had not been put in power as a Stalinist puppet, unlike most other communist leaders in the new East European satellite states. He did not depend upon Moscow for his authority. If not a war hero, he was a respected partisan leader. Only he was capable of uniting the amalgam of Yugoslavia, which consisted in 1946 of the six separate republics of Montenegro, Macedonia, Serbia,[13] Bosnia and Herzegovina, Croatia and Slovenia, and which without his leadership would certainly have fallen apart. In his personality he possessed that combination of charm and ruthlessness which those who wish for a parent/child relationship admire in a leader, and which is sometimes described by the word 'charisma'.

After the split with Moscow, which he survived by the skin of his teeth, things went very much Tito's way. Djilas, an intellectual and often an embarrassment to the party leadership for his tendency to ask awkward questions and challenge the 'party line', was imprisoned, together with other political detainees. Federal institutions were reformed or created from scratch. On smaller issues, the communist party was benevolent: older, traditional boundaries were re-created, and Bosnia became a republic once again, its internal boundaries precisely where they had been under the Austrians, or indeed under the Turks.

Economic reforms were experimented with, provided that they did not affect the sovereignty of the communist party; and a degree of liberalism was practised. 'Industrial democracy' was lauded, and indeed Yugoslavia's economy did develop, although probably not as a result of industrial democracy. Tourism grew and grew, especially on the Dalmatian coast, and many foreigners came to visit and admire Yugoslavia, with its attractive scenery and climate, its fascinating history (now safely in the past, or so it was believed) and its development of progressive socialism.

The 'Non-aligned Movement'

President Tito himself became famous for leading the 'Non-Aligned Movement', a move towards providing a respectable international alternative to the cold war bulwarks of communism and capitalism, as represented by the Soviet Union and the United States of America: rigid, monolithic structures which, like giant bull-dozers, crushed everything in their way. What was the alternative? States such as India, Egypt and Yugoslavia had freed themselves from their colonial masters. They did not brandish nuclear arsenals, submarines, strategic bombers, and the other paraphernalia of the modern super-state. They did not seek to dominate the world, whether by conquest or economic imperialism. And they were finding their own path to peace, prosperity and progress. It was a compelling vision. But in Yugoslavia at least, it was founded on a myth.

The Collapse of Yugoslavia

Tito died in 1980, and his myth died with him; for it was Tito who had held the new Yugoslavia together. It was found after his death that his new constitution, just when it was most needed, did not work; and that the notion of 'collective leadership' was incapable of realisation. Besides, the international context of politics was changing. The Soviet Union was no longer the force that it had been, and President Gorbachev, the man with whom Mrs Thatcher could do business, was experimenting with both *glasnost* and *perestroika*: economic and political reforms that were to lead to the collapse of the USSR. Communism did not work, and nor did its institutions; and it was time to face the truth.

The emergence of new states

In what was about to become the former Yugoslavia, <u>Slovenia</u> led the way. Slovenia had three advantages. It was next door to Italy, and had an acquaintance with life elsewhere. Its people were all Slovenes, with one language and one source of ethnic origin. Thirdly, it had achieved a sufficient degree of economic and industrial development to be able to exist on its own resources.

Slovenia claimed its independence from Yugoslavia, and after a short war obtained it. Slovenia is now a truly independent state, except that it has subjected itself to the constraints of the European Community, and is also a member of NATO. But those are features of a voluntary submission, and the advantages clearly outweigh the costs.

<u>Macedonia</u> obtained its independence from Yugoslavia about the same time as Slovenia, in 1992. It has since been bedevilled by inter-ethnic conflict and has still to resolve its nomenclature: it is in dispute with the Greek government, which has a province of the same name. As a result, the UN describes the former Yugoslav republic, logically enough, as the Former Yugoslav Republic of Macedonia; a name which does not find favour in the Republic of Macedonia itself.

<u>Montenegro</u>, an almost entirely Slav nation, remained attached to Serbia until 2006 as the rump of the former Yugoslavia, but has now detached itself from Serbia and is forging its own regional identity.

The remainder of the former Yugoslavia, which included <u>Serbia</u> with its two autonomous provinces; <u>Croatia</u>; and <u>Bosnia and Herzegovina</u>, has been subject to major conflict and international intervention, and a long-term settlement, it must be said, has yet to be achieved. We shall not attempt to summarise the whole of that conflict, but concentrate our intentions on Bosnia.

Bosnia after the collapse of Yugoslavia

When the former federal republic of Yugoslavia began to collapse in the late 1980s, there was no obvious solution to the problem of Bosnia. Would it be able to secede from the union, if it wished? If so, what about its divided population? No doubt if they had been left to find a solution for themselves, the Bosnians might have been able to do so. After all, as the sympathetic and knowledgeable commentator Noel Malcolm argues, Bosnia is not in itself an ungovernable entity. It may be small, comparatively poor, and divided on ethnic and religious grounds; but so are many of the constituent nations of the world to-day.

The Bosnians, however, were not left alone to sort out their own future. Both Serbia and Croatia had claims on Bosnia, either in whole or in part. The Bosnians were divided into Bosnian Serbs, Bosnian Croats, Bosnian Moslems or Bosniaks, and others, with the first three groups being numerically the most important. Bosnian Serbs and Croats might be expected to feel some affiliation with Serbia or Croatia. However, the preferences of the Bosnian Moslems or Bosniaks would be more difficult to predict; and any conflict in the Balkans would attract international attention—if not an international settlement at a new congress of Berlin or its equivalent.

Moslems in Europe

The Bosnian Moslems formed a third element in the Bosnian population at the collapse of Yugoslavia. They are the only significant Moslem population in Europe, with the exception of recent immigrants from Turkey, Pakistan and elsewhere. (Albania had a significant Moslem population under Turkish rule. But Albania under President Hoxha was the world's first state to be officially atheist; and besides, there is some evidence that at least some of the Albanian population had converted to Islam for tactical reasons, and their degree of 'Islamicisation' was never fundamental. Bosnia remains the exception in containing a substantial minority of practising, European, Moslems.)

221

Bosnian Moslems are not of Ottoman descent, and feel no allegiance to Turkey, ancient or modern. Their allegiance is to Bosnia, and presumably a Bosnia that offers religious tolerance, economic prosperity, and political choice: a modern democracy, in fact, and a worthy member of the European Community.

War 1992-1995

Bosnia was recognised as an independent state by the European Community on 6 April 1992. (Malcolm, 1996, Chapter 16, page 234: The Destruction of Bosnia, 1992-1993.) Independence, however, did not mean peace. War broke out between Serbian and Croat-backed forces, supported on some occasions and in some areas by elements of the regular armies of those states, together with the modern equivalent of the Bashi-bazouks: marauding gangs of criminals from Belgrade and Zagreb, prepared to loot, burn, rape and murder where they could do most harm, and not officially accountable as the representatives of any sovereign power.

The war in Bosnia was labelled a civil war, although the adjective is debatable, since this was a war fuelled by outside influences and forces. Siege is a better description for the assault on Sarajevo. The 1992-1995 war was a new outburst of the old and conflictual claims of Serbia, led by Slobodan Mihailovic, and Croatia, led by Franko Tudjman, over Bosnia. Meanwhile, the Moslem Bosnian Prime Minister, Goran Isetbegovic, sought to retain the integrity of his country. Neither aggressor was able to establish a mono-ethnic territorial area, since the population of Bosnia was indisseverably mixed; and 'ethnic cleansing' came into force.

Although something like half the normal population of Bosnia was killed, dispossessed, or driven into exile, not even a *de facto* settlement by right of conquest was achieved. Both random and systematic killings were commonplace, including the Srebenica massacre of several thousand Bosniak males by Serbian aggressors, which UN peace-keeping troops failed to prevent.

Sarajevo at war

The war was a disaster for Bosnia in general and Sarajevo in particular. Sarajevo became not only a real source of murder and suffering, but a symbolic location for the death and suffering in Bosnia which so appalled the rest of Europe and the world but which proved so hard to stop. One of the most civilised cities in the former Turkish empire, and the site of the 1984 Winter Olympic Games, became synonymous with the worst aspects of a war, if not of brother against brother, then of former neighbour against former neighbour. Serbian artillery and snipers ringed the town and opened fire as they chose, and normal life disappeared: to be replaced by the single goal of survival as a pressing and sufficient ambition.

International interventions, conferences and peace-keeping and restoring missions took place. UN and EC officials came and went. Private charities intervened. Outside troops were deployed in UNPROFOR. British infantry commanders who had served in Northern Ireland found the situation strangely familiar, and sampled the local slivovitz with the local warlords with the feeling that they might have been sitting down with the Ulster Volunteer Force in Portadown or Belfast, and that if their Prime Minister were to talk of ancient hatreds, he might have started nearer home.

Meanwhile, three years went by.

Malcolm argues that the war could and should have been stopped by firmer outside intervention, including the supplying of arms to the government of Bosnia in order to resist both Serb and Croat armed invasion. In fact an arms embargo was officially maintained for much of the war, but this was a policy that favoured Serbia as its army was fully equipped and it possessed weapons factories. In the end, NATO aeroplanes bombed the Serb armed forces into a cease-fire, and the modern great powers, led by the USA, once again settled the future of Bosnia without undue reliance on the wishes of its inhabitants.

The Dayton Peace Agreement

The upshot of American intervention was the Dayton Peace Agreement, upon which rests the present peace (2010). Under this complex and much criticised settlement, Bosnia was divided into two separate entities, the Republica Srpska and a Muslim-Croat Federation. A form of central government was set up over the two, with a rotating presidency and a High Representative with extraordinary powers, responsible for ensuring that the Peace Accord was put into practice.

The third holder of this office, from 2002 to 2006, was the former

British liberal democrat leader Lord Ashdown, who, a decade earlier, had been vehemently opposed to the non-intervention by the western powers in what was described as a civil war.

His views are conveyed in depth in what was intended as his exit interview as High Commissioner, published in The Guardian on 2 November 2005. Ashdown described Dayton as a superb agreement to end a war, but a very bad agreement to make a state. 'From now on', the aticle quoted him as saying, 'we have to part company with Dayton and try to build a modern democratic state, for which I have tried to lay the foundations.' Those foundations included what he described as a new human right: the right to return home after a war. 'It's a miracle that ten years after a war in which 250,000 people were killed—one sixteenth of the population—and two million displaced, that one million have gone home.'

Lord Ashdown was further quoted as saying that the Serbs needed to acknowledge their guilt for the Srebenica massacre. 'Truth and reconciliation are always combined, but I would split them: I don't think Bosnia is ready for reconciliation, but I do think it is ready for truth.'[14]

Princip's vision

We began this biography of Gavrilo Princip, the assassin who brought about the First World War, with a chapter on empire. Princip had intended that Bosnia be freed from the Austro-Hungarian Empire and gain a closer association with Serbia; but he did not intend that one subordinate relationship simply be replaced by another.

Gavrilo Princip was a Bosnian Serb, christened into the eastern Orthodox faith, and steeped in childhood with the heroic myths and achievements of the Serb 'folk' as expressed in its oral traditions and poetry. However, Princip was not only a Bosnian Serb but an active member of Young Bosnia. As a Young Bosnian, Princip wanted to see his native country transformed by both political and social change into a new entity.

In so far as Princip (and most of his colleagues) had formed a political vision it was for some form of romantic anarchism, in which women were liberated, races were equal, religion was kept in its place, centralised government was abolished, and such collective decisions as were necessary were agreed by the people as a whole.

Needless to say, that anarchist vision has never become a reality. Indeed, in some ways it was doomed to fail from the start. Vladimir Gacinovic, the Young Bosnian (and young Puritan) amazed the more worldly Trotsky with his assertion that relationships between the sexes in Young Bosnia were, to use an analogy from the study of mathematics, pure rather than applied. As we have said elsewhere, comment on this aspect of youthful idealism would appear superfluous.

Nationalism and identity

Rather more important is that Princip was not a dyed-in-the-wool nationalist, and did not wish to see a Bosnian Serb state for a Bosnian Serb people. Although the majority of members of Young Bosnia were Serbs, and had to struggle to repress what they would have seen as their involuntary Serb prejudices, they did attempt to do so. There would be an equal place in the new Bosnia for citizens of different origins, including Serbs, Croats and Moslems. Nationality and identity were linked; but the connection was neither necessary nor sufficient to determine statehood and citizenship.

Does that ideal persist? At the height of the Bosnian war of 1992 to 1995, clearly not; for in the middle of a quasi-civil war of conspicuous brutality, 'ancient hatreds' are very likely to be less than ancient, and people will naturally associate with what they perceive to be their primary group. Its possibilities in a post-war environment are harder to assess.

The 'ungovernable Balkans'

Such was the violence in the Balkans after the collapse of communism, which has included both ethnic cleansing and war crimes by members of one race or ethnic group against another, and which reached its most intractable condition in Bosnia, that some commentators concluded that Bosnia is intrinsically ungovernable: a sort of perpetual failed state, pre-programmed to self-destruct.

We do not agree with this conclusion, but are influenced by the views of commentators such as Malcolm, Glenny, Mazower and others that the Balkans in general and Bosnia in particular are not in principle ungovernable, and that their inhabitants are not genetically programmed to massacre each other at the slightest opportunity.

Supposed explanations that simply refer to the periodic revival of 'ancient hatreds', and 'ethnic cleansing' as if it were a cyclical activity which is only to be expected, are unhelpful. There is a tradition of ethnic cleansing by irregular forces in the Balkans, which goes back to the Bashi-Bazouks of the Ottoman Empire if not before, and which was not difficult to revive either in the Second World War or at the collapse of Yugoslavia. There are war criminals on trial at the International Court of Criminal Justice at the Hague in Holland, and there should be others. There are aspects of fanaticism, both individual and national, about the recurring conflicts in the Balkans which it would be naïve to ignore. However, it would be a mistake to assume that the normal state of the Balkans in general, and Bosnia in particular, is war.

Luttwak's perspective

We tend to agree with the astute if controversial political commentator Edward Luttwak (born in 1942 in Romania, and now an American citizen) author of *Coup d'Etat: a Practical Handbook* (1968), *The Strategic Command of the Roman Empire* (1976) and other works, that war is not a necessary state of human affairs, and that without outside intervention, war, even civil war, comes to an end (Luttwak, 1999: his article in *Foreign Affairs* is provocatively entitled: *Give War a Chance.)*

Warfare is an essentially irrational activity, in which the costs (almost) always exceed the benefits; and people are not essentially irrational. The objectives of any war are finite. They can be achieved. They do not include permanent war; and if war continues for too long, war-weariness will set in, and combatants will make peace. Interventions impede this process and do not expedite it.

The Dayton Peace Agreement achieved a cease-fire; but a cease-fire is not a permanent settlement. It imposed a complex federal structure upon a small country and population, in which there are incentives for those who wish to preserve an unsatisfactory *status quo* and to exploit ethnic and linguistic differences whether real or supposed, as well as to pursue ample opportunities for corruption.

Young Bosnians to-day are required to register themselves as Moslem (Bosniak), Orthodox (Bosnian Serb) or Catholic (Bosnian Croat) and hence acquire an identity. Bosnian Serbs and Bosnian Croats have the possibility of a dual nationality as a Serb or Croat, but the Bosnian Moslems or Bosniaks have no such escape. This may help to explain why young Moslem women are more likely to wear a head-scarf now than when they were Yugoslavs. (If the state has branded you as a Moslem, as it were, then be proud of it). In the meantime, the country is divided, economic development is uneven, and the past is all too evident in the present. Statesmanship is needed but not in evidence and factionalism prevails.

It is easily possible to be pessimistic about the future of Bosnia, and indeed a sort of cheerful fatalism is a local feature. As the 1914 conspirators did before them, the people of Sarajevo spend much of their time in street-cafés drinking their tiny cups of Bosnian coffee and exchanging political and personal gossip in which the misdeeds of local politicians feature freely. Meanwhile, the beggars beg forlornly, the street cleaners clean industriously, the young discover a new night-club, and the international bureaucrats make their way to the Hotel Europa. This was opened in 1882 under the ownership of a well-known Bosnian Serb; damaged in 1914 in an anti-Serb reaction to the assassination of Franz Ferdinand; damaged again in the siege of 1992-1995; and re-built thereafter. It is a symbol of a new Sarajevo arising from the old, where the conference rooms are always full and the taxis always busy—and real progress will perhaps take place to-morrow.

*

A few yards from the Hotel Europa is the museum of Sarajevo's most famous event (leave the hotel's main entrance, turn left, turn right, and you're there; no need to take a taxi, although an international bureaucrat would probably do so. The Latin Bridge across the Miljacka is just beyond you, and the National Library—once the Town Hall—is a hundred yards upriver on your left).

It is a very post-modern museum. Inside is an interesting collection of artefacts, including a very small automatic pistol, a pair of trousers once worn by Gavrilo Princip, and a good deal of information about the military occupation of Bosnia by the Austro-Hungarian army in 1879. (One can hardly call it a campaign, although lives were lost: the Austrians had very sensibly surveyed Bosnia before conquering it, and had thus anticipated and resolved their major problem before the fighting began.) There is also a photograph of the large monument put up to the murdered couple, which was later erected near the scene of the crime. The monument has gone: its image remains as a fading memory of a long-forgotten reaction.

A few feet inside the entrance is a paving stone with Gavrilo Princip's footprints set into the concrete, as he stood, feet apart, and fired the fatal shots. The footprints, however, are at least two stages removed from reality. Firstly, they cannot have been his actual prints, but a representation. Secondly, the paving stone itself is not where it should be. Princip fired his pistol from the pavement outside Schiller's café, in the street. That street, however was shelled during the 1992-1995 war; and the stone was moved. Will the paving stone be replaced where it belongs, and where a harassed chauffeur once reversed a vehicle that was not his own, in a city that he did not know, under the orders of a general who should have known better? History will tell.

On the wall outside the museum a video plays silently, night and day, in an endless depiction of the assassination. A few seconds show the real heir apparent descending the steps of the Town Hall, flanked by saluting officials. Then the picture changes to colour. An impossibly handsome assassin throws his bomb at the imperial vehicle and an impossibly handsome Christopher Plummer *catches* the smoking object and deftly lobs it into the street—whilst his impossibly beautiful wife gasps silently, for all the world like an auditioning actress exhibiting anguish. Anguish, however, is required for her next scene, as the fatal shots are fired.

Well! Bombs, shots fired from a paving stone which has been made into a work of public art, a damsel in distress, and Christopher Plummer! Gavrilo Princip has found his epitaph: but who is there to see it? The Sarajevans hurrying to work across the Latin Bridge (which no longer accommodates cars, as it did in 1914: Sarajevo has reversed history at least in this regard) or alighting from the helpful tram which will soon round the corner and go back to the centre on its own endless loop, are unlikely to stop and examine his impossibly handsome features, at least as depicted in film. Princip is history; but it is not a history upon which they care to reflect in any depth.

There are cafes across the river, with chairs under sun-shades, and people selling second-hand books near-by. For those seriously addicted to retail therapy, the former Turkish bazaar or Bascarsija is an easy walk. For anyone who wishes to see a really impressive fortification, the Jajce

Fortress overlooks the whole area from its lofty hillside just outside the city, to the south east of where we stand. (Like many other Sarajevo landmarks, it contains local, Ottoman and Austro-Hungarian elements and parts of it are seriously in need of restoration and development—which will happen). And for those seeking an example of the orientalist style of architecture as interpreted by a Czech, the old Town Hall—now the National Library—is being carefully and lovingly restored, just up the river. Poor little Gavro cannot compete with all of that, and he does not try. He has done his thing. Its consequences are still with us.

*

Perhaps, like the Austro-Hungarian empire, Bosnia is a cracked pot held together by rusting wire (of the Dayton Peace Accord) and any attempt at radical reform must result in its final destruction. Meanwhile, the people of Sarajevo get on with their everyday lives, as they must do, and hope for peace and prosperity; but the fulfilment of that hope does not not lie in their hands.

There is a more positive scenario. Sarajevo is a remarkable city. It has survived earthquake, fire, plague and conquest. It withstood the siege of 1992 to 1995, and the courage, humour and tenacity of its people remains undiminshed. Its reconstruction may be uneven, but it is taking place: and futuristic buildings like the Avaz Twist Tower with its suggestion of a gigantically swollen minoret designed by a madman, show that Sarajevo does not only offer nostalgia. Its traditions of cultural diversity and religious tolerance have much to show to a divided world, and there is a sense of resilence and a feeling of hope amidst the poverty, the building sites, and the remaining scars of war, which is a tribute to the human spirit.

Perhaps the best hope for Bosnia is as part of a larger community, in which it retains some identity, and in which it is not impossible that elected Hapsburgs, Princips and indeed Dimitryevics will play their part. An idle dream? News from nowhere? We hope not!

NOTES

1 Prisoners learned to take their chains to bed with them, to avoid awaking frozen to the icy metal: but such counter-measures were not enough.

2 One of Freud's case studies was of the treatment of a patient to whom he gave the psuedonym Anna O, who has been traced to a Viennese patient named Bertha

229

Pappenheim (1859 to 1936), who was treated for hysteria by Dr Josef Breuer. Breuer influenced Freud in the development of psycho-analysis, and the two men wrote a book together (Studies in Hysteria). Bertha Pappenheim was not related to Dr Martin Pappenheim, but both were products of the Jewish population of Vienna who contributed so much to the intellectual, cultural and economic life of the empire and of post-war Vienna.

Bertha Pappenheim was not cured of her hysteria by the new methods of Dr Breuer, but survived the experience and went on to emigrate to Frankfurt and to build a distinguished reputation in her own right, as a leading figure in Jewish and women's studies. To bring the story back to Princip, at the end: Bertha Pappenheim died after she was interrogated by the Gestapo, in 1936. The Nazis went on to close down the institute that she had created, and its Jewish population was transferred to Theresienstadt concentration camp in 1942, where they died.

[3] The opinion was expressed to this author, when visiting Saraejvo in 2009, that Gavrilo Princip had committed suicide in prison as a result of his accumulating revulsion over the consequences of the assassination. Was there any evidence for this belief? I asked. Everyone knows it, was the reply.

Gavrilo Princip, a Bosnian Serb, remains a controversial figure in Sarajevo, where the past is not yet past, and where he is identified by his ethnic background. Although the museum at the site of the murder is quite well attended, Princip's grave is not on the tourist circuit, and Sarajevo appears not quite sure what to make of its most notorious event.

[4] Both Popovic and Cubrilovic were to reach old age. Joachim Remak visited Eastern Europe in 1968, to find the two surviving conspirators of the 1914 assassination very much alive and well (Remak, 1968). Cvetko Popovic was curator of the ethnographic section of the Sarajevo Museum. Vaso Cubrilovic, who had briefly served Tito as minister of forests after the liberation, was chairman of the department of history at the University of Belgrade. Popovic thought that the assassination might have been called off, from Belgrade, but the countermand had no effect. "We were in no mood to follow any change in instructions. We would have gone ahead, no matter what. You know we did, in spite of Ilic's doubts." Cvetko Popovic died in Sarajevo on 7 June 1980 at the age of 84, and his obituary was published in The Times on 11 June of that year. Vaso Cubrilovic died in 1990, at 93.

[5] There is a memorable photograph in Jan Morris's book *Trieste* of the funeral cortege in that very Austro-Hungarian city, which was the naval base for its empire.

[6] A court official wrote in his memoirs that the emperor said: 'A higher force has restored that order which unfortunately I was unable to maintain.' This cryptic phrase—was the emperor implying that Franz Ferdinand had been punished for his unsuitable marriage, or did it have some other meaning?—seems an implausible one under any interpretation, as Franz Joseph was not given to cryptic utterances. The more likely explanation is that the memoirist improved on the occasion.

7 Artstetten was the private propery of the Archduke Franz Ferdinand and remains in private possession. Konopischt was seized by the government of the new state of Czechoslovakia in 1919, together with any other properties of the orphans Max, Ernst and Sophie Hohenberg, on the grounds that they were part of the ruling family of Austria. Franz Ferdinand's great grandson, Max Hohenberg (born 1970) comments that this was 'Quite ironic, particularly after so much had been done to make sure that they were no longer part of the Hapsburg family. The three children had a single day to leave their house and were allowed to take five kilograms of private property with them. In an act of particular cruelty this was closely monitored by the Czech authorities who made sure the children did not exceed that weight...... Today... Konopischt Castle, which was never looted by either German or Soviet troops, holds most of FF and his family's private property such as children's toys, clothing, private letters, family photos etc. (That property) is being displayed in a museum by the Czech state (which) owns the castle today. .. ' Both Artstetten and Konopischt provide a living memoir of the Archduke and his family.

8 This was not a unique achievement for the widow of a Hapsburg. Readers will recall that Franz Ferdinand's younger brother, Karl Ferdinand, had been forced to resign all his privileges after he married the 'commoner' Bertha Czuber in 1909. Karl Ferdinand died of tuberculosis, a broken man, in 1915—only one year after his older brother, whose funeral he had been given special permission to attend. His widow Bertha, born in 1879, outlived her husband by 64 years, and died in 1979 at the age of 100.

9 Both brothers died relatively young. Prince Ernst lived from 1904 to 1954, and his older brother Prince Max (Maximilian) from 1902 to 1962. Their older sister, Princess Sophie, lived from 1901 to 1990 and died at 89. She is remembered with great affection by Max Hohenberg (born 1970), the great-grandson of the murdered couple at Sarajevo, whom I consulted in researching this book and whose comments have been invaluable.

10 Strictly speaking, anti-Semitism could be taken to mean a prejudice towards anyone of Semitic origin, both Arab and Jew. However, Hitler's prejudice in this case was against the Jews, and that is how we shall interpret the phrase here.

11 Nazi Germany and communist Russia signed a pact in 1939 that each would not attack the other, in order that each might pursue its own ambitions. Germany promptly attacked and seized Poland. Hitler's attack on Russia, Operation Barbarossa, which began in June 1941, was originally planned for May 1941 and was delayed by the Yugoslav distraction as well as other reasons.

12 If Hitler had invaded Russia earlier in the year, the Wehrmacht might have reached and taken Moscow before winter set in. In addition, the Nazis might have been able to reach and seize vital oil supplies at Baku.

13 Serbia included the autonomous provinces of Vojvodina and Kosovo, which meant that there were eight elements of the new Yugoslavia. Some areas, especially Kosovo and Macedonia, contained substantial Albanian minorities.

14 An academic, journalist, Balkan visitor and now politician himself, Michael Ignatieff writes in *'The Warrior's Honor'* (Ignatieff, 1998) on the difficult relationship between truth, reconciliation and justice.

Bibliography

Books

Albertini, Luigi
The origins of the war of 1914
Volume Two
Oxford University Press, 1953

Anderson, Dorothy
Miss Irby and her Friends
Hutchinson, London, 1966

Bailey, Jonathan
The First World War and the Birth of the Modern Style of Warfare
Strategic and Combat Studies Institute, Staff College, Camberley, Surrey, GU15 4NP, 1996

Bailey, Jonathan
Field Artillery and Firepower
The Military Press/Taylor and Francis
Oxford, 1989

Brown, Ann
Before Knossos...
Arthur Evans's travels in the Balkans and Crete
University of Oxford
Ashmolean Museum, Oxford, 1993

Cain, P.J. and Hopkins
British Imperialism:
Innovation and Expansion
1688-1914
Longman, London and New York, 1993

Albert Camus
The Fastidious Assassins
Penguin, 2008

Cannadine, David
Ornamentalism: How the British saw their Empire
Penguin, London, 2001

Dalrymple, William
White Moghuls
HarperCollins, London, 2003

Dedijer, Vladimir
The Road to Sarajevo
MacGibbon and Kee, London, 1967

Dixon, Norman
On the Psychology of Military Incompetence
Jonathan Cape, London, 1976

Dolph Owings, W A
The Sarajevo Trial
Documentary Publications, 1984

Evans, Arthur John
Illyrian Letters
Elibron Classics, 2005
First published by Longmans, Green and Co, London, 1878

Ferguson, Niall
Colossus: the rise and fall of the American empire
Penguin, London, 2004

Ferguson, Niall
The Ascent of Money:
A Financial History of the World
Allen Lane, London, 2008

French, Patrick
Liberty or death:
India's Journey to Independence and Political Division
HarperCollins, London, 1997

Geifman, Anna
Thou shalt kill:
Revolutionary terrorism in Russia, 1894-1917
Princeton University Press, Princeton, 1993

Glendinning, Victoria
Rebecca West: A Life
Weidenfeld and Nicolson, London, 1987

Glenny, Misha
The Balkans 1804-1999
Nationalism, War and the Great Powers
Granta Books, London, 1999

Gray, John
Straw dogs:
Thoughts on humans and other animals
Granta books, London, 2003

Hart, H L A
Punishment and Responsibility:
Essays in the Philosophy of Law
Clarendon Press, Oxford, 1968

Hattersley, Roy
The Edwardians
Abacus, London, 2006

Hosking, Geoffrey
Russia and the Russians
Allen Lane, The Penguin Press, 2001

Ignatieff, Michael
The Warrior's Honor:
Ethnic War and the Modern Conscience
Chatto and Windus, London, 1998

Keegan, John
The First World War
Hutchinson, London, 1998

Malcolm, Noel
Bosnia: a Short History
Pan Books, London, 2002

Mazower, Mark
The Balkans:
From the end of Byzantium to the present day
Phoenix Press, London, 2001

Morris, James
An Imperial Trilogy (1968-78)
Heaven's Command
Pax Britannica
Farewell, the Trumpets

Morris, Jan
Trieste and the meaning of nowhere
Faber and Faber, London, 2001

Remak, Joachim
Sarajevo: The Story of a Political Murder
Weidenfeld and Nicolson, London, 1959

Runciman, Sir Steven
A History of the Crusades (Volume One)
Cambridge University Press, 1951

Sked, Alan
The decline and fall of the Hapsburg empire
Second edition
Pearson Education, England, 2001

Smith, David James
One Morning in Sarajevo
Weidenfeld and Nicolson, 2008

Van der Kiste, John
Emperor Francis Joseph:
Life, Death and Fall of the Hapsburg Empire
Sutton Publishing, Stroud, 2005

West, Rebecca
Black Lamb and Grey Falcon
Canongate Classics, 1997

Zweig, Stefan
The World of Yesterday
Cassell, London, 1943

Articles

Armstrong, Hamilton Fish
Confessions of the assassin whose deed led to the World War—the notes of
Martin Pappenheim
Current History, New York, August 1927

Luttwak, Edward
Give War a Chance
Foreign Affairs, USA, July-August 1999

Remak, Joachim
Journey to Sarajevo
Commentary July 1968

Index